AF606069

ART AND MORAL CHANGE: A REEXAMINATION

Recent Titles from the Moral Traditions Series

David Cloutier, Andrea Vicini, SJ, and Darlene Weaver, Editors

The Structures of Virtue and Vice
Daniel J. Daly

The Aesthetics of Solidarity: Our Lady of Guadalupe and American Democracy
Nichole M. Flores

Radical Sufficiency: Work, Livelihood, and a US Catholic Economic Ethic
Christine Firer Hinze

Tragic Dilemmas in Christian Ethics
Kate Jackson-Meyer

The Fullness of Free Time: Leisure and Recreation in the Moral Life
Connor M. Kelly

The Moral Theology of Pope Francis: Expanding the US Reception of the First Jesuit Pope
Connor M. Kelly and Kristin E. Heyer, Editors

Beyond Biology: Rethinking Parenthood in the Catholic Tradition
Jacob M. Kohlhaas

Growing in Virtue: Aquinas on Habit
William C. Mattison III

Beyond Virtue Ethics: A Contemporary Ethic of Godward Spiritual Struggle
Stephen M. Meawad

Reenvisioning Sexual Ethics: A Feminist Christian Account
Karen Peterson-Iyer

Tomorrow's Troubles: Risk, Anxiety, and Prudence in an Age of Algorithmic Governance
Paul Scherz

Wealth, Virtue, and Moral Luck: Christian Ethics in an Age of Inequality
Kate Ward

ART AND MORAL CHANGE

A REEXAMINATION

KI JOO CHOI

GEORGETOWN UNIVERSITY PRESS / WASHINGTON, DC

Library of Congress Cataloging-in-Publication Data

Names: Choi, Ki Joo, author.
Title: Art and moral change : a reexamination / Ki Joo Choi.
Description: Washington, DC : Georgetown University Press, 2024. | Includes bibliographical references and index.
Identifiers: LCCN 2023037938 (print) | LCCN 2023037939 (ebook) | ISBN 9781647124588 (hardcover) | ISBN 9781647124595 (paperback) | ISBN 9781647124601 (ebook)
Subjects: LCSH: Arts—Moral and ethical aspects. | Arts and morals. | Aesthetics. | Christian ethics.
Classification: LCC BJ46 .C48 2024 (print) | LCC BJ46 (ebook) | DDC 170—dc23/eng/20240416
LC record available at https://lccn.loc.gov/2023037938
LC ebook record available at https://lccn.loc.gov/2023037939

♾ This paper meets the requirements of ANSI/NISO Z39.48-1992 (Permanence of Paper).

25 24 9 8 7 6 5 4 3 2 First printing

Printed in the United States of America

Cover design by TG Design
Interior design by BookComp, Inc.

To ABC,
for her generous partnership

CONTENTS

ACKNOWLEDGMENTS

The ideas treated in this book have occupied my mind for many years, going back to my days in graduate school. (Well, if you count the days that I worked mightily to appreciate art history in college, tried my hand at writing poetry, and came to terms with my inability to sing, then it goes back much longer.) And given the extent to which my thinking on aesthetics and ethics has evolved from then to now, I suppose this book could be considered the maturation or fruition of my many years of wrestling with that relationship. But I think it would be better to characterize my thinking on aesthetics and ethics in this book as simply "this is where I am now." This is not a hedge against the coherency of and my own confidence in the book's arguments, a number of which are not uncontroversial. Rather, it is my way of acknowledging that while I have changed my mind in a number of respects on the question of what art can and cannot do for the moral life, I am not so foolish to think that further evolution of thought is not possible. I continuously find myself challenged by the increasing number of fellow theologians wading into the waters of aesthetics and ethics and pursuing a different line of argument, and my hope is that this present study offers an equally stimulating challenge to them. In other words, I would like to think of this book as a constructive conversation starter.

The idea of the book's main thesis was first entertained in a response I was invited to give to a plenary address at the Society of Christian Ethics in January 2019 in Louisville, Kentucky. Diane M. Yeager, president of the society at the time, displayed tremendous graciousness in extending that invitation to me. That unpublished response served as the foundation for the last section of chapter 2 of this book. Portions of chapter 3 are reappropriations of select parts of an essay titled "The Deliberative Practices of Aesthetic Experience: Reconsidering the Moral Functionality of Art," *Journal of the Society of Christian Ethics* 29, no. 1 (Spring/Summer 2009): 193–218. I say "reappropriations" because portions from that essay have been enlisted for this book in ways that diverge from the ends of the original essay. Those who are familiar with that essay will perhaps notice that in this book I am much more skeptical of the kind of community-building work that aesthetic experiences can play, which was the primary focus of the essay. This is not to say that my proposal for how art and beauty can generate focused attention across difference was mistaken but rather that I now believe that I overstated the extent to which such focused attention can do the kind of moral work that I entertained originally in the journal article. Some of that shift in certitude can be gleaned, a tad, in another essay from which this book draws, "The Priority of the Affections over the Emotions: Gustafson, Aquinas, and an Edwardsean Critique," *Journal of the Society of Christian Ethics*, 38, no. 1 (Spring/Summer 2018): 113–30. Only two sections of chapter 4 of this book are substantial revisions of parts of this essay.

There are of course a number of persons to thank starting with Kristin E. Heyer, who was the first to encourage me to pursue this book through the Moral Traditions series at Georgetown University Press. Thanks also to Lisa Sowle Cahill for always asking about the progress of the book (gentle pressure is always good!) and to Jonathan Tran for thinking that this was a project worth pursuing even after reading a rough (very rough) draft of the introduction way back when. I am also grateful to the current editors of the Moral Traditions series for the interest and support they have given to this book, especially Darlene Fozard Weaver who has shown incredible patience over the past few years with my multiple writing delays. I am especially indebted to Al Bertrand, director of Georgetown University Press, for sticking with this book project and providing the encouragement for its completion. It is a genuine privilege to be a part of a press that has published so many of the leading voices in contemporary Christian ethics. And then there are my amazing colleagues and friends at Seton Hall University and now at Princeton Theological Seminary who have sustained me intellectually. Last but certainly not least, there is my family to thank, especially Mandy, who has shouldered more than she should have just so that I could hide from parenting duties and pretend to be writing (this time, I was only partly pretending, "my aesthetics book" is finally done, more or less).

INTRODUCTION

ESTABLISHING A TRADITION OF INQUIRY AND ARTICULATING ITS CHALLENGES

I think the relative merits of supporting art museums versus saving people of diseases that are easily preventable or curable are pretty clear. Both are "good" causes, but one is likely to do a lot more good than the other.

Eric Friedman, *Reinventing Philanthropy: A Framework for More Effective Giving*

Let him take into a tenement block a handful of flowers from the fields and watch the brightened faces, the sudden abandonment of play and fight that go ever hand in hand where there is no elbow-room.

Jacob Riis, *How the Other Half Lives: Studies among the Tenements of New York*

Paint helps a lot, but sadly it can't change the reality of social problems. A mural isn't going to change whether you care about the woman being beat up on the corner.

Alejandra Atrisco Amilpas, 2021, quoted in Oscar Lopez, "Frida Kahlo, Aztec Gods: Can Art Lift Up a Poor Neighborhood?"

This book considers the question of the relationship between aesthetics and ethics. To be sure, part of the challenge of this kind of inquiry is making sense of the term "aesthetics." As Peter de Bolla observes, there is a certain opacity to the term given its multiple usage:

> In common speech one may, for example, speak of X's "aesthetic" as if such a thing were the distinct property of an individual. . . . When the term is used with respect to an artist it is usually taken to refer to something like the artist's principles or particular program of making art. The term also has currency in the history of philosophy or ideas; in this context philosophers and intellectual historians speak of a tradition of "aesthetics" that began, so that story is often told, in the eighteenth

> century with [the German philosopher Alexander] Baumgarten's coining of the word itself (where the derivation from the Greek, meaning "sense perception," is uppermost in its use). . . . Yet another use of the term "aesthetics" can be found in professional philosophy, where it is sometimes used interchangeably with the phrase "philosophy of art." But even here there are shades of meaning or differences in emphasis. . . . In another domain of contemporary inquiry—now standardly referred to as "theory"—"the aesthetic" most often refers to *a theory of aesthetics* whose most important thinker is generally assumed to be Immanuel Kant. . . . [And whether following Kant or not] in some hands a "theory of aesthetics" is taken to be completely independent of any instances of art.[1]

The sheer variety of how the term "aesthetics" is defined is bewildering. The arguments that will be advanced in this book will to some degree respond to and inform the various conceptual wranglings on what aesthetics is or ought to be. But sifting through these various schools of thought is not the primary interest of this book. For the most part, this book employs a different definition of aesthetics, one that is ahistorical and thus neither derives from nor refers to any specific lineage of the word. Aesthetics, as it is employed here, simply reflects what we might say are "ordinary" assumptions of it: that is, aesthetics as referring to what we generally assume pertains to the arts, art, or works of art and even beautiful art. So, in this book I refer to aesthetics and the arts (and its variations) interchangeably while recognizing that in the more technical literature on aesthetics such swapping of terms is not necessarily precise.

In conjoining aesthetics and the arts together in this ordinary sense, the moral salience of two general kinds of aesthetic activities or practices is of primary concern. The first is aesthetic creativity, that is, those acts or events of producing art, not only the visual arts but also art in a global sense: theater, dance, opera, sculpture, literature, painting, and so on. The second kind of aesthetic activity pertains to those who are the recipients or audiences of aesthetic creativity. On this front, we can include everyday experiences and practices of reading, listening, and touching, including what art historians often refer to as acts of looking at art as well as any object or image that is beautiful.

Given this twofold delineation of aesthetics, the primary question of this book can be narrowed or specified in the following manner. Is artistic creativity a morally relevant activity? And can the multivalent perception of or experience with art and beauty, visual and beyond, contribute to moral reflection and judgment and thus ultimately moral action, change, or transformation? In this book, I am primarily concerned with how theological ethics can help us to think through these questions in terms of both identifying the conceptual challenges to bringing aesthetics and ethics together and indicating constructive pathways to meeting those challenges. My motivations for such a consideration are at least threefold.

ART'S UBIQUITY

The first motivation is born from an acute curiosity over the ubiquity of the arts in daily human life, even while such ubiquity is often concealed by the inattention to or, at the very least, the uneven regard for the arts in mainstream media and public discourse. So, except for those newsworthy instances in which particular artworks and installations incite controversy over the nature of obscenity and the meaning of free speech, the arts struggle to gain widespread sustained public concern. Consider the various and fiercely contested art controversies in recent years: Robert Maplethorpe's *X Portfolio* series at the Contemporary Art Center of Cincinnati,[2] Chris Ofili's exhibit *The Holy Virgin Mary* at the Brooklyn Museum of Art,[3] Yale student Aliza Shvarts's senior art project,[4] the North Korean debut of the New York Philharmonic,[5] Columbia student Emma Sulkowicz's fifty-pound mattress performance art,[6] Dana Schutz's painting of Emmett Till's coffin at the Whitney Museum,[7] and the toppling of Confederate Civil War statues during the 2020 Black Lives Matter protests.[8] In these kinds of high-profile instances, art displays its power to generate awareness to itself and draws the focused, intense interest of diverse individuals and groups. But such moments of concern and debate are often fleeting, and questions of the importance of the arts fade into the background until the next localized instance of controversy.

Economic realities too contribute to the sporadic nature of public interest in the arts. The social significance of the arts, whether they are central to political flourishing, the stability and vibrancy of civic life, or the general formation of an informed and participatory citizenry, generate substantial publicity when arts organizations receive generous funding: the $100 million bequest to *Poetry Magazine* by Ruth Lilly in 2002, for instance,[9] and MacKenzie Scott's no-strings-attached multimillion-dollar donations to numerous small arts organizations as part of her pledge to give away much of her Amazon-derived wealth.[10] More typical, however, is when funding for arts education falls victim to cost-saving measures, usually at the expense of what are professed to be more pressing social and economic programs. Unless severe budgetary axes fall on museums, theater productions, and painting and choral classes at the local elementary school, the arts—the question of the social, communal significance of the arts—often goes ignored.[11]

And yet, the value of the arts, the significant role they occupy in daily human life at both the personal and communal levels, is clear even if that importance is not recognized in a sustained manner. We need only consider the extent to which we find ourselves surrounded by art, a great deal of it. We place sundry objects of art on our desks, hang them on our walls, and display their images on our clothing. On our way to and from work, school, or the grocery store, we drive past public sculptures, admire the architectural composition of a house, and catch glimpses of color and design on storefronts and even billboards (or, alternatively, we lament the lack of graphic flourish on streets and stores we pass daily and decry the ugliness of some of our landscapes), all the while listening to an audio novel or streaming playlists. We sometimes find ourselves with others debating, sometimes casually, sometimes passionately, the preferences of some for the architecture of a quaint New England town over the extravagance of Manhattan's Fifth Avenue and Park Avenue. Some find Carnegie Hall beautiful, while others see Lincoln Center as simply adequate. Some prefer Broadway shows, while others enjoy films more and insist on watching them in a traditional multiplex. Some—actually many—are thrilled by hip-hop, while others are devotees of country music or extol classical music above all else. And we—in this instance I mean academics, including theologians—find it hard to refrain from remarking on the art that graces or, with some frustration, the art that underwhelms our own books.

The extent to which art is a mundane part of our daily lives only underscores the larger point that art—its creation, dissemination, and enjoyment—is a universal human activity of immense importance, one that is collectively valued. As Nicholas Wolterstorff observes,

> The truth is that in discussing the arts we are discussing something universal to mankind. We know of no people which has done without music and fiction and poetry and role-playing and sculpture and visual depiction. Possibly some have done without one or the other of these; none to our knowledge has done without all. Indeed—to single out just one of the arts—none to our knowledge has done without visual depiction. "There were," says the anthropologist Paul S. Wingert, "no primitive peoples, however meager their cultural attainments, who offered no patronage to the artist."[12]

In short, without the arts, human life would not be what it is. Therefore, I contend, they deserve the intellectual seriousness that other questions deemed weightier and more consequential often receive.[13]

TOWARD ART'S MORAL SALIENCE

The second motivation of this book builds on the first and pertains to theological ethics more specifically, that is, the way in which certain sectors within theological ethics have moved to capitalize on the ubiquitous presence of the arts to demonstrate that they are indeed central to the moral life. The arguments go beyond familiar claims that the arts are morally relevant because they are morally useful in expanding the moral imagination and helping to get a point across (e.g., in illuminating or punctuating a point, offering alternative mediums for social commentary, or facilitating emotions and thoughts that may be more difficult to articulate or express through speech alone). Surely the arts can function in such ways and serve as part of a wider tool kit for moral discernment. But the notion that the arts are relevant because they have utility does not necessarily indicate why their utility is morally indispensable or essential. The sciences too can perhaps powerfully illuminate a point, concretize abstract ideas, or bring unrecognized or underappreciated social questions into view. (Consider the popularity of STEM education in this regard.)[14] However, contemporary theological-ethical discourse suggests that the arts are morally indispensable. Such discourse goes a step further than simply demonstrating that the arts are morally useful and argues that their utility is of the sort that the moral life is impoverished without them.

The details of this line of argumentation will be mapped out over the course of the first two chapters in this book. For now, it bears emphasizing that this book will rely heavily on the spirit and letter of these arguments, given my belief in their importance and the need to develop them further for wider consideration. There are at least two reasons for this belief. The first is that these arguments call into question popular cultural assumptions about the arts that impede their regard as vital to human flourishing. I have in mind here the pervasive assumption that the arts are simply matters of recreation or leisure and therefore of ancillary importance, even though in practice we may find it difficult to imagine life without them. To some extent, we can call this attitude a way of thinking about the arts as autonomous and thus separate from ethics.

The second reason is that these new theological-ethical arguments lend further support to the growing skepticism over formalist or modernist aesthetics, which since the early twentieth century has served as the prevailing framework for contemporary definitions of art.[15] Art *as art* produces what the famed modernist critic Clive Bell, who will be scrutinized closely later in this book, referred to as an aesthetic emotion; in other words, art in its fundamental forms makes its audience "feel something" that is distinctively aesthetic. Thus, art constitutes its own autonomous sphere in another sense, not a trivial sphere of leisure and frivolity but rather one that takes the arts rather seriously, so seriously that to see art as linked to any other so-called nonaesthetic sphere is to denigrate it. As the pioneering art critic Clement Greenberg is well known for proposing, autonomous in this sense means that art does not depend on other arenas of human life for its self-definition and understanding.[16] In short, the modernist strategy of sealing art within itself is meant to elevate its status.

Contemporary theological-ethical engagements in aesthetics do not necessarily give us reason to dismiss out of hand the autonomy of the arts in the two senses just described. It would be reductionistic in the opposite direction to contend that the arts are morally important without qualification. However, to insist that the arts are separate—or must be kept separated—from other spheres of life, especially the moral life, does more to denigrate than establish and maintain the specialness of the arts. As noted earlier, insisting on their separation neglects the ubiquity of art. It is their very universality that makes the arts remarkable and necessitates our sustained attention to them. Again, can we imagine life without the arts? What forms of experience command such a place in our social, cultural, and moral imaginations? Any serious response must include the aesthetic.

Maintaining separation between the arts and the rest of human life for the sake of the arts is misguided. The arts are a central part of life. But how so or in what manner are they central? In this book, I am particularly interested in the potential for aesthetics to transform the way we think about moral inquiry and the possibilities for moral and social change. What do we miss in regard to the nature of moral thinking if aesthetics' autonomy is maintained? I believe that contemporary theological ethics provides novel responses to such a question. Yet, there are also limitations to the way in which that pathway has been paved so far in recent theological-ethical arguments for both aesthetics and ethics.

ART'S MORAL PLURALISM

This brings me to the third and leading motivation behind this book. Despite the strides that recent works in theological ethics have made in advancing the moral salience of the arts, they leave open what I will argue is an enduring problem in aesthetics and ethics discourse: the problem of moral pluralism or, rather, the inconvenient reality that the arts lead to a multiplicity of outcomes. More generally, this problem centers on the question of the how: How is it that the arts effect moral concern, action, and change? Up to now, the contribution of recent theological-ethical works in aesthetics, I shall argue, resides primarily in the realm of the what, that is, making the case that what the arts are and do are more than simply aesthetical but also ethical. But the how of this what is still conceptually wanting.

In my estimation, the question of the how remains the largest hurdle to demonstrating credibly the vital relevance of aesthetics to ethics. Consider that it is one thing to observe that life without the arts is difficult to imagine, but it is another thing to claim that the arts are therefore integral to the task of ethics. While I have indicated earlier my belief that the former claim ought to motivate us to consider the latter claim, the former does not demonstrate the latter. We may need the arts to entertain us, to distract us from the labors of daily life, and to make our daily routines more colorful, pleasurable, and bearable. But those needs do not necessarily mean that they are also moral needs or that enjoying, creating, and contemplating artworks necessarily feeds into moral reflection, judgment, and social action and transformation.

As Russ Castronovo points out, one of the more influential American movements on behalf of the arts was initiated by social reformers in the late nineteenth and early twentieth centuries. These social reformers insisted that the arts were essential moral goods and were critical to the maintenance of American democracy and civic life. However, the American polity, with its continued struggles with poverty, labor rights, and social upheavals due in part to mass immigration from Europe and the industrial transformation of the US economy, was not so cooperative with respect to the social reformers' aims:

> If aesthetics are a starting point to ethical citizenship, it is worth remembering that starting points do not necessarily lead to their destinations and that the path from aesthetic perception to democratic sensibility is not always a straight one. Even when links between aesthetics and justice seem secure and predictable, subjects whose emotions and instincts are quickened by beauty often fail to arrive at their moral destinations, the ethical baggage misplaced and their capacity for civic obedience lost along the way. For philosophers and reformers of the late nineteenth century, no less than for contemporary theorists of the last half century, aesthetics have appeared as an experiential base to start laying a foundation for social justice, political unity, or other collective project. But because this base shifts in response to historical and economic pressures, it is always in motion like the flimsy rope suspension bridges found in action adventure movies.[17]

Later in the book I will revisit parts of this American tradition of linking arts advocacy with democratic renewal and assess the specific lessons it might provide. But for now, Castronovo's recommendation to not lose sight of this history underscores a more general worry about aesthetics' relevance to ethics.

While we may hope that a person who loves museums and Shakespearean sonnets is also a good and just person, we can just as easily imagine—buttressed by numerous examples of personal and communal experience and history—a lover of poetry or some other art form to be no lover of virtue. Moral rectitude as well as hubris, greed, and elitism may be prevalent among the aesthetically "rich" in terms of not only artistic skill but also opportunities to perceive and appreciate the arts in some manner. Given such pluralism of moral outcomes, the importance of the question of how the arts are morally relevant should not be underestimated. And to some extent, I do not think it is underestimated. Otherwise, ethics education, to take as an example, would be left to the purview of literature or possibly film courses or would center around the study of art history or maybe the promotion of studio art classes. But how ethically substantive and effective would such alternatives be? Could we primarily rely on reading literature, looking at art, and listening to music for moral instruction, even moral formation? That even we, professors of ethics, do not rely on art in such a way—even if we think that novels, theater, and music are morally salient and endeavor to incorporate them here and there in our courses—speaks to some level of recognition, explicitly or implicitly, that what results from the arts (their impactfulness) is not necessarily predicable or reliable.

Not only do we need better conceptual accounts of how the arts can both facilitate and hamper moral goodness, we also need constructive accounts of how the arts can indeed accomplish the former. Otherwise, arguments that the arts are simply a matter of recreation or leisure (or that they should simply be regarded that way) or, alternatively, that they ought to be safeguarded from the interests of other purportedly nonaesthetic spheres of human life will be even more attractive and persuasive than they currently are and should be.

PIVOTING TOWARD THE AFFECTIONS AND RECONCEPTUALIZING ART'S MORAL IMPORTANCE

To counter such separatist inclinations in light of the pluralism of effects that come from the arts and to do so theologically, I propose what perhaps will seem paradoxical at first: the need for an interdisciplinary engagement. By this

I mean more specifically the need to turn to art historians, art theorists, literary scholars, cultural historians, and moral philosophers for clues that help us make better sense of how the arts can effect moral action and change and why they necessarily effect morally pluralistic outcomes. Various non–theological-ethical sources will be consulted, however, in the service of a broader aim: to sharpen our attunement to aspects of and voices within the Christian moral tradition that receive, as of present, minor attention in aesthetic and ethics discourse and on the question of the arts' moral salience. Thus, in proposing an interdisciplinary engagement, I do so on the twofold conviction that such an engagement enlivens theological sources and facilitates their wider or "public" applicability (or relevance beyond theological circles) in ways that simply interpreting those sources on their own cannot.

The interdisciplinary path I undertake ultimately directs our reflective attention to the nature and role of affectivity, or the affections in human perception. This path begins with an assessment of how certain modernist, or formalist, approaches to art conceive of the nature of aesthetic experience as essentially affective and then moves to how a Thomistic-inflected account of affectivity in the thought of Jonathan Edwards expands and ultimately complicates such modernist conceptions.

One might wonder why modernist conceptions of art are worthy of the kind of attention I will give them. As I noted above and I will do so again in more detail later in this book, focusing on how modernists think about art in relation to affectivity is critical because of their outsize influence in shaping popular cultural perceptions of art as existing within a sphere of its own. Whether we are aware (and willing to admit to it) or not, so much of the general public's attitudes toward the arts are legacies of modernist aesthetics.[18] Directing reflective energies toward them is also important because they provide the opportunity to elevate and recast Edwardsean theological sources in ways that are not immediately obvious. (This therefore reiterates the kind of interdisciplinary convictions that I noted above as central to the methodological shape or logic of this book.) To be sure, Edwards is often admired for the way he anchors the language of beauty to his doctrines of God and creation. But how his theological vision is applicable or can be responsive to theories of art (or can itself be counted as a theory of art) is terrain that has been traversed lightly if at all. What I propose in this book is that Edwards is highly pertinent to contemporary discourses on the arts, a relevance that can best be discerned if we focus our attention on the centrality of affectivity in such discourses, especially in modernist aesthetics. In short, affectivity is what sets the arena for an interdisciplinary engagement between modernist and Edwards's accounts of art.

Edwards is arguably the premier theorist of affectivity, at least within the North American context. My aim is to indicate how an Edwardsean account of the affections not only complicates modernist accounts of art but also pushes a reassessment of how we in the discipline of theological ethics should talk about art's moral salience, more specifically its power to effect moral change and transformation. As I show in the opening chapters of the book, a number of contemporary theological-ethical studies (particularly those that focus on the concept of beauty) take affectivity as the primary linkage point between aesthetics and ethics; it is through affectivity, in other words, that these studies construe arts' importance for the moral life.

There is an intuitive rightness to this affective trajectory in contemporary aesthetics-ethics discourse: affectivity and its concomitant concepts of emotions and feelings are central to aesthetic experience by its very definition or nature. Therefore, I am not exactly sure how we can talk about aesthetic experience—that is, the experience of appreciating, encountering, and creating art—apart from the language of affectivity. So, if we want to talk about the moral salience of the arts, then we need to do so in a manner that takes the affectivity of aesthetic experience seriously. But what remains an undertheorized and thus an open question in theological-ethical discourse on the arts is how the affectivity of aesthetic experience explains what I have been referring to as the problem of art's moral pluralism: Why do some people find particular artworks offensive and others inoffensive? Why do some find offensive art (say, art that depicts violence or is sexist, racist, or bigoted) beautiful and good while others do not and vice versa? In general, why does art elicit differing judgments and move persons in conflicting directions, even if its intention may have been to move its audience toward a specific moral destination? Or, why do works of art created with no specific moral intent engender particular moral judgments and actions anyway?[19] To address or resolve these rather vexing questions requires, I propose a different way of talking about affectivity in relation to the arts (and thus art's connection with ethics). This different way is informed by an Edwardsean account of affectivity, and it comes to light most vividly and constructively when contrasted with modernist accounts of affectivity and aesthetic experience.

An Edwardsean account of affectivity flips the lines of causality in the relationship between aesthetics and ethics. What I shall entertain in this book, particularly in the second half, is the extent to which the moral pluralism of the arts reflects the ways in which the affections govern our perception of and response to the arts rather than the other way around, which is the more typical way of thinking about affectivity in aesthetics discourse. The more typical path, to be more precise, is to regard affectivity as expressions or manifestations of how art is felt; affectivity, in other words, is a response to art, or art is something that elicits or moves our affections. In the context of theological-ethical discourse, more specifically, such a way of thinking about affectivity is key to conceptualizing how art might deepen our capacities for moral discernment, that is, how art facilitates embodied ways of knowing. But such a way of thinking about affectivity can too easily ignore how our affective responses to art are oftentimes made possible because of prior affective commitments: we are moved because we are already affectively formed to move accordingly. In my saying as much, one might think I am ultimately delimiting the power of art; in a way, I am. That is not to deny, however, the reality that the experience of art—its perception, appreciation, and even participation in its creation—can have profound affective influence on persons' lives (again, via facilitation of embodied knowing, impressing on its audience alternative visions of life by enlivening the imagination and so forth); I do not dispute such influence throughout this book. But the point I hope to also make clear is that such affective impact is never a unidirectional process. If art is indeed morally impactful—and thus moves us in particular moral directions—it does so not only on account of art's "intrinsic" moral power but also in constitutive relation to its audiences' particular and prior affective formation. My claim is that unless we pay closer attention to the formative role that prior affective formation plays in how one perceives, receives, or responds to art, then we lack the conceptual tools to better account for how any single art object can lead to radically divergent reactions. It is rarely the case that art objects are received universally, even rarer for such objects to move persons in ways intended (if the art object was indeed created with such intentionality).

In various points of the book I highlight multiple instances of art installations or particular art pieces leading to unexpected outcomes. Such instances do not imply that art is morally irrelevant (and thus should be kept to its own so-called aesthetical sphere), but it does require that we shift and expand our understanding of how art is morally important. The argument that I advance in this study is that art's moral importance requires that we first understand the extent to which persons' opinions about aesthetic activities (whether positive or negative) and their moral responses to art (or maybe even lack of a response) are on account of what one believes are important for a life that is good. Central to the force of this claim is that the affections are more than the emotions. More accurately, the affections are the moral life, or the constellation of dispositions, habits, or experiences that inform, shape, or constitute moral judgment and action, and thus make the moral life what it is. In short, aesthetics gains its moral meaning and power precisely because the affections are not necessarily the same as the emotions, which complicates notions of affections that are strictly aesthetic (e.g., modernist notions). This way of conceptualizing the affections, as distinguishable from the emotions, also challenges theological-ethical discourse on aesthetics to think beyond art's capacity to embody knowledge and to pay greater attention to (and ultimately have greater appreciation for) art's capacity to engender difference and argument.

So long as we appreciate the fuller sense of the affections that I have just invoked, then disagreement is best regarded as a constitutive feature of art's moral power, or so I argue. We should expect a pluralism of responses to art if responses to it cannot be untethered from its audiences' particular affective (or, more precisely, moral) formation. Such normative expectation does not diminish art's moral salience but instead augments it by reframing the nature of moral disagreements and misunderstandings that the arts generate: rather than regarding such disagreements as simple differences in personal taste and aesthetic style, misunderstandings of what the art object is about, or a matter of some people "just not getting it" while others do, such disagreements are, more significantly and constructively, reflective of competing visions of the good life, about which forms of life are meritorious and which are less so. From this vantage point, we can think of the arts as arenas for moral communication and contestation (even if they are created, produced, or put on display without such intentionality). Correlatively, this transforms the arts into indispensable sites through which we gain a sense of what is morally possible for society. In short, to ignore the arts is to ignore one of the more vivid lenses through which society can understand and assess its moral condition and its prospects: the limits and possibilities for community, mutual understanding, and solidarity and the virtues and practices necessary for a society—one that is expectant of difference—to flourish.

OUTLINE OF CHAPTERS

So far, I have made a good deal out of recent theological-ethical efforts at retrieving aesthetics for ethics, but I have only done so in the abstract. The task of naming these efforts more specifically falls primarily on chapters 1 and 2. Approaches to aesthetics in contemporary Christian ethics can be delineated along the following lines: the turn to literature and the turn to beauty. Both turns can be conceptualized as framing the arts (activities of artistic creation and perception or enjoyment) as forms of ethical practice. For the turn to literature (chapter 1), it is the aesthetic activity or practice of reading—especially the reading of narratives and novels—that is an integral or formative practice of moral discernment and ultimately judgment and action. For the turn to beauty (chapter 2), the focus is less on reading than on the broader practices of aesthetic perception: reading as well as looking at, listening to, and, more generally, experiencing the arts.

The turns to literature and beauty can also be specified as "consequentialist" accounts of aesthetics and ethics, following the nomenclature of Marcia Muelder Eaton.[20] I follow her characterization to underline a kind of directional momentum that the turns to both literature and beauty assume. Aesthetic practices such as reading and looking are not just parallel to the skills and practices of moral discernment. More strongly, the arts effect moral formation and moral change; they are morally efficacious. And while the specifics of how aesthetic practices effect such moral change and transformation will differ from the multitude of proponents of each turn (whether from postliberal, platonic, liberationist, or Catholic social teaching proponents, among many others), what weaves them together into a single tapestry is the following twofold theme. First, aesthetic practices are reflective of the nature of moral knowing, which is more than what Kantian forms of rationality assume or allow, and second and more provocatively, aesthetic practices are integral to how we in fact know what is morally required and good. Thus, while reading, looking, and listening are morally consequential activities, this is to say more accurately that aesthetic practices are morally necessary.

In outlining the consequentialist character of contemporary aesthetics and ethics discourse in Christian ethics, my aims are twofold. First, it is an attempt to assemble notable approaches to aesthetics in Christian ethics into a more definite discursive tradition (or tradition of inquiry) and to weave between them interpretative threads that show the questions and themes that are driving this tradition.[21] This attempt is the first of its kind, and that such an attempt has not been pursued before is remarkable given, as I noted above, the multiple moves toward literature and beauty in contemporary Christian ethics. But as I shall show, a tradition is indeed discernable, and this tradition warrants wider appreciation and consideration. In that respect, the two opening chapters of this book are my efforts at identifying the main interlocutors of this tradition and defining its central thematic parameters and connections to the wider concerns in theological as well as religious ethics. I see this present study as not only coalescing and drawing attention to this tradition of moral inquiry but also adding to it constructively, pushing its boundaries. Second, in articulating this tradition of inquiry, my aim is to also affirm the general intentions of the turns to both literature and beauty (that art effects moral change and in that regard is morally consequential) while identifying a specific line of inquiry that needs to be taken up in order to move this discourse forward. If the arts can indeed offer alternative points of view and complicate mindsets and preconceptions, all toward facilitating concrete moral action, then what kind of moral action? Can the arts engage our imagination and move our emotions and will in the specific direction of justice, mutuality, and solidarity, or, conversely, do they make us more susceptible to uncritical moral visions, to illiberal prejudices and values?

These questions mapped out in chapters 1 and 2 underscore the challenges to a consequentialist casting of the arts, but they do not necessarily show that such a casting is wholly suspect and that aesthetics and ethics must remain separate. A consequentialist account is possible, but as I indicated earlier and as chapters 1 and 2 will demonstrate further, such an account will require a precise, nuanced description of the mechanics of the movement from aesthetic experience to moral experience, with a sustained focus on reconstructing the nature of affectivity as something including but also more than the emotions.

The groundwork for this reconstruction begins in chapter 3, where I turn to a number of theorists of aesthetics including Elaine Scarry (on her idea of beauty and aesthetic perception as that which elicits focused, repetitive attention through artistic mediums) and Eaton (on her idea of the arts as requisite moral skills for democratic community and citizenship). The importance of these two thinkers is rooted in their efforts at paying close attention to how aesthetic objects (and, correlatively, aesthetic perception) function or operate in the concrete, or the ways in which various art objects and forms interact with their audiences. They in large part can be seen as pushing the descriptive question of the kind of work that art objects in themselves can accomplish before attempting to theorize why the arts can do whatever it is they can in fact do.

With that in mind, we will see in chapter 3 that art in itself is capable of a good deal of moral work. Yet, it is striking that both Scarry and Eaton are unable to articulate the moral work of aesthetic perception independent of a particular conception of the moral life or theory of the good. In other words, description and theory run into each other, wherein one cannot engage in the former without also assuming the latter and to an extent vice versa. So, while the arts in themselves are capable of substantive moral work, that work is inherently limited; art alone can only do so much (even art that is created with a specific moral intent, that is, to encourage, incite, or move persons toward a definite end). Instead, what explains the many normative claims that we might have about the moral power of the arts is dependent on seeing the arts in a particular way within a larger account of the good. This claim is given concrete visibility in the role the arts play in US political life as agents of remarkable social transformation and inter- and intracommunal disagreement, division, and violence.

In chapter 4, I propose further that if accounting for the moral work of aesthetic perception apart from a theory of the good is an untenable project, then we will need to revisit and revise the claims we will have first encountered in chapters 1 and 2 regarding the relationship between the arts and emotions. A focus on aesthetics alerts us to this relationship with particular urgency, underscoring the limitations of accounts of moral reasoning that tend to curtail rather than elevate the cognitive role that emotions can and should play. (This point is underscored especially by theological-ethical studies that advocate for the moral power of beauty, as we shall see in chapter 2.) However, the relationship between the arts and emotions run aground if it reflects the misunderstanding that emotions can be moved independent of a person's disposition of character. As I will demonstrate through a critical reading of select texts in aesthetic formalism or modernism (from Clive Bell and Peter de Bolla in particular), this misunderstanding often arises in part from the common practice of referring to emotions and affections interchangeably, but they ought not be referred to in this manner.

On that last matter, Thomas Aquinas's account of emotions and affections, specifically the distinction between the two, proves instructive. Aquinas's insights are sharpened when we turn to Jonathan Edwards's emphasis on affections over emotions. In his delineation between notional knowledge and affective knowledge, Edwards demonstrates that our emotions fail to recognize and support moral goodness unless our agency is disposed in a particular way. Disposition in this context signals the significance of virtue and character, but for Edwards the affections, with their connotation of the unity of heart, mind, and practice, capture more fully what it means to be persons who are disposed toward a particular moral vision more so than the familiar language of the virtues. Such a position sharpens the descriptive observations of the limitations and possibilities of the kind of moral work the arts are capable of, as mapped out in chapter 3. While the arts are capable of substantive moral work, which is enabled by moving the emotions of their audiences, that work is ultimately ambiguous or, more specifically, leads to a pluralism of effects precisely because the affectivity of those perceiving, reacting to, or otherwise engaging with the arts vary. Just as what we perceive, feel, value, and ultimately do are inextricably tied to our affectivity, so too is the moral force of the arts in our lives; it is inextricably tied to our affectivity, to the moral vision we are disposed to.

Chapter 4's account of the arts, emotions, and affectivity illumines why the arts can lead to indifference or even violence (even if certain artworks are intended for the opposite) and why the arts can also lead to solidarity (even if certain artworks are intended to divide and exclude). The intention of an artwork matters less inasmuch as perceivers of art are emotionally moved not so much by the artwork itself but instead by the perceivers' affectivity, which is to say the larger valuational motivations through which one's emotions are formed. That art leads to a pluralism of outcomes does not undermine the moral power and significance of the arts but rather the opposite: the very fact that individuals and communities of persons react to art so fervently one way or another is indicative of how important aesthetics (or a particular account of what is good and bad art, appropriate and inappropriate art) is to our various views of the good life. As I noted earlier, life is difficult to imagine without the arts, and thus we should not be surprised that the arts—including debates about them—are front and center in all arenas of our lives.

If the arts are morally powerful because they are central to so many of our conceptions of the good life and if that explains why the arts can move persons toward both division and unity, violence and cooperation, then how should we think about aesthetics as a source in Christian ethics? Chapter 5 responds to this question by assessing the relationship between the arts and social capital (or the norms, networks, or goods that facilitate social cooperation, mutuality, and community) and conceptions of art as sources of moral lessons. My argument will be that the constructive contributions of both ways of thinking about art are limited, given their inattention to art's inherent moral pluralism. Thus, rather than viewing the arts as necessarily promoting social capital or, as others will argue, pivotal to moral education, the arts are best regarded as case studies on the kind of moral limitations that difference imposes on communities.

This argument specifies what I noted earlier about what is missing in much of contemporary theological-ethical discussions on aesthetics. What is missing is the notion of the arts as the cultural medium through which we can better understand what is morally possible and not possible. To see specific aesthetic objects (especially particular perceptions, reactions, and responses to the arts) as snapshots of a particular community's perspectives on the good life offers glimpses into not only the kinds of competing moral visions within society but also the extent to which those competing moral visions are incommensurate. In that respect, the arts, as the final chapter will conceive of them, provide a way of assessing the limits and possibilities of moral reasoning, the contextuality of moral discernment, and the need for moral thinking that is dialogical and dialectical. While the kind of moral pluralism that art effects, as I argue, underscores the contingent nature of moral reasoning, such pluralism also underscores the extent to which the possibility of mutual understanding and agreement and the idea of "public deliberation" will be dependent on particular habits and skills of moral attention, reflection, and discourse that take seriously such pluralism.

In sum, while the arts, as the final chapter will argue, do not necessarily prove that an aesthetically rich community is one that is richer in social capital or has greater access to moral insights, an aesthetically rich community ought to be encouraged and supported inasmuch as it reminds us of the kind of world we in fact inhabit and what it takes to live faithfully in such a world. This ultimately points to a theological statement on the human condition—its fallenness—and the need therefore to theologically prioritize moral humility, fallibilism, tolerance, and generosity. Those are the virtues appropriate to a world of competing moral visions. Art is neither inherently countercultural nor progressive and democratic. But the arts—their moral pluralism—can instruct us on the challenges to moral transformation and solidarity, the persistence of moral conflict, and the requisite habits of mind and speech that allow us to navigate, with realistic hope, a fallen world, fragmented and tribal.

Before moving on to the chapters themselves, it bears noting what I have avoided so far: the term "theological aesthetics" and characterizing this book as one in that genre. The reason for this avoidance is not that theological aesthetics is unimportant; while this book is a study in aesthetics and ethics, it is also a study in theological aesthetics. As we will see especially in chapters 4 and 5, my response to the kind of question and problem that I have outlined in this introduction, which I will outline further in the opening chapters of this book, will be rooted in a particular rendering of Edwards's theological aesthetics.

It is well known among Edwardsean scholars that central to Edwards's theological vision is the beauty of God's being. So, it may be odd that I am intentionally shying away from describing this book as a work in theological aesthetics. By the time we get to chapter 5, however, it will be clear, or so I hope, that a theological aesthetics, one that is indebted to Edwards, has been operative throughout the book. It will also hopefully be clear that my response to what I propose is the central problem in the contemporary theological-ethical turns to literature and beauty cannot necessarily do without a kind of Edwardsean theological aesthetics, or an Edwardsean-shaped theological account of art, especially on what art can or cannot do.

But that only raises the question of why not couch what I am doing in this book as a study in theological aesthetics, especially a study in Edwardsean theological aesthetics. First, as will be apparent by the time we get to the end of chapter 4, my turn to Edwards's theological aesthetics will not follow the usual playbook. I will feature less-trodden aspects of his theological aesthetics. The dimensions of his thought that I believe are critical to the kind of question that contemporary theological ethics underappreciates—the question of art's moral pluralism—is his delineation of affections and emotions and thus, more broadly, his theological account of the self (or anthropology). The Edwardsean theological anthropology that will anchor this book begins with some distinctions that Aquinas makes and builds on those distinctions by way of Edwards's vision of divine sovereignty and the nature of religious and moral knowledge (in other words, the affections). Edwards's delineation of affections from emotions and his account of the self are usually not the focus of or, at least, the starting points in studies of his theological aesthetics, formally speaking; the more typical starting point is his doctrines of God and the trinity and then moving to their implications for virtue.[22] So, in "avoiding" his theological aesthetics, I am in actuality attempting to draw attention to it but in a new light. This alternative way of approaching his theological aesthetics, I believe, underscores the constructive relevance of Edwards for contemporary theological ethics and especially modernist discourses on aesthetics in a manner that the more conventional renderings of his theological aesthetics perhaps make opaque.

This brings me to the second reason for avoiding theological aesthetics talk, which is that theological aesthetics in its more traditional construals, unlike this present study, focuses typically on a combination of at least three kinds of questions. The first is what we can call the relationship between Christianity and representation. For instance, is the Christian tradition anti-icons, images, or material representations of the divine? To what extent should Christian faith and imagination be textually, visually, and aurally oriented? Is Christian belief better expressed aesthetically rather than propositionally? Are there specific kinds of artworks or genres that are more appropriate to belief and worship?[23] A second set of questions can be cast as more doctrinally focused: Are there aesthetic concepts that are more fittingly descriptive of who God is? Is God knowable through art, whether natural or artifactual? Are certain kinds of art forms more revelatory or disclosive of who God is?[24] A third kind of question pertains to the form of the Christian life. For example, is there a particular style or aesthetic to the Christian life? More specifically, can the Christian life be accounted for through the aesthetical language of form, and what difference would doing so make to our understanding of the Christian life? Additionally, are there particular artworks or art forms or, more broadly, a particular "aesthetic" or specific aesthetic experiences (of beauty wonder, awe, and so forth) that speak to what the Christian life is or ought to be or that helps us to better discern the nature of the Christian life, what it means to be persons of faith, to love God and neighbor?[25]

The point in mentioning at least these three sets of questions is to indicate how my approach to theological aesthetics in this book reflects perhaps a fourth set of questions that moves beyond examining the appropriateness and meaning of aesthetics for theological reflection and Christian existence and toward the lived mechanics of aesthetics' moral capabilities. In other words, I am primarily interested in the shift from whether art is theologically and ethically relevant to how belief and practice (specifically moral action and change) are in fact actualized through art. There have been some in theological aesthetics who have taken up the challenge of this shift in questions (and these voices I will refer to in various chapters of this book), but for the most part, pursuing this shift has not been the principal work of contemporary theological aesthetics, if I may be so bold to claim. *Art and Moral Change: A Reexamination* demonstrates why such a shift is necessary, however. And in so doing, works to expand the range of questions that should concern theological aesthetics and thus reframe what theological aesthetics might mean (or how it should be approached) for ethical discourse. When it comes to the problem of art's capacity for moral action, change, and transformation, we will need to approach it from different angles of inquiry, ones that ultimately focus less on determining the theological status and content of art and more on the ways in which our actual lived experiences of art complicate our theological understanding of what art can or cannot do. Such a way of proceeding, then, circles us back to what I noted earlier: that an Edwardsean account of the self will be key to making sense of what art can and cannot do in the sphere of the ethical. More generally, if we want to move beyond the question of whether art is relevant to ethics and focus on the question of how art changes minds and actions, then we will need to reimagine theological aesthetics through the lens of theological anthropology.

Finally, for readers who are looking to see if I provide a guide on what counts as good art or bad art and, specifically, what theological rubric (or, again, theological aesthetics) can provide such assessments, there will be some disappointment with this book, especially among those who may be caught up in our current culture wars and those who may feel that "traditional" faith is under assault by secularization. This is not a book that will provide a practical guide for such judgments.

This is not to say that I do not think that there is such a thing as good art and bad art or offensive art and edifying art and that Christians should refrain from advocating for and embracing certain kinds of art and art forms over others. But delving into those questions, I believe, often leads us astray, by which I mean they distract us from a fundamental reality. I will say more about this in detail toward the end of this study, but for now, suffice it to say that my primary interest is in drawing our attention to the question of why we react to art the way that we do. What is particularly interesting to me is the extent to which so-called good art and bad art lead to plural responses, even if the intention of the artwork is to elicit a particular response (or at least hopes for a particular response in its perceiver). My contention will be that understanding the nature of such pluralism necessarily leads us to the primacy of disposition or affections in our response to art. Thus, if there is such a thing as good or bad art, it cannot be determined apart from one's disposition or affections. If this is so, then we must be ready to expect not only pluralistic conceptions of good or bad art (since affections are plural, not singular) but also heated disagreements (maybe even conflicts) over what is good or bad art or what makes an artwork offensive or inoffensive, religiously and morally speaking. In that respect, while we should not feel restrained from making judgments about artworks as either good or bad and trying to intellectually persuade others of the rightness of our judgments from our own dispositional or affective angle of vision, only focusing our energies on what is good or bad art is too naive, maybe nostalgic, and inevitably counterproductive. We perhaps do better by focusing our energies on discerning which social virtues and practices will help us to better live with the kind of pluralism and disagreement that art—of all sorts—inevitably engenders.

NOTES

1. de Bolla, *Art Matters*, 5–7. See also Baumgarten, Ästhetik; Kant, *Observations on the Feeling of the Beautiful and Sublime*; and Kant, *Critique of Judgment.*
2. See Wilkerson, "Trouble Right Here in Cincinnati."
3. See Niebuhr, "Anger over Work Evokes Anti-Catholic Shadow, and Mary's Power as Icon."
4. See Arenson, "An Artwork at Yale May Not be Real, but the Furor Is"; and Yabroff, "The Arts: Exhibits Designed to Shock."
5. See Huizenga, "The New York Philharmonic Plays Pyongyang."
6. See Smith, "In a Mattress, a Lever for Art and Politics."
7. See Kennedy, "White Artist's Painting of Emmett Till at Whitney Biennial Draws Protests."
8. See Rodriguez and Collins, "Statues Toppled throughout US in Protests against Racism."
9. See Kinzer, "Lilly Heir Makes $100 Million Bequest to Poetry Magazine." Or, consider the publicity received for the Italian fashion designer Giorgio Armani's $1 million donation for the creation of the Armani Arts Institute for the New York public school system on February 17, 2009.
10. Kaufman, "MacKenzie Scott's Multimillion-Dollar Message."
11. For instance, in 2009 the former governor of New Jersey, Jon S. Corzine, in response to historic projected state budget deficits, proposed cutting about $6 million in arts funding, a 27 percent reduction, in violation of New Jersey law on state funding for arts and culture. The response from both New Jersey Democrats and Republicans was severe. See Friedman, "Corzine Proposes Cutting Arts Funding below Required Minimum." Similar

responses reemerged on a more national scale with proposals by the Trump administration to eliminate funding for the National Endowment for the Arts. See, for instance, Bowley, "What If Trump Really Does End Money for the Arts?" The threat of governmental cuts to the arts was exacerbated by the COVID-19 pandemic, from New York City and Philadelphia to the West Coast, including cities such as San Diego. See, for example, Dafoe, "Bill De Blasio's 2021 Budget Would See a Significant Decrease in Funding for New York's Museums, Already Hit Hard by the Lockdown"; Dafoe, "Arts Leaders Fear Philadelphia's Planned Budget Cuts Will Completely 'Decimate the Grassroots Cultural Scene'"; and City News Service, "San Diego Proposes Major Budget Cuts to Offset COVID-19 Revenue Losses."

12. Wolterstorff, *Art in Action*, 4.
13. While chapters 1 and 2 of this book will highlight the number of theological-ethical studies on aesthetics, their numbers are minuscule compared to the number of essays and books that are published dealing with the ethics of war, economic ethics, health care, and biomedical ethics, among other areas in social ethics.
14. For instance, a popular website on middle school education asserts that "a STEM lesson provides a perfect kickoff for an ethics discussion, since a scenario generally accompanies the real-world problem kids are trying to solve. From there, ethics principles and practices can be built naturally into the lesson." Jolly, "Teaching Ethics Should Be a STEM Essential."
15. See, for instance, Dziemidok, "Artistic Formalism." Postmodern critiques of aesthetic formalism has been especially influential. See, for instance, Gall, "Aesthetic Problems, Realist Solutions."
16. Greenberg was one of the earliest art critics to have employed the term "modernism." See Gaiger and Wood, *Art of the Twentieth Century*, xx. For a helpful survey of the various schools of aesthetic formalism, see Curtin, "Varieties of Aesthetic Formalism."
17. Castronovo, *Beautiful Democracy*, 29.
18. Wolterstorff, *Art in Action*, 24. Our views of art are "bewitched" by them, he asserts. Wolterstorff's views on this will be discussed further in chapter 3.
19. For instance, consider the paintings by John Sonsini of Spanish-speaking day laborers in California and his disavowal of what others think are statements of anti-immigration policies of the Trump administration. "In the current climate, people sometimes see themes of immigration in Sonsini's work. Men leaving home—working hard for money to send back to their families, separation for sustenance. Sonsini denies it. His art, he says, is not political. 'I definitely am not trying to make statements,' Sonsini says. All he's making are paintings." Stamberg, "Artist Says His Portraits of Day Laborers Are Paintings—Not Statements."
20. See Eaton, *Aesthetics and the Good Life*, chap. 7; and Eaton, *Merit, Aesthetic and Ethical*, chap. 5. As I will note, not consequentialist in the utilitarian sense but rather in the sense that they do something specific in the realm of ethics, they are morally efficacious.
21. In this way, I follow Susan Moller Okin's notion of tradition as a "'not-yet-completed narrative'" or "living argument" about particular goods as opposed to a tradition revolving around a set canon of texts. Okin, *Justice, Gender, and the Family*, 61; and Stout, *Democracy and Tradition*, 135–39.
22. See, for example, Crisp and Strobel, *Jonathan Edwards*, chap. 2. See also Delattre, "Religious Ethics Today," 70–71; and Delattre, *Beauty and Sensibility in the Thought of Jonathan Edwards*.

23. See, for example, Brown, *Religious Aesthetics*; and Dyrness, *Visual Faith*.
24. See, for instance, Viladesau, *Theological Aesthetics*; Sherry, *Spirit and Beauty*; Farley, *Faith and Beauty*; Barbeau and McGowin, *God and Wonder*; and Thiel, *Now and Forever*.
25. See, for instance, García-Rivera, *The Community of the Beautiful*; and Weichbrodt, *Redeeming Vision*.

1

LITERATURE AND THEOLOGICAL ETHICS

Is the ubiquity of the arts in daily life indicative of widely held assumptions that the good life entails having certain kinds of experiences, specifically aesthetic ones? Marcia Muelder Eaton thinks so and has observed further that such assumptions suggest an inherent connection between aesthetics and ethics and that without the arts the moral life would be impoverished.[1] Yet, what that connection might be, or why we might assume a good life to be one that is also an aesthetically rich one, is not necessarily clear if even acknowledged at all. Even if the pandemic lockdowns of 2020 and their consequent shuttering of bookstores, movie theaters, concert halls, music festivals, art galleries, and museums have revealed the extent to which we desire, love, and enjoy the arts, that revelation did not necessarily include a finer, more explicit sense of why the arts are important to the good life. "Crises makes art even more crucial to people's lives," an art critic wrote in assessing the future of classical music concert halls and dance venues in the wake of COVID-19. "'We are a necessity, not a luxury,'" proclaimed Christine Goerko, a soprano with the Metropolitan Opera, in the summer of 2020. "'Congregating and creating art together is one of the more human things we do,'" added the president and CEO of Lincoln Center.[2] But if the arts are important because they bring persons and communities together, then that is also true of sports and restaurants, hence the collective laments over their suspension or restricted operation too during the COVID-19 pandemic. But if communities have mourned the closing, some temporary but many permanent, of art venues, sporting arenas, coffee shops, and food halls alike, then what makes art uniquely important to the good life? What makes art important in ways that distinguish itself from a baseball game or dining out? While the ubiquity of the arts, or at least the ubiquitous desire to enjoy them, may intimate a collective sense of their importance to our lives, that sense remains unexamined, and the challenge in articulating that importance persists. Does arts importance necessarily mean that the good life is dependent on opportunities to enjoy art, including opportunities to create art? More generally, does it mean that without aesthetic experiences, a good life is not possible or, at the very least, less available? If so, then how might we explain that necessity? What is it about aesthetic experience that makes it a constitutive feature of the good life?

In this chapter, I begin assessing potential resources to address these questions within theological ethics. Two trajectories in theological ethics readily recommend themselves. The first is, as I shall refer to it, the turn to literature. The second is the turn to beauty. They are not mutually exclusive trajectories, but they are not identical either. At the very least, the multiple voices that constitute each trajectory respond to the question of whether aesthetics is necessary for the good life (and, more specifically, the task of ethics) in the affirmative. This affirmation in the turn to beauty will be assessed in chapter 2; this affirmation in the turn to literature is addressed in the present chapter. In each case, I will attend to the nature of this affirmation and whether it is ultimately successful.

The turn to literature in theological ethics can be categorized as consequentialist, as opposed to separatist, in its approach to aesthetics and ethics.[3] This turn is consequentialist in the sense that aesthetic experiences—particularly the practice of reading—is taken as effecting a particular way of thinking and ultimately a particular way of being in the world. The works of Stanley Hauerwas and Diane M. Yeager, specifically their advocacy of the novel as an indispensable site for moral learning, are two important consequentialist conceptions of aesthetics and ethics, or so I will propose. My aim is neither a systematic overview nor a sustained critique of their advocacy of the novel but rather to stress particular features of their advocacy as points of departure for examining other key accounts and thus to open up a broader view of the kind of concerns, commitments, and problems framing the conversation on literature's moral efficacy in theological ethics. What we will see is that while the turn to literature broadens our understanding of ethics and the resources (aesthetic resources) that are essential to the task of ethics, the turn to literature runs into two interrelated questions that underscore the type of challenge that confronts the project of linking aesthetics to moral thinking, action, and change. The first question is whether reading masks literary instances of illiberalism and thus threatens the reinscription of such values in the lives of its readers. The second question is whether the turn to literature sufficiently accounts for those instances in which reading (and, by association, other aesthetic practices) indeed leads to illiberal outcomes despite expectations to the contrary. The first question can be construed as one internal to the conversation on literature's moral efficacy in theological ethics, revealing the diversity and critical interaction of positions within this conversation. The second question might be construed as more external to the conversation insofar as it is one that is addressed ambivalently if at all.

NOVELS, VIRTUE, AND MORAL DISCERNMENT

Discourse on the moral import of aesthetics has been traditionally muted in Christian ethical reflection. But with the renewal of virtue ethics and the desire for alternative accounts of Kantian-based moral agency, the moral salience of literature, particularly the literary form of the novel and the correlative practice of reading, has gained heightened attention. Maria Antonaccio offers a helpful summary of this attention given to the novel. First, many "claim that the novel allows us to identify with characters unlike ourselves." Others claim that the novel "permits us to regard our lives and conduct from a changed perspective."[4] Both are versions of the claim "that by engaging our moral sensibility and judgment, the act of reading itself is 'exemplary for conduct.'" Stanley Hauerwas's and Diane Yeager's treatments of literature and ethics are typical of this claim, or so I will propose. Both will diverge slightly with respect to their views on the novel's effect on the reader, that is, on what kind of exemplary conduct the novel presses on the reader and how the novel effects such exemplary conduct. Nevertheless, both will maintain that the novel is hardly neutral and immaterial when it comes to forming moral knowledge and ultimately moral action in part because of the nature of moral reasoning itself and also in part due to the kind of moral content that particular kinds of novels communicate.

Hauerwas, one of the pioneers in the retrieval of narrative for contemporary Christian ethics, argues that through stories agency is made possible:

> To be agents requires a directionality that involves the development of character and virtue. Our character is the result of our sustained attention to the world that gives a coherence to our intentionality. Such attention is formed and given content by the stories through which we have learned to form the story of our lives. To be moral persons is to allow stories to be told through us so that our manifold activities gain a coherence that allows us to claim them for our own. The significance of stories is the significance of character for the moral life as our experience itself, if it is to be coherent, is but an incipient story.[5]

How stories form our character and thus bring coherence to our moral agency, that is, dispose us to a particular mode of life, is parsed out more specifically in Hauerwas's discussion on how reading novels can provide an account of morality that takes constancy and forgiveness as its primary virtues. In this discussion, we are given a glimpse into how Hauerwas's retrieval of narrative for Christian ethics can be counted as a more specific retrieval of aesthetics—albeit a specific kind of aesthetic experience, that of reading—for Christian ethics.

Novels not only serve an epistemological function but also enable performative capacities, having "the power to elicit our sympathy and thus change our attitudes"[6] The novel, therefore, is instructive and formative of virtue:

> Thus, the very reading of the novel is a moral training. By forcing our eyes from one word to the next, one sentence to the next, one paragraph to the next, we are stretched through a narrative world that gives us the skills to make something of our own lives. To make something of our own lives requires our being able to locate our story in an unfolding narrative so that we can go on. Without such a story, we lack the means of constancy, and without forgiveness we lack the means of making our lives our own. . . . Novels are the means, though not the only means, to be sure, that we have to attain the skills of locating and telling our individual stories, not as instances of some grand schemes, but as uniquely ours. Just to the extent they are ours, they make constancy possible.[7]

Emphasis on the last clause—"they make constancy possible"—is warranted as a strong indication of the consequentialist undertones of Hauerwas's conceptualization of the novel, for "possible" in this context is not a straightforward connotation of maybe or perhaps. Instead, the underlying sentiment is that the novel is an indispensable site for constancy's acquisition. As Hauerwas claims in the first half of the citation above, without the narrative of the novel, the skills of living lives of constancy and forgiveness are elusive; "the very reading of the novel is a moral training."

Though Hauerwas does not make such a claim unqualifiedly, the extent to which he is willing to ascribe such moral power to the novel is striking. Inasmuch as they make constancy and forgiveness possible, Hauerwas is unwilling to entertain seriously what he observes as the "fashionable [denial that] the novel has any direct [moral] import" and that novels should be written and read as "ends in themselves rather than attempts to help us be good." Furthermore, he finds specious criticisms of mediocrity and sentimentality in art and literature when they are "subjected to moralistic purposes" rather than "depict[ing] life as it is."[8] For Hauerwas, that distinction is a false one and too easily dismisses the formative power of the novel. Finally, Hauerwas finds the novels of Anthony Trollope as well as Jane Austen as exemplifying the dual commitment to both reality and moral relevance without sentimentalism.

Hauerwas tells us that Trollope understood himself as a "realistic novelist," endeavoring to offer characters "with their good and their bad."[9] In so doing, Trollope thought that he "in no way contradicted the moral purpose of his art."[10] Rather, in portraying characters in their full reality, Trollope hoped to "instruct us morally" by drawing us to identify with his characters "and thus learn some of our own proclivities." Moreover, in this identification Trollope hoped that his readers would gain a clearer picture or sense of how the virtues, particularly constancy and forgiveness, are in reality operative. "Novels such as Trollope's are possible only when they manifest the forgiveness which he commends through their pages. His ability to depict characters 'realistically' entails a spirit that has the power to form an art sufficient to shape our response to forgive in a similar fashion. We are able to do so because we have learned literally to see another sympathetically rather than sentimentally or with resentment."[11]

To the extent that we can identify with Trollope's characters, following their lives occasions the opportunity to learn about particular virtues. But it is not a simplistic identification—in the sense of the novel's characters' lives are just like ours—but rather identification insofar as they engender a way of seeing the lives of the characters as worthy of our response and commitment. Thus, in this way the characters' lives become a means of making particular virtues meaningful to the reader, teaching us the skills that allow us to live lives of virtue that are, as Hauerwas states, similar to those depicted in the novel but in a way that is particular to our concrete here and now.[12]

Yeager's account of the novel and ethics resonates with the consequentialist spirit of Hauerwas's advocacy of the novel, but she accounts for the novel's moral efficacy in a slightly different way in terms of its ends. For Yeager, the novel provides moral knowledge that is essential to social action and transformation and emphasizes less the formation of a life of virtue. In other words, the novel clarifies and widens moral thinking so that we can be more sharply attuned to the kind of moral decisions that are required of us. But such moral work is not possible with any kind of novel; the kind of novel she has in mind is the social novel, which, she states, "advances . . . social solidarity and social change."[13]

For an example of a "good social novel," Yeager draws attention to the 1889 novel by William Dean Howells, *A Hazard of New Fortunes*, a tale of several New York families' literary and business travails in the Gilded Age. Though she resists a strict consequentialist approach to the novel and ethics in her persistent denial that mass exposure to social novels can by itself solve various social ills of the day, Yeager is steadfast in her belief that the social novel has a formative role to play in advancing social solidarity and change.

The social novel—the good social novel—"shows . . . the complex social movement by which a community's sense of justice and duty is revised."[14] As such, the good social novel reveals the necessary ingredients for moral revision or change. But the good social novel also facilitates that very change—it "actively contribute[s] to that revision in the social world of its readers"—by "contribut[ing] to the creation of social conscience."[15] To be more specific, when morally successful, the social novel informs moral discernment by relaying to our conscience what we had not grasped (or did not want to grasp and confront or refused to do) previously. Thus, the good social novel not only clarifies or reinforces what we ought to do but also gives access to moral priorities that cannot be had or, at the very least, cannot be obtained easily apart from the novel. Consequently, the good social novel displays the "simple power of story," that is, "the power to plunge us into worlds we otherwise would not know, thus pushing back our moral horizons, laying bare the forces to which we are subject, and drawing us into sympathetic identification with people unlike ourselves in situations we might wish to avoid."[16]

Yeager does not expressly discuss the novel's role in forming character and instilling particular virtues; it is unclear whether such a way of thinking about the novel is a primary concern. Still, Yeager's description of the moral force of the social novel does share some basic features with Hauerwas's approach to the novel, particularly his discussion of Trollope. So, Yeager's reference to the novel as "drawing us into sympathetic identification with people unlike ourselves" resonates with Hauerwas's claim that the realistic novel's moral force is in its capacity to "see another sympathetically," as we saw above. And just as that sympathetic identification, for Yeager, clarifies as well as reminds us of the kind of moral posture that we ought to commit to, whether we knew this prior to reading or not or whether we just lacked the will to do so, so too for Hauerwas in his advocacy of the novel as that which reveals the truths about ourselves and our communities despite our tendency to ignore them. As he asserts in reference to another novel, one by the English author Richard Adams, *Watership Down* (1972), "the necessity to hide the dangers of our world make it impossible to confront those aspects of our social order which impose unequal burdens on others. Our conspiracy for safety forces us to see our neighbor as a stranger. Good and just societies require a narrative, therefore, which helps them know the truth about existence and fight the constant temptation to self-deception."[17]

Common to both Hauerwas and Yeager is the emphasis placed on the moral force of literary depictions of reality as it is. According to Yeager, Howell, as "a major force in the shift in American literature from 'romance' to realism,"[18] rejected the tradition of Christian social novels of the Gilded Age that "falsified human experience" as a means of eliciting the moral response of its readers:

> The conventional assumption was that fiction, particularly if it was to be morally inspiring, must show life as it ought to be rather than as it is. The protagonist should be a hero or heroine readers would strive to emulate. . . . What he [Howell] objected to were their fictional strategies, which he considered to be incompatible with the end they sought. In defending his critical judgments and defining an alternative model of narrative fiction, he defended "art for humanity's sake" against both art for art's sake and lying sentimentality—the first because it retreated from responsibility into "unmoral" aestheticism and the second because it falsified the human condition.[19]

Drawing lessons from Howell as well as from the novelist Jonathan Franzen, whom she regards as a modern-day compatriot to Howell, Yeager argues that the social novel is morally relevant inasmuch as it illumines the complexity of human life, individual and communal, in a fictive style. The thesis motivating this position is that the powerful portrayal of such complexity contains within itself the power to elicit the difficult questions about the nature of our social circumstances, our life together. For Franzen, according to Yeager, it is this power that "lay[s] claim to [the] lasting attention" of the good social novel. Thus, in an almost similar way to Trollope's emphasis on the priority of portraying characters realistically—in their "good and their bad"—according to Yeager, Franzen as well as Howell "believed that change begins in understanding; . . . [and this] requires a meticulous, true representation of what is actually the case."[20] "To know what is the case is to want and envision something better; to envision it is to try to bring it about."[21] Hauerwas might add that one successfully envisions the story when one makes that story one's own; as he famously asserts with respect to the story of the Gospel, Jesus's story is a social ethic, and the Christian's task is to inhabit that story and be formed by it.[22]

The confidence Yeager places on the power of the social novel for moral understanding is underscored further in her final appeals to Henry Sidgwick's moral thought. In those appeals, Yeager argues firmly that the good social novel is able to direct or move—or, as she explicitly puts it, cause—us to the kind of social sympathies Sidgwick thought were necessary for living well.[23] Turning to the end of Sidgwick's *Methods of Ethics,* Yeager concludes her reflections on the social and moral weight of Howell's 1889 social novel in this way: "If Sidgwick is right, as I think he is, in insisting that to live well we require social support and 'the sympathy of other human beings,' then perhaps what is most important of all is the way in which these stories *cause* the 'judgments and sentiments of others' to echo in our minds, thus sustaining our own ability to discern the fitting and to judge humanely—and lending us courage in the face of moral duty."[24]

SOCIAL HIERARCHIES AND THE LIMITS OF LITERATURE?

The commonalities between Hauerwas's and Yeager's approaches to the moral importance of literature underscore the general trajectory of the consequentialist conception of aesthetics and ethics. Their differences underscore the various expressions of this trajectory. To reiterate, reading—specifically novels that confront the reader with a truthful picture of reality—moves us toward particular notions of goodness, either the life of virtue or a form of moral deliberation that supports and facilitates social solidarity and change. Such movement for Hauerwas is tied to our participation in the truthfulness of the story itself, while for Yeager the movement from reading to social solidarity and change is primarily a function of how the realism of the social novel transforms our understanding, specifically our conscience and thus our sense of right and wrong. Either way, what binds them is the attempt to minimize sentimentalism, a critique that is often leveled against reading and the fictive world of novels. We can also see their accounts of reading as pushing back against critiques of reading as ephemeral and therefore of little lasting impact on the reader. From their vantage points, reading is not necessarily a self-terminating experience as some aesthetic formalists or modernists have claimed, as we saw in the introduction. Nor is such an experience merely entertaining, a matter of leisure and play.

Furthermore, the practice of reading broadens our conception of ethics, that is, what it means to engage in moral reflection and to translate that reflection into action. On this front, Hauerwas and Yeager are certainly not alone. For Marianne Jennings, stories are what brings to light the multidimensionality of ethical decision-making, without which the urgency and weightiness of ethics is absent. "Stories haunt. Stories remind. Stories are examples that move us and inspire fortitude. Without stories of ethical choices, good and bad, we learn ethics in a sterile void. Those trained in a sterile void behave with all the compassion, foresight, and conscience of automatons. Stories—both fictional and nonfictional—breathe life into ethics. They also breathe ethics in the lives of students who have learned these stories well."[25] Similarly, for Patricia Lamoureux, stories remind us that ethics is something more than a skill or technique for resolving moral dilemmas:

> The goal of moral living includes not only right thinking, feeling, and acting but also becoming authentic persons and building genuine communities. This understanding of the moral life suggests there is more to it than conformity to rules or applying principles to cases. Overemphasis on duty, rules, and obligation in the Christian life has been accompanied by a view of moral theology that has stressed cognition divorced from the emotions and a reductionistic view of the moral person as a clever problem solver. But the moral life is not a science to be worked out by computer calculations, even with the most elegant and complex software. Employing the arts as tutor in the moral journey, particularly the narrative arts, can help us appreciate the complexities of forming good character, building a just community, and choosing rightly.[26]

Hauerwas would certainly agree with Lamoureux and specify further that stories are important because they are in fact the shapes our moral lives take. Thus, stories do not simply illumine the complexity of moral decision-making but rather illumine the very nature of the moral life itself. As Hauerwas argues, "in more Kantian and utilitarian moral theories the attention paid to the concepts of character and virtue has clearly been subordinate to accounts of obligations,"[27] but the moral life is not intelligible simply as a series of obligations; those obligations are only intelligible if they take the form of a narrative or are expressed narratively.[28] However, it is erroneous to think that only certain forms of moral reasoning (e.g., deontological and utilitarian) are narratively lacking; it is that some are more thickly and coherently constituted than others. At any rate, the more pertinent point with respect to the relationship between aesthetics and ethics is that so long as all forms of moral reasoning are narratively constituted, then the practice of reading is itself a moral practice. And this matters for a number of reasons, not the least of which is that for Hauerwas, we should not expect moral agreement to be possible by appealing to common moral denominators or abstracted moral baselines.[29] That issue underscores the prospects for moral change unless appeals are made beyond simply relaying facts and statistics. As Yeager writes regarding the role that aesthetics can play in ecological advocacy, "Factual truth, by itself, does not always have the power to convince and mobilize. . . . 'No important change in ethics was ever accomplished without an internal change in our intellectual emphasis, loyalties, affections, and convictions.'"[30]

Whether Yeager would go as far as Hauerwas in claiming that reading is a moral practice is arguable. As explained earlier, her primary interest in the social novel is tied to its ability to challenge its readers to confront the social ills that such novels illumine. Thus, her emphases move more in the direction of literature's ability to elicit our sympathy and thus change our attitudes and sense of justice and obligation toward others. Such an account of literature is one that Hauerwas, while not dismissing it ("That is no small matter," he claims),[31] suggests misses the larger ethical consequence of literature: how it envisions a particular mode of life that invites us into it (that invites our participation in the story itself), thereby enabling a sense of unity, direction, and meaningfulness to our lives. Despite their differences, we can approach Yeager and Hauerwas as both agreeing, at the very least, that literature can and must play a role in making persons morally perceptive. To live rightly requires being able to see ourselves, others, and the world we inhabit correctly or truthfully. But if reading makes us morally perceptive, one question that arises is whether that kind of perception is sufficiently critical or simply imitative. To be more specific, does a consequentialist formulation of literature and ethics give sufficient allowance to the possibility that the moral force of the novel can facilitate the assimilation of dubious values and worldviews, wittingly or not? Antonaccio casts this question in terms of whether the aesthetic experience of reading literature can be too morally consoling, in other words, whether it makes "moral thinking seem less difficult, more immediate, than it really is." She states that "the danger . . . is that the pleasures of reading, along with the sense that we ourselves are 'characters in a story,' may convince us that we have already arrived at our moral destination."[32] But it could very well be the case that such a destination is not necessarily the one we ought to seek and inhabit.

This danger, one might argue, is less pertinent to Yeager's advocacy of the social novel, since its moral power is in moving the self to the other in solidarity; this is not a moral destination that ought to raise our suspicions. But what are we to do with the fact that the social novels to which Yeager turns (Howell's specifically) are situated in a particular cultural milieu of the late nineteenth and early twentieth centuries? This question is amplified and made more worrisome when we turn to Hauerwas, who values the novels of

Trollope and Austen, among others of the Victorian era. In these novels, do they not depict characters—and thus stories within which Hauerwas thinks we should locate ourselves—of a time in which rigid and often stifling social hierarchies, stratification, and segregation prevailed?

These are questions that Annette Baier asked of Alasdair MacIntyre's appeals to the virtues embodied in Victorian novels as well as more ancient communities of Greek thought. And given MacIntyre's importance to at least Hauerwas's articulation of the relationship between narrative and the virtues,[33] Baier's concerns are especially instructive. The concern is not whether reading novels of a particular era will lead to a straightforward endorsement and adoption of illiberal values and social hierarchies that may constitute the cultural fabric of those novels' worlds. Rather, the concern is what happens when such values and hierarchies are not named explicitly and confronted head-on, which in appealing to them leads to more subtle but nevertheless problematic reinscriptions of those worlds' illiberality. As Baier observed, "MacIntyre's version of moral virtues and the good life in Homeric times, in Athens, in the England of Jane Austen's heroines, does successfully veil the power relationships constitutive of those social worlds. The concept of power plays no important role in his analysis."[34] Consequently, MacIntyre's response to modernity's moral legacy of autonomy and individualism over and against more communal, constitutive forms of life risks swapping one form of social disempowerment (modernity) for another (Homeric virtues and their Victorian reincarnations).

Baier was sympathetic to MacIntyre's critical assessment of modernity's moral legacy. Though drawing on David Hume's moral thought rather than MacIntyre's retrieval of Aristotelian virtue, she, like MacIntyre, found modernity's emphasis on the autonomous will problematic. In Hume's concept of social artifice and the necessity of mutually agreed customs, Baier found affinities with MacIntyre's claim that the notion of an autonomous will—and thus the moral life itself—can only be arbitrary. This is also a familiar Hauerwasean criticism of liberalism, particularly its forms in liberal Christianity. MacIntyre's remedy, which Hauerwas follows, rests on recognizing the need for the will to be informed, shaped, and habituated into a tradition that initiates the moral agent into a meaningful life story, one that cannot be self-generated, since that is impossible to begin with. So too for Baier in that significant elements of Hume's moral philosophy "can be seen as an ancestor of MacIntyre's (or Wittgenstein's) concept of a practice, a form of life with its own standards and internal goods, an activity that one can learn only by being taught by those already initiated into it."[35]

But Baier approached MacIntyre's enthusiasm for premodern forms of life as alternatives to modernity's moral incoherence as too easily masking their inherent social, structural inequalities. This is where Baier found Hume more helpful. Hume is interested in not only the moral importance of "being taught by those already initiated into" certain cultural practices but also the variety of cultural practices, particularly those concerned with publicly recognized goods such as "political power" and the kind of privileges sustained by differing power distributions in society.[36] Does the possession of power of a particular elite class result in social, political, and economic privileges residing in themselves, or does it allow for the possibility of such privileges to be distributed in more "'oblique directions'"?[37] While Baier claimed that MacIntyre, in his *After Virtue*, is willing to "raise the question 'To whom does power accrue?' of modern societies—the manager and the therapist profit from our moral malaise, get power over us," MacIntyre nevertheless fails to take more seriously the kind of social, political, and economic privileges that result from the power that "the old style managers and therapists," namely "kings, popes, and priests," possessed. "What gave them their power may have been what MacIntyre sees as the moral health rather than the moral malaise of those over whom they exercised power, but the fact of privilege and superior power remains."[38] While modernity's commitment to autonomy may be confused and unintelligible and ultimately less liberating than promised, our present sensibilities toward equality of persons, democratic participation, social mobility, and the rule of law are for many hardly trivial features of modern society and in many respects are foreign to the forms of life MacIntyre prefers over and against those of modernity's.

Whether Hume provides a more adequate and compelling account of tradition and narrative-based moral inquiry than MacIntyre's is an open question. But Baier's comments on the insufficient appreciation for the nature of power and privilege in the forms of life MacIntyre champions are noteworthy. Her observations raise a flag of caution on those such as Hauerwas who appeal enthusiastically to Victorian exemplars of the realistic novel in their capacity to initiate us into narratives that form in us the virtues of constancy and forgiveness, virtues that would be otherwise beyond our reach. Thus, Baier's reservations with MacIntyre's account of the virtues serve to further underscore the urgency of the question Antonaccio raises with respect to consequentialist approaches to literature: the pleasures of reading "may convince us that literature can teach us self-knowledge and concern for others. But what if the education that novels offer actually prevents a more rigorous scrutiny of the linguistic forms we are so eager to inhabit (including our very eagerness to inhabit them)?"[39]

LITERATURE AND MORAL REASONING: A REAPPRAISAL

Are consequentialist accounts of literature fated to the kind of criticism that Baier leveled against such accounts? Noël Carroll observes that "we seem to fall effortlessly into talking about" art, including novels, "in terms of their ethical significance."[40] Moreover, our ethical assessments of them are variable:

> That is, we find some artworks to be morally good, while some others are not; some are exemplary, while some others are vicious and perhaps even pernicious; and finally other works may not appear to call for either moral approbation or opprobrium. So, though we very frequently do advance moral assessments of artworks, it is important to stress that we have a gamut of possible evaluative judgments at our disposal: from the morally good to the bad to the ugly, to the morally indifferent and the irrelevant. And it is this availability of different judgments that I am referring to as the variability of our moral assessments of artworks.[41]

In accounting for this variability in our moral assessments of artworks, Carroll is not disputing the moral consequences of art. He is in fact trying to make the case that artworks do not simply have "its own purposes" and are thus irrelevant to ethics.[42] But what Carroll is attempting to underscore more specifically is that it would be mistaken to think that our reactions to art will always be in the direction of finding them morally rich in one way or another, for it is the case that we think of the moral value of art in variable ways, even in those artworks that are intended for a particular moral end. (This also means that the reverse is the case, wherein artworks that are not specifically intended toward a specific moral purpose will not necessarily escape moral assessments and responses.) One point in calling attention to this variability is that while art may indeed serve as a moral instructor or provide moral training to some degree or another, the way in which it does may be less of a straight line than some accounts, such as those of Hauerwas and Yeager, can come off as suggesting. In other words, the nature of our understanding of artworks is marked with greater cognitive and emotive wrestling and conflict.

To some extent, Antonaccio's reflexive approach to the practice of reading can be regarded as reiterating the way Carroll sees variability operating in our understanding of artworks. Calling it a reflexive account, Antonaccio's aim is to underscore the importance of approaching literature evaluatively rather than regarding it as moral exemplars. In other words, what Antonaccio is interested in is highlighting the importance of reading as a critical assessment of the moral worlds novels portray.[43] To think of a reflexive approach to literature is to conceive of the relationship between the novel and its reader with a sufficient distance between them. Such distance is what allows the work of moral evaluation to manifest itself on the part of the reader. "Reflexive distance would require the reader not simply to submit to the social reality of the narrative. . . . Rather, it requires the reader to engage in a critical scrutiny of linguistic forms through the reflexive structures of consciousness. On this view, the novel is not simply a school for virtue or an education in moral sentiment; it is also an occasion for the transformation of consciousness in relation to the real."[44]

Antonaccio's advocacy for a reflexive model of aesthetic experience in the foregoing quotation relies on the nature of individual consciousness articulated by the moral philosophy of Iris Murdoch. As Antonaccio describes, Murdoch believed that "egoism is the primary dilemma of the moral life."[45] This egoism is the source of illusions and fantasies, masking or veiling the truthful perception of reality. Human consciousness, insofar as egoism is a tenacious feature of it, is engaged in the struggle against its own illusions, its fantasy producing impulses. More importantly, however, this struggle "takes place in and through the linguistic mediations of human consciousness"; consciousness itself "is constituted by diverse linguistic processes through which human beings 'picture' reality." For Murdoch, language is the medium of moral reflection, deliberation, and ultimately moral change. It is through language that we struggle to resist egoism. Thus, while the human person is incapable of thinking apart from language, our selves are not solely languages we inhabit. Rather, language is the forum through which the human person becomes conscious of the world in which she inhabits in its actuality, and in this consciousness she gains a sense of who she is as an individual human person, as one who deliberates, evaluates, and struggles, possessing the capacities of moral effort.[46] Thus, language, especially a particular language scheme, is never a moral destination but instead is the road that, if traveled well, leads to a truthful vision of reality, of world and self. As Murdoch put it, "We are all story-tellers. . . . We have in our activity as story-tellers a way of judging, a way of evaluating the world that surrounds us, and this gives us in return a sense of our own identity, our separateness, our own self-being."[47]

In light of her reading of the Murdochean relationship between language and moral consciousness, Antonaccio claims that literature, the novel in particular, plays an important role in the "struggle to see the real beyond the veil of personal fantasy," that is, in the struggle against egoism.[48] So, Antonaccio states of Murdoch that "for the artist, the primary test of the struggle with literary form is the creation of character."[49] Art that depicts this struggle in its character portrayals can aid in our own struggle to see the real. Such depiction, then, may constitute the heart of artistic excellence: in good art we perceive acutely "'the existence of other people and their claims.'"[50] Accordingly, Antonaccio asserts that reading participates in the same struggle as ethics. So long as there is this similarity to be drawn between the two, reading, like moral inquiry, is a reflexive event. In reading, we engage in the task or responsibility of moral struggle alongside the text.[51] Thus, literature "becomes an occasion for a confrontation with one's own capacities for self-deception, fantasy, and self-aggrandizement in one's use of language."[52]

Antonaccio provides an important alternative to consequentialist conceptions of literature, not so much as a counterpoint to them but rather as a corrective. If reading is to be a morally beneficial practice, then it must be a practice that allows for the sufficient evaluation of the very content of what is being read. In other words, the moral import of reading cannot be so direct that the moral world of the readers is shaped uncritically by what they are reading. Too susceptible is the self, then, to reinscribing a moral world left insufficiently appraised. Antonaccio believes that this susceptibility is high in Hauerwas's turn to the novel and concludes similarly with respect to Martha Nussbaum's advocacy of narrative fiction as models for moral reflection.[53]

Antonaccio's concerns find company in other accounts of aesthetics and ethics that attempt to tie literature and ethics together but not too tightly. A prime example is the kind of connection that William C. Spohn draws between reading and moral goodness. Initially he voices similar Hauerwasean notes, his argument centering on the formation of perception, "the threshold of moral experience." As Spohn elaborates, "We have to notice the features of experience that make for human flourishing or suffering before we can begin to respond emotionally and deliberately. Being attentive or indifferent to the claims of others is more a function of moral development and character than raw intelligence. Those who are acutely perceptive of the moral potentials of experience are people who have developed virtuous habits of empathy, fairness, respect, and love. Moral oblivion is fed by their opposites."[54] While Spohn will claim that literature is crucial to the formation of moral perception, it is interesting that he insists that such formation is indirect or, more precisely, must be indirect. By indirect, he is not necessarily suggesting that literature is more powerless than powerful in forming moral perception; rather, he is concerned primarily with how literature is presented to the reader, whether in a too obviously moralistic fashion or with a kind of eagerness to elicit moral responses. Both modes of presentation can fail to engage in the kind of evaluative dynamic that is necessary for literature to be ultimately morally formative. So, Spohn notes:

> When teachers try to use them [e.g., novels, though not exclusively, but also films, photographs, poems, etc.] only to make a point, it is usually frustrating for all concerned. Students fix on facets of the poem or story that are tangential and yawn at the insight the instructor hoped to convey. The literature majors in class may cringe at a story being used "didactically," an enterprise that they have learned to hold in low esteem. They have been warned that a poem should not mean but be.[55]

The alternative, Spohn proposes, is to use literature in a way that invites engagement and appreciation of "it on its own terms."[56] He continues:

> Making a story exhibit A for courage or exhibit B for the pitfalls of greed [for instance] prevents the student from entering the strange world present in the work. When the reader takes the leap of imagination to enter into the metaphors of the poem or the world sketched in a story, meaning opens up indirectly. A liberating education has always used stories and other artistic products to stretch students' experience by helping them imagine life from angles of vision very different from their own. Literary critic Wayne C. Booth writes that we learn to relate to literary characters as virtual friends who expand our sympathy and moral range. Keeping company with them enriches our lives by enabling us to see the world through their eyes and to ask fresh questions about our own perspective.[57]

In the above, Spohn ends up sounding a lot more like Yeager than Hauerwas; perhaps, then, Antonaccio's criticism of Hauerwas's turn to the novel is less applicable to Yeager's. At any rate, the pertinent point here is to recognize Spohn's emphasis on the indirect role of literature. That emphasis leads him, interestingly, to employ a modernist characterization of art (that it has an integrity of its own and thus lacks a formal connection with anything pertaining to ethics, what Carroll refers to as the autonomist position on art),[58] but Spohn does so in a subversive way, which is to say in a manner that does not predetermine or bias the reader into expecting a particular moral communication from an artwork. This matters to Spohn because it serves to promote rather than prematurely curtail the evaluative assessment that is needed for art's moral salience to come into view. Such evaluative assessment or "reflective engagement" is made possible when readers are invited to assess literature as it is.[59] Stories then become "moral resources" rather than predetermined moral destinations, sharpening moral perception and "our ability to discern our own moral choices."[60]

At times Spohn, instead of sounding like Yeager, can flip back to sounding a lot more like Hauerwas. Not only does literature sharpen our ability to discern our moral choices, but such heightened discernment also results from being formed or schooled by the narrative itself through repeated identification with its characters and, correlatively, to the vision and values of their creations, both of which "reshape our own pattern of desires."[61] In other instances, Spohn switches back to a more reflective account of our relationship with reading/literature in the mold of Antonaccio's approach. In addition to the indirect ties that Spohn draws between moral perception and literature as we saw above, he will also propose that reading, specifically "reflective reading," allows us to try out lifestyles that are admirable as well as ones that are banal or appalling.[62] "It permits us to appreciate ways of life without paying the full price of living them out."[63] In so allowing, reading facilitates our imaginative capacity to consider what kind of life is morally responsible or reprehensible, analogically. The analogical imagination that reading engages "trains readers to project forward the several trajectories their lives could take."[64] Reflecting on the merits of those trajectories is a critical feature of reading's moral work and effects on us.[65]

Gregory Currie refers to this kind of reflective appraisal as a form of planning, or the ability "to plan our lives." It is not that all our moral choices are results of such reflective considerations, but insofar as anyone hopes to make good moral choices, such conduct requires at the very least "[anticipating] circumstances, the consequences of actions, the reactions of others." That kind of planning or thinking and attentiveness involves the cognitive work of the imagination, which Currie, like Spohn, believes that reading fiction "can enhance."[66] Currie describes the "planning function of imagination" in the following way: "We imagine ourselves undertaking the contemplated action, and we see, in imagination, what the consequences are. . . . You imagine how these events might turn out and then review the imagined outcome, redoing the projection when you realize you need to take into account more or other circumstances." This work of imagining then aids in deciding "what strategy to adopt in solving a problem or attaining a goal" and improving our abilities to adopt the better strategy. Reading, according to Currie, thus provides more than simply propositional knowledge and also supports the "knowing-how of [moral] skills and abilities."[67]

Currie will claim that the kind of imaginative thinking that is enhanced by the practice of reading is distinct from other forms of planning that the imagination supports. In other words, the imaginative projection into the lives of others can be had more readily through the reading of fiction. He suggests that such imaginative projection could, "in principle, be provided by something else." So, he suggests, instead of reading George Eliot's novel *Middlemarch* (1871/1972), he could "imagine the lives of people of my own invention."[68] But that has the disadvantage of requiring a level of creativity that one (actually, most people) might not possess; "good fictions give us, through the talents of their makers, access to imaginings more complex, inventive, and instructive than we could often hope to make for ourselves." Thus, he concludes, "Better on the whole to listen to the narrative of another, more competent teller of tales." Currie is willing to admit that we might be able to imagine what it is like to live in the shoes of another without literature (or with the aid of something other than literature), but literature holds special status in facilitating that task of the moral imagination. For Currie, fiction, by its very definition, revolves around characters, which makes fiction especially important since ethics is in essence about human relationships. Imaginative evaluation of fictive characters broadens and refines our capacity to evaluate how we should relate to characters in real life as well as what kind of character one ought to be in the real world. In short, what matters to Currie is the power of storytelling—of narrative—in getting our imaginations to work in a manner that necessarily spills over to the realm of ethics.

Currie's belief in the irreplaceable ethical role of literature is also shared by Spohn.[69] It is perhaps shared by Murdoch too.[70] However, the influence of the art movement known as Expressionism might suggest that literature is not as morally exceptional as it is sometimes claimed to be.[71] Regardless, the point in highlighting Currie's emphasis on how reading enhances the role of the imagination in moral decision-making and action as well as its resonance with Spohn's emphasis on what he calls, as we saw above, the indirect relationship between reading and the moral life, is to underscore how consequentialist approaches to literature need not necessarily fall into the kinds of traps that Antonaccio delineates through her advocacy of a Murdochean-based reflexive account of reading. If her primary concern is that consequentialist accounts can too easily be taken as drawing a too direct line between reading and right action, then such accounts may lack the critical distance that is needed for reading to support deep moral thinking, the kind that can assess critically which actions or which forms of life one ought to commit to. Otherwise, reading is no more than one step toward morally dubious imitation, making the reader susceptible to the kind of lives that, as Baier suggests in her critique of MacIntyre that we saw earlier, are less than liberating. Currie and Spohn (at least in his non-Hauerwasean moments) point to a conception of reading that is more akin to an evaluative process, one that allows us to imagine ways of moving forward as morally responsible persons as well as paths to avoid. Which paths are which, however, is not directly made available to the reader but is left to the reader to determine through reflective struggle. In other words, in reading, we confront the very definition of moral terms rather than simply being tutored in predetermined definitions of them.

READING AND ITS MORAL (UN)RELIABILITY?

Antonaccio's advocacy of a reflexive model of literature is helpful in attuning us to the potential moral naivete of some consequentialist construals of literature's relevance to ethics. Rather than simply informing us and drawing us into exemplary forms of life, reading asks the question of what is so exemplary (or perhaps less than exemplary) about the forms of life a novel depicts. Therefore, the moral salience of reading need not simply reside in the establishment of a sympathetic connection between the reader and the novel's characters, nor should reading's moral salience be conceived in that way. We might be scandalized by a novel, or we might simply find it puzzling and upsetting or shallow and saccharine. The variety of reactions that reading elicits informs our evaluation of a novel's characters and thus the forms of life and courses of actions those characters embody.

However, if reading is a reflexive experience in the way just described, does that necessarily mean that the evaluative process that novels support is reliable? Is the kind of evaluative process that reading supports necessarily supportive of humanizing values? Consider the following from Murdoch in her essay "The Sovereignty of Good over Other Concepts": "Art, and by 'art' from now on I mean good art, not fantasy art, affords us a pure delight in the independent existence of what is excellent. Both in its genesis and its enjoyment it is a thing totally opposed to selfish obsession."[72] But Murdoch is not always as definitive as those lines suggest. Later in the essay she writes, "Art transcends selfish and obsessive limitations of personality and *can* enlarge the sensibility of its consumer."[73] She then reiterates that art "*can* stretch the imagination, enlarge the vision and strengthen the judgment.[74] That such an effect is a possibility—"can"—rather than a surety is noteworthy. It is one thing to assert, as a normative point, that art, especially the practice of reading, tugs our consciousness toward selflessness, pity, justice, or compassion, but it is another thing to assert that the moral tug of art will indeed be successful. Even Murdoch, despite what she claims so assertively about the evaluative importance of art—that "art reveals reality," that it "combines just modes of judgment and ability to connect with an increased perception of detail"—hesitates to be definitive at least in terms of actual outcomes. "The good artist is not necessarily wise at home, and the concentration camp guard can be a kindly father," she admits. However, she immediately hedges a bit by saying that "at least this can seem to be so, though I would feel that the artist had at least got a starting-point and that on closer inspection the concentration camp guard might prove to have his limitations as a family man."[75] But at what point does this hope misalign with the kind of realistic vision of human life that she so adamantly thinks we all need to attend to?

Murdoch's hedge reveals the kind of inevitability that colors much of the contemporary turn to literature in ethics. Baier, as we saw earlier, worries that reading too easily allows readers to ignore the illiberal cultural mores of certain kinds of novels. One can make the case, as Baier does (rightly, in my opinion), that overlooking the social assumptions and asymmetrical power relations that are taken for granted in particular literary genres distracts from, if not diminishes, their moral usefulness. But Baier's critique presumes that reading will have an effect, and depending on what one reads, the effect may be morally dubious. But is it not entirely possible that reading will not have the kind of effect that is expected? Will reading a Victorian novel necessarily lead to a reinscription of (or at least an obliviousness to) its gender inequalities and patriarchy in the daily life of its readers? Is reading as effective a practice as it is made out to be or, in Baier's case, as it is feared?

The reflexive model of literature aims to recast reading as a critical moral practice. In other words, it aims to be less Manichean. It is not that bad novels will lead to bad people and good novels will lead to good people; instead, novels, with the diversity of characters they employ, provide the evaluative frame to assess lives worth pursuing or not. But still, what reason is there to expect reading to engender the kind of evaluative work that the reflexive model claims? Is it not entirely possible for persons to end up being unaffected by what they are reading? (This assumes that they bother to read in the first place, which is increasingly unlikely.)[76] But if they do bother to read and end up being affected, will the ensuing evaluative work necessarily inspire or support the kind of liberal values that Baier prefers or the kind of selflessness that Murdoch champions? What is to prevent the reader from ending up choosing wrongly or wanting subsequently to read novels that introduce morally dubious worlds? Surely, finding a novel's character lacking need not provoke a kind of moral resistance to the character's questionable behavior. It is entirely possible to think that a novel's character is, say, pedestrian or maybe even scandalous and still love the character and perhaps even want to be or be with that character (consider the popularity of contemporary romance novels).[77] And while reading a novel under certain kinds of conditions (i.e., reading a novel on "its own terms") might, as Spohn suggests (as we saw earlier), lead to readers reading critically, even he is unwilling to go so far as to claim that all will therefore read critically under such conditions.[78] It is the potentiality that literature possesses that maintains his general enthusiasm for literature's evaluative importance.[79] But potentiality is often just that, and it frequently goes unactualized despite our best efforts at reading carefully or despite the quality of the novel before our eyes. For every example of success there is a counterexample and a counterexample to the counterexample, and so on. Because of this diversity of outcomes, we might rightly wonder, then, whether reading is ordinarily a reflexive experience and whether we can therefore rely on literature and expect to work our way to the moral life from there.

NOTES

1. See Eaton, *Aesthetics and the Good Life*, chap. 7.
2. Davidson, "High Culture Brought Low."
3. I am relying on Eaton's nomenclature in *Aesthetics and the Good Life* and Eaton, *Merit, Aesthetic and Ethical*, chap. 5.
4. Antonaccio, "The Consolations of Literature," 623.
5. Hauerwas, *Vision and Virtue*, 74.
6. Hauerwas, *Dispatches from the Front*, 53.
7. Hauerwas, 55–56.
8. Hauerwas, 53.
9. Hauerwas, 53, 54.
10. Hauerwas, 54.
11. Hauerwas, 55.
12. This is a point he makes in reference to another novel in Hauerwas, *A Community of Character*, 12. Cf. Anthony Savile's account of the ethical consequences of literature: "We cannot give a coherent account of planning for the future unless we have available notions like 'desirable,' 'valuable,' or 'estimable.' . . . This can come about only if we find things in the world to be of value and to be worthy of our esteem, and that will happen only if we frame a vision of the world that sees it from a point of view that we share with others and that generates descriptions of it cast in terms of, and responsive to, our common interests." As quoted by Eaton, *Aesthetics and the Good Life*, 159.
13. Yeager, "'Art for Humanity's Sake,'" 474.
14. Yeager, 475.
15. Yeager, 475, 476.
16. Yeager, 476.
17. Hauerwas, *A Community of Character*, 18.
18. Yeager, "'Art for Humanity's Sake,'" 452.
19. Yeager, 450–51.

20. Yeager, 455.
21. Yeager, 456.
22. Hauerwas, *A Community of Character*, 37. That the Gospel takes the form of story is part of Hauerwas's larger argument that narrative is central to theology: "The argument is not that some theology may be expressed via narrative, but the 'stronger suggestion that narrative or story is a means of expression uniquely suited to theology or at least to Christian theology.' This does not mean that all theology must itself assume the form of narrative, but rather whatever form theological reflection may take, one of its primary tasks is reminding us of a story [namely, the story of Jesus]." Hauerwas, *Truthfulness and Tragedy*, 71. As such, theology's task is to show how "the gospel is a story that gives you a way of being in the world," which allows us to see "how other kinds of stories form our lives truly or falsely" (73). Thus, what makes particular stories or novels critical to moral formation is that they are measured against the story of the Gospel that we must inhabit to begin with. This reflects Hauerwas's general conviction that "the 'facts' that are to be known can be known only by having stories that form and thus provide appropriate knowledge of the world" (74).
23. See Yeager, "'Art for Humanity's Sake,'" 471–73.
24. Yeager, 477 (emphasis added).
25. Jennings, "The Absence of Stories," 166.
26. Lamoureux, "Introduction," 4–5.
27. Hauerwas, *A Community of Character*, 97.
28. Hauerwas, 98–99. Compare "We cannot account for our moral life solely by the decisions we make; we also need the narrative that forms us to have one kind of character rather than another. . . . As our stories . . . they will determine what kind of moral considerations—that is, what reasons—will count at all" (Hauerwas, *Truthfulness and Tragedy*, 20); and "Our morality is more than the adherence of universalizable rules" (Hauerwas, *Vision and Virtue*, 35).
29. Hauerwas, *A Community of Character*, 97–99.
30. Yeager, "'Art for Humanity's Sake,'" 122. Cf. Hauerwas, *Vision and Virtue*, 35: "Our morality is more than adherence to universalizable rules; it also encompasses our experiences, fables, beliefs, images, concepts, and inner monologues."
31. Hauerwas, *Dispatches from the Front*, 53.
32. Antonaccio, "Consolations of Literature," 623.
33. Hauerwas, "Agency," 187.
34. Baier, *Postures of the Mind*, 247.
35. Baier, 251.
36. Baier, 252.
37. Baier, 252.
38. Baier, 251.
39. Antonaccio, "The Consolations of Literature," 623.
40. Carroll, "Art, Narrative, and Moral Reasoning," 126.
41. Carroll, 126.
42. Carroll, 135.
43. Antonaccio, "The Consolations of Literature," 639.
44. Antonaccio, 639–40.
45. Antonaccio, 640.
46. In her more systematic study of Murdoch's moral philosophy, Antonaccio asserts at the very start that "against the displacement of the notion of consciousness in favor of the

authority and primacy of language, Murdoch retrieves consciousness as the fundamental mode of human moral being. In doing so, she seeks to defend the reality and value of the human individual as irreducible, and thus to resist its absorption into linguistic and other impersonal systems. What makes this attempt so distinctive is that Murdoch does not simply ignore the contemporary turn to language [including Hauerwas, who Antonaccio places in the camp of communitarian critics of liberalism]; rather, she takes language with the utmost seriousness." Antonaccio, *Picturing the Human*, 3–4. That seriousness reflects her belief that "moral identity is constituted by a prior framework of value. . . . Yet on Murdoch's view, the appeal to a narrativist or communitarian conception of identity runs the risk of denying the self's capacity to transcend its social roles, and thus may fall prey to the distortions of the social totality, or may cede too great a measure of its responsibility to the authority of existing arrangements. Murdoch's conception of the self attempts to preserve the self's integrity without isolating it from a world of others that defines its normative claims and purposes. In effect, she charts a middle course between what she sees as the dangers of a model of autonomy by which the self wholly transcends contingency (its relations to nature, history, and others), and a model that dissolves or assimilates the self into these contingent relations" (10).

47. Murdoch, "Art Is the Imitation of Nature," 253.
48. Antonaccio, "The Consolations of Literature," 640.
49. Antonaccio, 641.
50. Murdoch, "On 'God' and 'Good,'" 57, as quoted by Antonaccio, "The Consolations of Literature," 641.
51. Antonaccio, "The Consolations of Literature," 639.
52. Antonaccio, 641.
53. See Nussbaum, *Love's Knowledge*.
54. Spohn, "The Formative Power of Story and the Grace of Indirection," 16.
55. Spohn, 15.
56. Spohn, 15.
57. Spohn, 15–16.
58. Carroll, "Art, Narrative, and Moral Reasoning," 134.
59. Spohn, "The Formative Power of Story and the Grace of Indirection," 16.
60. Spohn, 19, 20.
61. Spohn, 20.
62. This suggests a moral exceptionalism to reading and literature. See notes 69–71 below.
63. Spohn, "The Formative Power of Story and the Grace of Indirection," 20.
64. Spohn, 22.
65. Eaton expresses a similar sentiment. Reading a novel entails both imaginative identification and role-play with its characters—that is, you find character X so compelling and attractive that you see yourself (or desire to see yourself) as character X or find yourself daydreaming about such a life—as well as imaginative evaluation and assessment of the characters in a novel as a means of self-evaluation and assessment in reality. Eaton writes, "We may imagine that we are a character in a book, for instance, and what it might be like to act some way. But we may also ask ourselves whether we might *in fact* be someone like this, whether the reasons we get into the trouble we do might really be that we are like this character. We imagine not that we are so-and-so but whether if we acted like this we might find ourselves in a comparable mess." Eaton, *Merit, Aesthetic and Ethical*, 153.
66. Currie, "Realism of Character and the Value of Fiction," 165.

67. Currie, 166.
68. Currie, 171.
69. While nonliterary forms of art can be morally consequential, Spohn's emphasis on reflective reading signals a hierarchy of morally consequential art. "I believe that ethics' closest allies in the world of the arts are not the fine arts but the several varieties of narrative arts: short fiction, the novel, film, theater, and autobiography. While there is nothing automatically humanizing about stories, they have a greater formal potential to affect our moral vision and values than painting or sculpture, for example. Nonnarrative forms of art can also enhance our appreciation of moral realities, but in a less direct way because human characters are not central, or when they are, as in dance, their reality is not defined verbally. Architecture and sculpture can lift the human spirit, but they do not have the potential to pattern lives as do the narrative arts. It is easier to identify emotionally with the characters of a novel or film because narratives have the shape of human existence: we are all unfolding unfinished stories" (Spohn, "The Formative Power of Story and the Grace of Indirection," 20). Compare Spohn's comment to Hauerwas's: "a story at least seems to involve 'an imputed pattern of human relationships richer, more throbbing and intense than appearances may actually justify.' But it is not just any imputed pattern, but a pattern that takes the form of narrative. . . . [A]n essential aspect of narrative . . . is a connection between non-necessary, contingent events. . . . [I]t is only through narrative that we can catch the connections between actions and responses of men that are inherently particular and contingent. . . . A story, thus, is a narrative account that binds events and agents together in an intelligible pattern. We do not tell stories [in narrative form] simply because they provide us a more colorful way to say what can be said in a different way, but because there is no other way we can articulate the richness of intentional activity—that is, behavior that is purposeful but not necessary. For as any good novelist knows there is always more involved in any human action than can be said. To tell a story often involves our attempt to make intelligible the muddle of things we have done in order to have a self." Hauerwas, *Truthfulness and Tragedy*, 75–76.
70. For Murdoch, the question of literature's distinctive import is perhaps more complicated, though, as I have noted above, Antonaccio suggests that Murdoch places special emphasis on novels as a privileged art form. That would certainly explain in part Murdoch's efforts as a novelist. Yet, Murdoch complicates rather than clarifies the issue of what constitutes good art. First, "The good artist, in relation to his art, is brave, truthful, patient, humble; and even in non-representational art we may receive intuitions of these qualities" (Murdoch, "The Sovereignty of Good over Other Concepts," 84), hence Murdoch's cautious nod to various forms of modern art of the early and mid-twentieth century. For instance, when Murdoch writes that "one sees in paintings by Mondrian . . . the way in which what in a first painting in a series looks like a tree becomes something much more like a lot of squares or oblongs in the final version. Good abstract paintings are not just idle daubs or scrawls, forms wandering round at random in spaces, they are somehow about light and colour and space, and I think that this is something that the abstract painter is very conscious of, he is not in a state of total freedom, he is relating himself to something else and his paintings exist for us in a world where we normally take colours to be parts of objects. . . . Formalism draws our attention to the extent to which we are responsible for what we see. . . . We bestow significance but we also constantly test it and we incorporate the tests, the tests of truth, in the work itself" (Murdoch, "Art Is the Imitation of Nature," 256–57). But second, Murdoch will also suggest that certain art

forms are more capable than others: "These arts, especially literature and painting, show us the peculiar sense in which the concept of virtue is tied on to the human condition" (Murdoch, "Sovereignty of Good over Other Concepts," 84). Also, "But fictional literature has a *special* moral dimension because it is about people, and I venture to say, it is in however covert, unclear, secret, ambiguous way, about the struggle between good and evil" (Murdoch, "Art Is the Imitation of Nature," 255, emphasis added). She then calls attention to J. R. R. Tolkien's *Lord of the Rings*. In an earlier passage from the same essay, Murdoch proposes, "Yet, we must also, in reaction, tell ourselves how ordinary and how natural and how instinctive art is. Literature, which might seem more sophisticated than painting or music, is just as natural—perhaps, given the existence of speech, *more natural*" (252, emphasis added). And to make matters murkier, Murdoch is willing to admit that disciplines other than art may indeed relay the notion of virtue she has in mind. As she surmises, "An intellectual discipline can play the same kind of role as that which I have attributed to art, it can stretch the imagination, enlarge the vision and strengthen the judgment" (Murdoch, "Sovereignty of Good over Other Concepts," 87–88).

71. Spohn may have a point (see note 69 above), to a certain extent, that sculpture and architecture are not story-bound. But that observation may be less applicable to music, dance, and the visual arts and especially to particular movements within those art forms such as Expressionism. According to the art historian Norbert Lynton, "the only true innovation that modern Expressionism can show was the discovery that abstract compositions could serve at least as effectively as subject pictures. The subject, having served as the vehicle for expressive gestures (to some extent as the acceptable sugar coating round the pill of meaning), could, it was found, be abandoned entirely. The expressive power of colours and shapes, of brushstrokes and texture, of size and scale was shown to be sufficient. This last development was stimulated by artists' awareness, increasing since the early nineteenth century, of the directly affecting character of music. Here was a form of creativity that communicated *without benefit of narrative or description*, without even any appeal to associated reflexes." Lynton, "Expressionism," 30 (emphasis added). Even without the benefit of narrative, as Lynton describes, nonverbal forms of art within the modern Expressionist movement were not without impact; they were, in fact, deeply influential in the shaping of cultural and sociopolitical attitudes of much of the twentieth century.
72. Murdoch, "The Sovereignty of Good over Other Concepts," 83.
73. Murdoch, 85 (emphasis added).
74. Murdoch, 87–88 (emphasis added).
75. Murdoch, 94.
76. Crain, "Why We Don't Read, Revisited."
77. Braidwood, "The Love Boom"; and Schwartz and Sullivan, "Gen Z Is Driving Sales of Romance Books to the Top of the Bestseller Lists."
78. Spohn, "The Formative Power of Story and the Grace of Indirection," 16.
79. Spohn, 18.

2

BEAUTY AND THEOLOGICAL ETHICS

If the turn to narrative and literature in theological ethics represents one major trajectory in the theological-ethical approach to aesthetics, the turn to beauty represents a second. To the extent that both turns to the aesthetic are concerned with expanding moral reasoning beyond Enlightenment-Kantian frameworks, both trajectories intersect and share mutually reinforcing ends. Yet, recent works that focus on beauty and theological ethics move along a slightly different track inasmuch as they belong to a more explicit attempt at reimagining the essential relationship between theological ethics and theological aesthetics. As Susan Ross observes, while there are important crosscurrents between virtue ethicists, especially those who emphasize the importance of narrative (as we saw in chapter 1) and those in ethics working to retrieve theological aesthetics, the work of the latter constitutes a kind of corrective to the former on the view that virtue ethics does not highlight the role of beauty in moral formation.[1]

As we saw in chapter 1, I have referred to the turn to literature in theological ethics as a kind of consequentialist approach to aesthetics and ethics insofar as they see literature as having value beyond its own realm (i.e., beyond aesthetics for its own sake or the pleasure of reading simply for its own sake) to the arena of ethics. One key way in which reading is consequential to the moral life is how literature can expand conventional accounts of moral formation and discernment, which is to say beyond strict rationalist accounts. The moral life is not simply about following abstract rules. Again, the turn to beauty in theological ethics shares this basic premise. However, the turn to literature raises a number of questions. These questions do not necessarily undercut the basic premise that reading is morally important, but the challenge of these questions is whether the defense of this premise is adequate. If literature is morally formative, then how do we avoid literature that assumes, uncritically, illiberal values? And relatedly, if literature is claimed to be morally formative, then can we indeed expect and rely on literature to effect moral change and right moral practice?

In this chapter, I assess how the turn to beauty in theological ethics might respond to the kind of questions that the consequentialist positions on aesthetics and ethics in chapter 1 raise (or whether they acknowledge and grapple with those questions at all). While a number of theologians whose work I will turn to in this chapter are not necessarily theological ethicists per se or do not work out of the specific discipline of Christian ethics, my attention will be on those whose advocacy for beauty necessarily entails the advocacy for a particular way of thinking about the moral life. Thus, I will refrain from engaging those accounts that aim primarily to serve as a corrective to the Christian tradition's relative ambivalence toward the image, the arts, and form, however important such correctives are. (These accounts therefore might be best categorized as, strictly speaking, works in theological aesthetics.)[2] My main interest will be with those whose support for theological aesthetics takes the additional step of explicitly linking that support to a reconsideration of fundamental questions pertaining to moral agency. Two such exemplary accounts are from Susan Ross and Roberto Goizueta. Theirs will be the primary focus of this chapter with the intention of highlighting select features of their accounts as base points indicative of the various emphases and goals that the many theologians who advocate for beauty and ethics share in common either implicitly or explicitly.

Ross's and Goizueta's accounts of beauty and moral agency, I propose, are instructive instances of how articulating a moral aesthetic or an aesthetics of ethics (as I call it) is taken up as the primary task of the larger turn to beauty in theological ethics. This task entails enlisting beauty to elevate the role of affectivity and the senses in the moral life, that is, emotions, feeling, delight and pleasure, seeing or looking, hearing or listening, and touching, and a theological anthropology that prioritizes relationality and community over individualism. That way of approaching beauty, as I suggest below, bypasses or averts the kinds of questions that the consequentialist approaches to literature and ethics find difficult to address, at least on the question of reading and illiberalism (or the avoidance of unjust power relations). As such, their primary contribution is to illustrate how a focus on beauty changes or redirects the terms of debate in ethics away from focusing primarily on the nature of moral thinking per se to focusing more on how beauty offers the theological language to underscore and elevate underappreciated but essential dimensions of the moral life, the embodied underpinnings of moral reasoning.

However, there is an unresolved tension in the turn to beauty inasmuch as Ross and Goizueta are unable to forgo or escape completely the question of how aesthetics leads to ethics in their emphasis on affectivity. This is not to dispute the basic premise of the argument that beauty underscores the importance of the emotions and senses for the moral life. But it is to ask how those feelings and senses are trained so that they are indeed actualized in a manner that is beautiful or appropriate to the form of life that beauty reflects and calls us to (i.e., justice). To appreciate this question is to recognize one of the more difficult challenges that the attempt to bring aesthetics and ethics together faces: the problem of aesthetic perception and moral failure. This is a challenge we broached at the conclusion of chapter 1 in the turn to literature, and, as we shall see, a challenge that is only magnified in the turn to beauty.

BEAUTY AND THE AESTHETICS OF ETHICS

Bringing beauty and ethics together is of course in keeping with the traditional theological unity of the good, beautiful, and true. But what is meant by their intrinsic connection is another matter. Two of the more notable attempts at retrieving beauty for ethics are from Susan Ross and Roberto Goizueta, and a map of their basic premises will be necessary before assessing how their retrievals provide a measure of the contributions of and challenges to the larger turn to beauty in theological ethics.

Ross's aim, as stated in one of her earlier attempts at retrieving beauty for ethics, is to secure beauty as a "central dimension" to right action.[3] What this means more specifically, she states, is that "beauty is found in an ordering, intentional or not (as in nature) of material in a way that presents a unique vision of some dimension of the experienced world that gives the beholder both pleasure and a sense of deeper meaning."[4] Such pleasure and sense of meaning are intrinsic features of being responsive to beauty in our built and natural environments. Furthermore, such aesthetic responsiveness outlines the kind of moral life that is beautiful. While Ross agrees with Hans Urs von Balthasar that theological aesthetics calls attention to how being responsive to the beauty of God "is important for directing moral action," she calls for an amendment to this Balthasarian position by mapping an image of divine beauty that is more sensitive to feminist concerns and experiences of women in community.[5] Two interrelated features of Ross's account of divine beauty in a feminist theological key are worth noting in particular.

First, drawing especially from Elizabeth Johnson and Sallie McFague, Ross advocates for an image of divine beauty that promotes "concrete models of human life" that are fully participatory of both men and women.[6] In such an image of divine beauty, a mutuality that models God's love for all persons in full friendship is central. Also central is an invitation to "human creative engagement" that is reflective of an understanding of God as "dynamic mystery." With these features of divine beauty in mind, Ross emphasizes that from a feminist theological perspective, the language of God is not meant to be "simply descriptive"; its task is to empower a responsive, active relationship with God that translates similarly (or becomes embodied) at the interpersonal level or within human community.[7]

Second, for Ross, a feminist theological construal of divine beauty is necessarily contrastive to Balthasar's theological aesthetics, which "emphasizes revelation *over* experience," prioritizing "the language of surrender and obedience as the human person perceives the glory of God in the story of Jesus Christ."[8] While Ross is careful to say that Balthasar's theological aesthetics does not demand "pure passivity" on the part of the person who receives the revelation of God's glory, such receptivity, she claims, is such that it "seems to downplay seriously the role of human autonomy" in responding and ultimately living the beauty that is central to God's glory. So, while Ross can agree with Balthasar that "speaking adequately of God *is* a moral task," inasmuch as "moral action is dependent on an adequate vision of God," she parts with his stress on contemplation and praise of God as "the ultimate end of the moral life." Instead, her feminist approach to divine beauty "focuses on the concrete, lived experiences of women and men as the location of the human relationship to God."[9]

My aim here is not to adjudicate between Ross's feminist conception of divine beauty and moral agency and that of Balthasar's neo-orthodox account. The point is to notice that Ross, in her critical engagement of Balthasar's theological aesthetics, emphasizes the importance of aesthetic perception for moral action. Specifically, for Ross, to speak of God's beauty is to speak of how God is revealed and then experienced and understood in a manner that affirms the affections or calls attention to the theological import of the affective dimensions of human agency. The perception and then the response to divine beauty is not simply an intellectual event but one that is embodied, enlisting the senses. "Theology's work is not just in the rational and moral dimensions of the person but in the affective as well," she remarks.[10]

Ross also emphasizes, as part of her response to Balthasar, how the aesthetic language of beauty is a crucial means of appreciating, noticing, and validating theologically lived experiences that have gone unnoticed or at the very least underappreciated. For instance, Ross calls attention to the aesthetic practices of a community of Ndebele women in South Africa, how they "have painted their homes in decorative colors and produced beautiful beadwork."[11]

Their works are not simply aesthetic but also reflect a moral quality; in fact, they are inseparable. So, Ross says,

> Their work is beautiful in and of itself. Yet what struck me as I read of these women's efforts was their persistence in maintaining these practices in the midst of apartheid, of war and social and economic pressures from their own countries, including massive displacement and even genocide. There is a quality to these artifacts that is instructive in considering the relationships of beauty and justice. These aesthetic practices are these women's ways of maintaining their community's identity. They offer continuity from one generation to the next, yet they are particular and even individual expressions of each woman's skills and vision. Yet their context, I suggest, gives them a deeper significance than simply being beautiful artifacts. These artifacts are more than just beautiful paintings, weavings, or beadwork. They are also profound statements about the transformative quality of beauty.[12]

Ross reiterates these points with "the joint basketmaking efforts of Tutsi and Hutu women who had lost their husbands in the Rwandan genocide of 1994."[13] In both cases, Ross's emphasis is on how these aesthetic practices, their beautiful works of art and craft making, are also moral practices, specifically works of justice. They preserve community and promote it in the midst of war and its devastating aftermath; their aesthetic works and practices subvert ugliness and squalor that demoralize and devalue a sense of their worthiness. In short, these African women's aesthetic lives model a form of justice that goes beyond obeying rules, submission to hierarchical authority, and seeing choices through an instrumental calculus. As Ross reiterates, the artwork and craft making of these African women are practical but not simply practical and mere objects of consumer desire.[14] They serve particular domestic functions in the daily routines of these women's lives, but "they are not simply tools."[15] Contrastively, their aesthetic practices and objects exhibit the values of a community rooted in mutual cooperation and affective connectedness and affirmation of life.

Like Ross, Goizueta insists on a tight correspondence between the beautiful and the good but through an interpretation of human agency exemplified in the popular religiosity of US Hispanic Catholicism.[16] I will draw primarily from his groundbreaking *Caminemos con Jesús: Toward a Hispanic/Latino Theology of Accompaniment*. There he writes that "the symbols and rituals of [Hispanic Catholic] popular religion are prime examples of the intrinsic value of beauty, and, hence, the intrinsic value of human life as beautiful, i.e., as an end in itself."[17]

The emphasis on "as an end in itself" is the key to understanding Goizueta's meaning of "human life as beautiful." First, note his careful emphasis on the dramatic details of the Good Friday procession rituals of the San Fernando Cathedral in San Antonio, Texas. He refers to the observations of one parishioner-participant in the procession:

> Reflecting afterward on his participation in the procession and crucifixion, he remarked: "Every year, the procession and crucifixion are basically the same. Every year I participate and, several times, I've played the part of one of the soldiers who crucify Jesus. I know the part almost by heart. And yet, each year when the time comes for me to pound the nails into Jesus' feet, I feel chills running down my spine and tears come to my eyes." God is revealed in the doing, in the active participation, in the hammering of nails. It is in the act of walking alongside Jesus and all the others on the Via Dolorosa, and in the act of hammering the nails into Jesus' feet, that this man encounters God—in the most concrete, physical way possible. The only end, or goal, of the man's action is simply the action itself. What makes the man's participation sacred is not the end result, i.e., the completion of the drama, but his active involvement in the evolution of the drama. That is why, though he clearly knows how the story will end, he continues to find it revelatory—because the revelation occurs not at the end, but in the process itself, in the acting itself, in the performance itself. Consequently, his relationship with God is re-enacted whenever he participates in the ritual.
>
> The same is true of all the other participants: the singers, the musicians, the clergy, the children who joyously run down the aisles tossing flower petals during the Easter Vigil, the women who scrupulously dress Mary and Mary Magdalene. . . . God is revealed less in the song than in the singing and playing, less in the sermon than in the preaching . . . and, therefore, . . . in the passion, the living of that life [Jesus's life] itself.[18]

In addition to his detailed attention to the dramatic, aesthetic form of this Good Friday procession, Goizueta calls specific attention to how in this ritual divine revelation is received and experienced in the participants' aesthetic performances, all of which are actions characterized as producing nothing.[19] "More precisely, they are not undertaken primarily *in order to* achieve a result. Their value to the participant derives from the fact that these are not fundamentally the actions of one individual by him or herself, but actions between him or her and God, Jesus, Mary, the saints, and other members of the community, both living and dead." Thus, divine revelation is received "*in the process*" of the participants' relationality and not as an achievement of their relationality.[20] As Goizueta observes, "religion *is* relationship," which US Hispanic popular Catholicism—its narratives—exemplifies. Correlatively, "what *defines* human action as such is praxis, or interpersonal action, i.e., relationship."[21] In US Hispanic popular Catholicism, human action is always depicted and reenacted as interpersonal action, or what Goizueta calls "aesthetic praxis."[22]

Following the work of the Mexican statesman-philosopher José Vasconcelos, aesthetic praxis, Goizueta tells us, contrasts with poiesis.[23] Poiesis describes a form of praxis or human interpersonal activity whose end is not internal to the activity itself but rather external to it. Praxis, based on those terms, is understood to have no intrinsic value or end. Human relationships are only instruments or means to particular ends, and consequently, the measure of human activity (and ultimately the value of human life) is in what it can produce, that is, "in its usefulness."[24]

For Goizueta, Marxism and capitalism provide ready examples of poiesis. Though capitalism is typically understood as antithetical to Marxism, both presuppose the notion that "production is the prototypical human activity."[25] As such, the fundamental difference between the two amounts to no more than divergent opinions on the criteria of production or the ends of human activity. Thus, from the vantage point of Marxism or capitalism, "human life is viewed and valued as the means or instrument through which we produce a desirable product, whether that product is income and profit, food, or the classless society."[26]

Alternatively, from the vantage point of US Hispanic popular Catholicism, human life is viewed and valued in terms of "praxis-as-an-end-in-itself."[27] This means that human interaction and relationships constitute activity between whole persons, which is to say nonobjectified, nonabstract persons. Human interpersonal activity in these terms is not possible from an instrumental view of human action such as those of Marxism and capitalism. In defining human activity in terms of a means-end calculus, human persons are reduced to objects, and human interpersonal activities "become[s a source] of oppression wherein persons use and manipulate one another."[28] Thus, according to Goizueta, what neither capitalism nor Marxism "appreciates is that to make life an object to be worked upon is to instrumentalize life and thus, inevitably, to kill life."[29]

Modernity in its many guises kills life by alienating ourselves from our own actual bodies. However, in US Hispanic popular Catholicism, because praxis is always aesthetic praxis, human action is not just interpersonal action but also interpersonal action that "is rooted in our bodiliness itself, since life is always corporeal. . . . [O]ur interior life, the life of the heart . . . is never disembodied."[30] This stress on embodied relationality resonates with Ross's advocacy of beauty and moral agency. In a later article on aesthetics and ethics, Ross refers approvingly of Mark Johnson's claim that "how we know and what we value are rooted in our bodily experiences."[31] She explains that while "language allows the representation of reality in conceptual terms," Johnson's "more significant point is that these same conceptual terms are based not purely 'in the mind' but rather are rooted fully in embodied experience."[32] This is not to suggest that our intellect simply resides in our bodies and no more but rather to specify that our intellect is more fundamentally affective in nature; this is why our knowing and doing "operate on a fundamentally aesthetic level," Ross notes of Johnson's argument.[33] Similarly, Goizueta argues that "without affect, human praxis is simply physical matter in motion and is, thus, no different from the 'interaction' of billiard balls or bowling pins. . . . Thus, to treat subjects like objects is to ignore the interior dimension of human life, i.e., the emotional, affective, and spiritual dimension."[34] Quoting Vasconcelos, Goizueta affirms that ethics must therefore be aesthetics: "'In its highest form, ethics is aesthetics, that is, service out of love, not out of duty.'"[35] Reason alone distorts human action as a thing or simply as an act.[36] But that amounts to a disembodied moral life.[37]

But Goizueta adds that human praxis is not embodied in just any physical body. In other words, human praxis is not mere physical movement.[38] To be engaged in aesthetic praxis is to interact with others in "empathic fusion," which is to say "truly relate to the other as a person."[39] A mark of such empathic fusion or true relationality is the freedom to express feelings. When one can risk expressing one's feelings to another without fear of "estrangement and alienation," then one knows that one is in relationship with others where persons are treated as ends and not as means.[40] This is a relationship in which the desire or need to control the other is relinquished. This, in other words, is a relationship in which a "basic level of justice" is established.[41] Nichole Flores specifies this claim by suggesting that aesthetic solidarity is the prerequisite for justice. She takes the intersubjective relationality of Goizueta's aesthetic praxis as essentially the blueprint for authentic solidarity. Persons stand with one another in solidarity only when their interactions "affirm human dignity."[42] Such a form of human relationship contrasts with what she refers to as "consumptive solidarity," or commercialized, commodified forms of relationality wherein persons' lives and experiences are commodified for profit, business interests, and the like.[43] Only when we engage one another in a manner that resists such commodification can justice be a possibility. From Flores's perspective, then, we can think of Goizueta's account of aesthetic praxis as the preparatory work that makes justice real in community.[44]

BEAUTY AND THE QUESTION OF MORAL MOTIVATION

To be sure, what I have provided thus far is only an initial sketch of Ross's and Goizueta's turn to beauty. We need to also attend to how for Goizueta the specific language of mediation is critical to the linkage between beauty and aesthetic praxis or noninstrumental relationality and ultimately justice. His focus on Our Lady of Guadalupe is especially important in this regard. For Ross, we also need to attend to the role that she ascribes to arts education in supporting the affective dimensions of moral agency and the life of justice. Both of these matters will bring into relief a critical question that lurks underneath the larger turn to beauty in theological ethics. Before parsing out this question, I want to pause for a moment to reiterate more precisely at least two features that bind Ross's and Goizueta's accounts of beauty and ethics. These two features are noteworthy especially in the way they position the turn to beauty contrastively to the turn to literature.

Affectivity, Moral Vision, and Beauty, Both Natural and Artifactual

The first feature is how the retrieval of beauty for ethics—and thus the advocacy for our material, cultural realities, especially the arts, as nontrivial human pursuits—underlines the need to recognize the affective, embodied dimensions of moral discernment and action. The second feature, which is a correlate of the first, is that a focus on the beautiful is what alerts us (in a way that simply focusing on ethics cannot) to the affectivity of right moral action, drawing particular attention to the value of mutuality, participation, and community. Beauty therefore constitutes a critical way of articulating the good, or the measure of what it means to be good: how we ought to live a life that is beautiful. "In the interplay of justice and beauty, we are drawn to the beautiful because it is a good and right ordering of life; we are drawn to do the good because it makes the world more beautiful," as Ross states.[45] Without beauty, then, we miss the fullness of what constitutes the good if all that we focus on are rules, norms, obligation, and rationality. Note that for Ross it is not that virtue and duty are unimportant: "Clearly, the need for obediential, virtue, or deontological approaches cannot be ignored."[46] But our understanding of moral action is deficient if that is all there is to the moral life; it misses the deep connection between moral action and form (the form of the good) or moral vision.

In these two features, two potential points of contrast emerge between the turn to beauty and the turn to literature in theological ethics. First, while we saw in chapter 1 a favoring of narrative arts over nonnarrative arts, the focus on beauty necessarily demands a broadening of aesthetic expressions or mediums, inclusive of literature but beyond it as well. Thus, Ross's examples of African women's craftwork and artistry are beautiful; so too are the more formal art disciplines, as we will see shortly when turning to Ross's discussion of the promotion of arts education by Catholic nuns pre–Vatican II. And for Goizueta, as is discussed below, beauty cannot be adequately grasped unless we turn to the beauty of popular religious celebrations. We see this broadening of aesthetics in others who turn to beauty to include not only artifactual forms of beauty (e.g., works of art) but also to the beauty of the natural environment. Indeed, for Kathryn B. Alexander, the turn to beauty cannot preclude natural beauty lest we ignore the fact that the Christian tradition, despite its moments of deep suspicions of images and the corporeal, never jettisoned the redemptive possibility of the beauty of the natural world.[47] So too for Patrick T. McCormick.[48] McCormick will go as far as to say that the turn to beauty must go beyond nature to also include the beauty of the stranger and, more specifically, in the act of welcoming, in being hospitable to the stranger.[49]

In short, in the turn to beauty, theologians appear less apt to privilege one form of aesthetic form or medium over another. If, to follow Ross, God is revealed in human creative engagement, then God will be revealed in all expressions of beauty, whether natural or artifactual and, importantly, in human action, that is, in the moral responses to the perception or experiences of such revelation.[50] So, not only is there beauty to be found in the arts and in nature, but there is also beauty in just relationality and the way in which forms of community are rooted in affirmations of life. As Ross proposes, there is beauty in generosity, which is requisite of mutuality.[51] The central insight operative in the turn to beauty in ethics is not that any particular aesthetic medium or form is more morally salient. Instead, the point is to be attentive to those aesthetic practices (whether creating, appreciating works of art, experiencing the beauty of nature, or living justly) that reflect and manifest the form of the good and ultimately the true.

Second, to the extent that beauty is the form of the genuinely good life—that it calls us to seek out or be attentive to those aesthetic expressions that reflect such a form—the turn to beauty avoids the criticism of illiberality, or the concern that a focus on or an attraction to aesthetics can too easily lead to an uncritical acceptance of values that may be more corrosive to human agency rather than liberating. Goizueta's emphatic contrasts between aesthetic praxis and the poiesis of capitalism and Marxism is a striking example in this regard. The value of Hispanic popular Catholicism is in its beauty, which is to say in its resistance to forms of agency and interrelationships that do not promote the value of the person as person but simply as a means to an illiberal end.[52] So, not all aesthetic expressions can count as beautiful (though multiple aesthetic forms or mediums can, as just noted, be revelatory of God's goodness); particular aesthetic expressions or works of art can only be counted as beautiful if reflective of a particular moral vision. The integration of moral vision into beauty as an in-built aesthetic standard is an important implication from what was articulated at the top of this section as a central feature of the turn to beauty in theological ethics, that beauty attunes us to a particular (true) form of the good.

From Seeing to Doing

But there is tension in this claim, a tension that we have encountered implicitly but requires more explicit articulation now. Is beauty fundamentally an experience of a particular form of the good (or the theological language that most accurately attunes us to the truly good), or is beauty that which facilitates or moves us to experience or live that particular form of the good?

To specify the issue that is at stake in this subtle distinction, consider first McCormick's proposal on the necessity of beauty for justice. This necessity, he claims, is not only in the moral vision it delineates, a moral vision that is biblically warranted, he claims.[53] But the necessity of beauty for justice also pertains to beauty's inherent capacity to actualize justice, the "beauty of the righteous community," borrowing from Martin Luther King Jr. So, notes McCormick, righteous community is not only beautiful (and thus something to appreciate, delight in, and affirm), but the beauty of such a conception of justice is the means of its self-actualization in human action: "If beauty unselfs and decenters us with its attractions, so too a vision of justice can offer itself as a thing of beauty that draws us out of ourselves and into harmony with others. Radiant with its own integrity, harmony, and clarity, the dream or vision of the righteous community pulls us beyond the chaos and violence of our disordered communities and draws us to the light of justice."[54]

Given the moral power of beauty, to bring about justice, McCormick will also claim that persons have a "right to beauty." More specifically, "all humans have a fundamental right to live and work in some modicum of beauty," since beauty in our natural and built environments offers "the contemplative and self-transcending rest . . . essential to achieving our full humanity as persons." This also means, according to McCormick, that the opportunity to create beauty is a fundamental human need, "without which we cannot fulfill our potential or vocation."[55] In contrast, environmental, industrial, and urban "ugliness disfigures our planet" and "disfigures persons and communities."[56] Such ugliness denies the transformative power of beauty to do its work in the everyday lives of persons. Inasmuch as creation's beauty, expressed in both the arts and nature, are more often than not inaccessible to the socially marginalized (ugliness prevails rather than beauty in many economically disadvantaged or underresourced communities), McCormick will go on to claim that the right of beauty must also mean that "the poor" have a "special claim" to beauty.[57] McCormick therefore anticipates similar claims made by Pope Francis in his social encyclical *Laudato Si'*.[58]

What is so striking in McCormick's advocacy for beauty's moral necessity is the systematic detail he provides in delineating what a beautiful community should look like and the kind of ethic that beauty demands. From the perspectives of scripture and Catholic social teaching, beauty calls for a society that takes seriously the option for the poor, pursues environmental activism, and holds a renewed appreciation for urban planning.[59] For McCormick, without beauty around us, that is, without having the ability to create beauty through craft and the arts and without the opportunity to enjoy the beauty of nature, whether in the wild or even in something as simple as a garden, the actualization of a beautiful community—a righteous community—is not only diminished but also insidiously feeds and empowers injustice. But what is left underdeveloped is how beauty in our built and natural environments actualizes such beauty in moral action beyond the claim that beauty unselfs us. Surely, unselfing, decentering, or relativizing one's interests and ego is a critical piece to actualizing justice; Iris Murdoch, Simone Weil, and, more recently, Elaine Scarry have all claimed as much, and McCormick's account of the intrinsic connection between beauty and righteous community relies heavily on their claims.[60] So, McCormick will assert, "Caught in the sudden grip of beauty, we are momentarily unconcerned with ourselves or with defending our ego. . . . Beauty dethrones us and renders us one of the crowd."[61] But how an individual experience of beauty's unselfing power then translates into loving, desiring, supporting, and participating in righteous community is less clear.[62] That movement, from personal experience of beauty to one of justice, is even less clear in Scarry's account of beauty, a matter I will take up more specifically in chapter 3.

A more definite moral psychology underlying this kind of aesthetically induced unselfing is provided by Alexander, whose focus, as we noted earlier, is demonstrating the Christian tradition's openness to both artistic and natural beauty as sites for religious insight. Drawing from Josiah Royce's post-Kantian idealism, Alexander asserts that beauty is something that "we need to experience."[63] Why? Her response:

> *Without* beauty we consider the prospect of a radically diminished life. Take, for example, a child in a dense urban area who never experiences green or wild spaces. Imagine a child who is not exposed to museums or cultural events. Surely these are real scenarios for far too many. And so we ask, what is the dilemma of a life without natural beauty or the arts? There seems to be an obvious diminishment. We would assume that such a life comes with greater challenges for striving for one's highest aim or finding ultimate meaning. And if we use Royce's language about insight into the need and way of salvation, a life without beauty is one that might miss this insight.[64]

For Alexander, such insight is characteristically religious (or is best interpreted as religious), since it alludes to the need "for salvation from a power greater than ourselves." Moreover, such insight is powerfully felt in our experiences of natural beauty, though not exclusively. But religious insight is also and perhaps ultimately moral insight, the realization that "we cannot achieve salvation on our own" but only with others in community.[65] The experience of natural beauty adds the insight that our redemption requires "a community committed to ecological restoration and well-being." Alexander will also characterize such insight as "drawing us into" such community.[66] Note the kind of step-by-step progression that ensues from the experience of beauty, especially in nature:

> Following the individual experience [of beauty in nature], we then realize that we cannot achieve salvation on our own [step 1]; at the same time we long to share such experiences of wonder in the natural world, so we turn to social experience [step 2]. We are drawn into community. We then try to analyze the connections we come to see through our reason [step 3]. The will comes next, for we then want to get in touch with the bigger picture and strive for higher aims in life [step 4].[67]

Yet, what is so significant about the moral insight and desire for community we gain through a religious insight that is at first engendered by an experience of beauty? Could not such moral insight and inducement for action also be had from being simply told about their importance or maybe listening to a lecture or reading a textbook on environmental justice?

If Alexander provides a specific moral psychology that maps how it is possible to move from religious insight and then ultimately to moral insight and embracing community, then Ross provides the conceptual frame for why such a progression of insight and ultimately moral discernment and action must necessarily include if not begin with aesthetic experience. While we saw that for Ross beauty attunes us to the importance of vision or form for the moral life and, correlatively, its affective dimensions, an underlying intent in making such claims is to call attention to the matter of moral motivation. Earlier we noted Ross's appreciation for Mark Johnson's emphasis on human knowing and doing as fundamentally embodied realities. She follows up on that insight by citing Jane Bennett, who argues that "without engaging bodily affect, ethics remains a set of rules without an impetus to act. Without the body, ethics is only a disembodied idea."[68] For Ross, all of this is to call attention to the notion that agency and action are matters of being felt. In other words, our affectivity must be cultivated in the direction of the beautiful, or to put it the other way around, it is beauty that, to borrow from her articulation of Bennett's work, "'organizes affects into a style and generates the impetus to enact'" right action, or action that is beautiful. Like Ross, McCormick notes, "beauty also has a special power to change and enlarge hearts and to motivate us to care about and act on behalf of a world that is larger than and creatures that are different from ourselves."[69] What Ross adds, however, is that such enlargement of heart is more akin to a kind of training or schooling of the heart toward an affective affirmation to care for the world and humankind[70] as much as it may be a kind of intrinsic "lure" or pull that "awakens within us a joyous attention to and care for the larger world."[71]

That beauty trains our moral vision and, correlatively, our affectivity toward the good is demonstrated, Ross proposes, in the history of arts education, especially in all-female schools sponsored by Catholic sisters such as Mundelein College and Dominican University, mostly pre–Vatican II. A small sampling of Ross's observations is sufficient to capture the essential connection she draws between beauty and its capacity to train and thus motivate us to moral action. Ross refers to the Religious of the Sacred Heart educator Janet Erkshine Stuart, who emphasized as a frequent theme "the idea of art as having the capacity to 'transfigure' the commonplace. . . . [T]he point is that education in the arts allows the person to see the revelatory potential in what would otherwise be unremarkable."[72] But it was not simply seeing but also performative: for Stuart, "in the disciplined training in the arts, students learn self-control but also how they are to live."[73] Thus, arts education was not simply something that women were expected to pursue (because being an artist or being artistically capable was more appropriate of the feminine and not the masculine); rather, "education in the arts was also a means of training girls and women in virtue."[74] That same idea is also found in the architectural intent of Mundelein College in Chicago. Sister Justitia Coffey, who spearheaded the design of the college's Skyscraper building (completed in 1930), insisted on an Art Deco design "'to boost student's self-esteem.'"[75] Thus, its Art Deco beauty and the artistic performances that were to be held in the college were meant to "elevate" its female students, to move them to a particular form of life. "The incorporation of the arts into educational curricula, the aesthetic dimensions of educational and social practices, and the ability to take on leadership roles in these activities were not primarily intended to make women 'more refined' but rather sensitive and thoughtful moral agents."[76]

Beauty and Mediation

Ross's phrasing "intended to make" goes to the heart of the tension that exists in the turn to beauty in theological ethics. Beauty attunes us to the moral significance of the affective; this is why theological ethics must also be seen as a theological aesthetics. But the claim, as we see with Ross, goes further: beauty informs and directs our affectivity so that we are moved to right action and a life of the good. The turn to beauty, then, ultimately is not far removed from the turn to literature, as we saw in chapter 1. The primary difference here is the more explicit emphasis on the critical role that affectivity plays in moving from aesthetics to ethics. That beauty makes us good moral agents is emphasized and reinforced more strongly in Goizueta's linkage of beauty and justice when he talks of the mediating capacity of popular religiosity in Hispanic Catholic communities.

Consider Goizueta's account of the Our Lady of Guadalupe story, what he deems as the central story of Hispanic popular religion. In this story, he observes the mediating power of beauty, in its fullest expression, in the relationship between Mary (la Morenita) and the commoner Juan Diego, who is instructed by Mary to speak to the bishop:

> A central theme of the Guadalupe story is the revelatory power of beauty. The story itself begins with music, the singing of the birds, and ends with flowers, the roses that Juan Diego takes to the bishop. The

> extended dialogues in which the Lady identifies herself as Mary are circumscribed by symbols of beauty which make that identification credible for Juan Diego. If Juan Diego believes what Mary tells him, it is not because her statements are self-validating or self-evidently true, but because they are preceded by beautiful, heavenly music and corroborated by beautiful, fragrant roses. The truth of Mary's statements is mediated by and revealed in the beauty of music and the flowers. Without the singing birds and the fragrant flowers, Juan Diego would not have encountered Mary and, even if he had, would not have believed her. It was in the music and flowers that he knew her. Here, interpersonal action [between Juan Diego and Mary] is defined and mediated by beauty.[77]

In this story, two sets of interactions emerge: one between Juan Diego and what Goizueta refers to as "symbols of beauty" and one between Juan Diego and Mary. These interactions, however, are not discontinuous. Rather, one leads to the other; as Goizueta states, "*Without* the singing birds and the fragrant flowers, Juan Diego *would not have* encountered Mary." It is Juan Diego's concrete, definite experience of beauty that "becomes the model for Juan Diego's own relationship with *la Morenita*."[78] The experience of beauty—the hearing of the beautiful music of birds and the seeing and smelling the beautiful flowers—captivates Juan Diego to beauty and prompts his surrender to it. This experience, then, allows him to enter "into a genuine union with another," in this case Mary.[79]

The experience of beauty moves or draws us to act justly (draws us to aesthetic praxis). "When we are in the presence of beauty, we *lose* our control and are swept up into the experience" or become "one" with the experience (e.g., with beautiful music).[80] This experience of surrendering ("affectively, through empathy" or simply "empathic fusion")[81] in turn prepares us for or opens us up to interpersonal activity in which the need or desire to control the other is precluded. Thus, according to Goizueta, experiences of beauty, at least from the view of the Guadalupe story, transform us to an aesthetic understanding of human action, that is, to justice.[82]

In large measure, the Guadalupe story reflects the "logic" of US Hispanic popular religion, including the Holy Week celebrations discussed in the previous section. It is in the very participation of the symbols and rituals of popular religion that one experiences beauty and correlatively aesthetic praxis. As Goizueta describes,

> The symbols and rituals of popular religion are prime examples of the intrinsic value of beauty, and, hence, the intrinsic value of human life

> as beautiful, i.e., as an end in itself, for the goal of the community's participation in the stories, symbols, and rituals of popular religion is nothing other than that participation itself. The goal of the interaction among the participants, and the interaction between them and Jesus, Mary, and the saints, like that between Juan Diego and *la Morenita,* is nothing other than the interaction itself—which is to be enjoyed and celebrated.[83]

In the participation of the stories, symbols, and rituals of popular religion, the participants perceive, behold, experience beauty: the beauty of the songs sung, the music played, the dances performed, and the crafts/folk art worn and displayed. And it is in this experiencing of beauty, in being swept up into the experience of beauty, that the participants interact with each other in such a way that the goal of the interaction is nothing other than the interaction itself; it is affective, aesthetic praxis.

BEAUTY AND MORAL CORRUPTION

For Goizueta, beauty, at least from the perspective of Hispanic Catholic popular religiosity, does not simply identify the mechanics of right moral action (i.e., affectivity, emphatic fusion) but also identifies the material space through which such action is made possible. This again recalls Ross's reference to Mark Johnson: "how we know and what we value are rooted in our bodily experiences and responses to the material realities we encounter."[84]

That Goizueta as well as Ross will shift back and forth between thinking about beauty as the proper language of theological ethics and thinking about beauty as the impetus or ground for doing the good is noteworthy because it also infuses a kind of ambivalence in their accounts of beauty and justice. While there is a rhetorical robustness to their characterization of the mediating power of beauty, that is, in its power to move persons to act for the good, there is also a modicum of restraint in their positions.

To be more specific, consider the claim that Goizueta makes toward the end of his discussion on beauty and justice: that there is, drawing once again from Vasconcelos, moral ambiguity in beauty's power to mediate aesthetic praxis or emphatic fusion, or what he also calls mestizaje. As Goizueta states, "we cannot address adequately the aesthetic character of human praxis if we do not, at the same time, retrieve the particular manifestation which aesthetic praxis takes in the history of the Latino community."[85] What are the particular historical manifestations?

> In Latino popular Catholicism, human action is mediated by physical symbols. These, however, are not only religious symbols but also *products* of our labor: e.g., the beautiful dresses which the women of San Fernando so carefully placed on Our Lady and Mary Magdalen to prepare them for Good Friday, the pieces of bread distributed to the congregation at the end of the Holy Thursday liturgy, the Eucharistic offering itself, the gifts we exchange with each other, the house which, through a family's interpersonal action (praxis), becomes a "home." Before these physical objects are religious symbols, they are economic products. Their religious meaning is mediated not only by their physicality in general, but by the specifically economic character of that physicality. The bread is not merely a physical object like any other; it is "fruit of the earth and *work* of human hands."[86]

The central point in this illustration of religious symbols as products of labor and particular economic relationships is to illumine the reality that "art is always susceptible to political and economic manipulation. . . . Indeed, the most 'revolutionary' abstract art is much more likely to be found in corporate offices and suburban mansions than in the houses and apartments of an inner-city barrio. Political propaganda and commercial advertising are clearer examples of instrumentalized art; these are forms of aesthetic praxis that, in the service of political economic goals, have been reduced to forms of poiesis, or productive activity."[87]

To the extent that "cultural symbols and practices are *always* mediated by political and economic structures and relationships,"[88] Goizueta claims that if the beauty of popular Hispanic Catholicism is to affirm and mediate aesthetic praxis as "life as an end in itself," then Hispanic popular Catholicism must take root "most firmly in those lives that are, in every way, most 'useless' to our society, i.e., most economically and politically superfluous. The very emphasis on beauty, aesthetics, and celebration then—and only then—becomes, *de facto*, a subversive act in a society geared toward the accumulation of economic and political power."[89] In other words, if beauty is to affirm its mediation of aesthetic praxis and resist or subvert poiesis, then it can only do so if there is an affirmation of aesthetic praxis first, and only then would the moral power of beauty be effectual. This is an extraordinary claim given, as I noted earlier, the robustness of the connection between beauty and justice that Goizueta makes initially in *Caminemos con Jesús*. He begins by proposing that beauty mediates aesthetic praxis. But then he ends with the claim that beauty mediates aesthetic praxis not because of its inherent power but instead because its inherent power emerges only when we commit to aesthetic praxis first. This conceptual reversal, or perhaps more fairly his way of accounting for the fact that beauty does not necessarily mediate aesthetic praxis, at least in the way that it is normatively conceived of doing, makes sense; Goizueta needs to move in this direction, given that his account of beauty is not simply a theological aesthetics but instead employs theological aesthetics as the ground for moral action.

Ross too will admit that beauty's power to motivate moral action is not without ambiguity. "Given the recalcitrance of human nature—its tendency to be lazy, to avoid the hard choices, to simply not do anything in the face of a call for action—it is impossible to say that the motivation for doing what ought to be done is always and primarily tied to the aesthetic. Indeed, sometimes we need to ignore our feelings or our aesthetic response to a situation in order to undertake some kind of moral action." So, she makes the following qualifications: "This is not to say that ethics by definition is always *primarily* engaged with the aesthetic. . . . But it is important to note that the aesthetic, in the broadest sense, is never entirely absent."[90] Similar to Goizueta, Ross also notes, drawing from Robin James's reflections on Jacques Rancìere, that "'the aesthetic is the *primary* medium in which privilege and oppression are maintained'" as well as "encountered."[91] Ross then makes the following speculation about the kind of relationship women religious (Catholic sisters of pre–Vatican II) had with the arts:

> From this perspective, one could say that women religious both represented the maintenance of privilege, particularly in their role as educators of women through the arts, yet also resisted the oppression of women. They did this by both cooperating with an aesthetic/political system that marginalized and idealized women while also using this system as a way to further their educational goals within it. This system was also one that privileged whiteness and wealth, whether implicitly or explicitly. . . . There is no question that Catholic women's educational institutions were places of white privilege.
>
> However, I suggest that the very aesthetic practices that women religious and their students were engaged in during the pre–Vatican II years worked to empower many of them to take on new roles in a post–Vatican II world. Their understanding of the aesthetic was broadened in an awareness of its social context and power.[92]

As a historical point Ross may indeed be correct to point out that the aesthetic practices of women religious did not simply reinforce and perpetuate white privilege. Yet, it is interesting that Ross will suggest that such a historical fact was possible because women religious and their students broadened their understanding of the aesthetic through "an awareness of its social context and power," which motivated action toward a more inclusive vision of justice and the good.[93] So, "women religious looked for new opportunities to educate children, particularly those in marginalized areas. Many of them came to understand their own privileged context critically and engaged in acts of ritual and moral agency in public ways." This elaboration is curious, since it would mean the need to slightly revise one of her earlier claims pertaining to the beauty of African women's aesthetic practices. "Contemplating the beauty of these African women's work opens the beholder to the creative potential for community-building in the humble tasks of 'women's work.'"[94] Yet, if the power of beauty is not without ambiguity, then we will also need to be open to the possibility—the real possibility—that contemplating such beauty will do no such thing to the beholder. The beauty of these African women's work to open the beholder to the creative potential for community building would require that the beholder first be aware of the social context of the African women's work as well as the beholder's own social context.

In a series of lectures that builds on her earlier essay "Women, Beauty, and Justice," Ross posits that such awareness of social contexts—of the beholder's and beheld's—may be more readily forthcoming when the aesthetic practices of African women are placed in contrastive relationship to forms of aesthetic expression that are (in her judgment) of dubious moral consequence:

> There are certain dimensions of the appreciation of beauty that writers on this subject emphasize, quite justifiably. Philosophers and theologians have stressed certain habits and attitudes. These include attentiveness, particularly attentiveness to detail, a heightened awareness, a sense of reverence, and the obligation to behold and enjoy.
>
> Yet, it seems that those of us who live relatively comfortably in the developed world live in a world where beauty is often up for sale. Not only can one pay to get one's wrinkles, age spots, and cellulite removed, it is also possible to decorate one's home in the style of Martha Stewart, Ralph Lauren, Calvin Klein, or any number of other famous designers by shopping at discount stores. It seems that almost every week there is a new television show about home design, and I confess that I enjoy watching some of these shows. In some interesting ways, at least some of the virtues listed above can be applied to the world of home design: attentiveness to detail—anyone who has ever watched Marta Stewart make a holiday decoration can only be amazed by the details she includes; a heightened awareness—how many of us, after

> having watched a television show or read a decorating magazine now look at a piece of furniture or a wall color only to see it as tired, passé, and in desperate need of change; even the obligation to behold and enjoy can be exercised with the purchase of a few magazines or fabric samples, or by window-shopping at the local mall. Yet, I doubt that a sense of reverence, of a decentering of the self, of a turn to others, are most characteristic of how we feel when we have finished a decorating project. It seems to me that perhaps some of us may well be in need of a little decentering, a little humility about the relation between beauty and justice. A comparison between the women of Africa and the women of the home decorating shows can be sobering and decentering as well. Perhaps such a decentering—the kind that we experience when we behold the art and craft work of these women—might help in engaging us more intensely in the struggles for justice, especially justice for women, in the world.[95]

It is worth underscoring how Ross accounts for the morally transformative power of African women's craft making and artistry, which flexes its moral muscles to the extent that we see their work—we attend to their details and appreciate and enjoy them—within a larger socioeconomic, political frame, when we are "more aware of our place in our own world and in the universe."[96] It is interesting therefore that Ross, in her critique of Balthasar's theological aesthetics, claims that "Balthasar's theological aesthetics does appear to be less equipped than feminist theology to appreciate the aesthetic and moral quality of these artifacts [from African women]" because of "his inattentiveness to the social and historical context of human life. . . . Ultimately, an adequate theological aesthetics will be attentive to the theological message, the media in which the message is conveyed, and the context in which it is found."[97]

With that in mind, it is perhaps not surprising that when Ross turns to studying the importance of arts education for pre–Vatican II religious sisters, she concludes her study by speaking less of the formative power of beauty and reemphasizes the importance of theological aesthetics in illuminating a fuller account of moral agency:

> The work of women religious shows how attention to the whole person—intellect, emotions, and bodily sensations—needs to be at the center of ethics. Too often, the theological anthropology that undergirds ethics fails to account for the multidimensionality of people, whose social, historical, and familial contexts have powerful influences on responses to issues that require a moral response. Although an

aesthetic approach is not a sufficient element to moral education, it is nevertheless a necessary part of this process.[98]

But if aesthetics is necessary, then in what way is it necessary? If the normative claim is that beauty moves us to justice, then how does the power of beauty manifest itself in the direction of moving the affections toward right action rather than corruptibility? That Ross as well as Goizueta will soften this normative claim with the reluctant acknowledgment that social interests, location, and dynamics often shade us from perceiving, valuing, and living the beautiful suggests the difficulty and complexity of articulating what it means to say that beauty is morally necessary, that ethics cannot do without beauty.

BEAUTY, MORAL FAILURE, AND THE AMBIGUITY OF AFFECTIVITY

One of the more notable retrievals and defenses of theological aesthetics can be found in David Bentley Hart's *The Beauty of the Infinite: The Theological Aesthetics of Christian Truth.* While the focus on the book is less on developing a theological aesthetics for theological ethics, elements of the book distill the spirit of the turn to beauty in theological ethics that I have endeavored to outline above and in a manner that brings to the fore more pointedly the kind of problem that confronts the turn to beauty in theological ethics.

If, as I have tried to illustrate with Ross and Goizueta, the turn to beauty draws attention toward a more holistic account of moral agency, Hart too moves in this direction but by emphasizing the nonviolence of the beauty of God. So, he proposes that sustained attention to beauty necessarily positions Christian thought contrastively to the vision of life that we have inherited through "the great project of modernity." Christianity as rooted in the beauty of God made present in the form of Christ is contrastive to modernity's logic in at least two ways. First, the beauty of the form of Christ radiates in judgment of perhaps what we might say is the power-centered politics that defines statecraft in the modern era.[99] As such, the beauty of the form of Christ is fundamentally one of peace rather than violence. The inherent violence that marks the political authority of the modern state marks "the authority of thrones, dominions, principalities, and powers whose role is violence."[100]

Second, insofar as beauty rather than violence characterizes the form of Christ—the truth of Christianity—beauty offers an alternative to the Enlightenment "myth of disinterested rationality."[101] If beauty is at the heart of Christian thought, then Christian thought, in its very nature, is about proclamation, exhortation, bearing witness, and persuasion rather than about appealing to epistemological foundations by way of universal reason. Put slightly differently, if Christian thought is recast as theological aesthetics, then Christian thought is basically not one of rational explication but instead is rooted in story, which is to say that Christian thought "[makes] its appeal first to the eye and the heart, . . . the only way it may 'command' assent." Therefore, he concludes, "the church cannot separate truth from rhetoric, or from beauty."[102] Echoing Ross's and Goizueta's stress on affect for moral action, Hart's argument also echoes Meryl Westphal's defense of heteronomy and, consequently, his preference for testimony above and beyond so-called rational argument.[103] The intelligibility of Christianity is a kind of testimony or, as Hart prefers, witnessing not only because Hart finds foundationalist metanarratives a fool's errand but also primarily because Christian thought, if rooted in beauty, will necessarily demand a form of reasoning that is no more and no less than bearing witness. Bearing witness is not only in keeping with the beauty of the form of Christ, but as such, bearing witness is in keeping with the intrinsic peace that the form of Christ communicates, and thus so too is martyrdom.

That the beauty of the Christian story, its intrinsic nonviolence, demands martyrdom is proposed in the last chapter of *The Beauty of the Infinite,* and while it is made primarily with the question of hermeneutics in mind—that is, how Christians ought to communicate truth, evaluate truth claims, evangelize about the truth, and so forth—the linkages he makes between beauty and martyrdom are the closest he gets to articulating the salience of theological aesthetics for theological ethics, particularly as it pushes into the realm of war and peace. This articulation culminates in the following passage:

> Christian rhetoric can only be a declaration of witness, a gift. A gift of martyrs—which is the name that must, finally, be given to the Christian practice of persuasion—can never be returned violently, as the Same; because this gift is always peace and beauty, violence can "receive" the gift, but never return it.
>
> This means, perhaps tragically, that Christian peace has no prudential or universal or systematic way of averting war (though neither has anything else), but can overcome violence only though conversion [through persuasion]. . . . Christian thought should be aware always of the risk of war, but should still nonetheless never consent to the illusory peace of "neutrality." Hermes, the messenger and exegete of the gods, always crosses an alien distance to bear tidings, always traverses a *chorismos;* but Christian thought announces a God who is himself the distance of all things, the impossibility of exile, the peace

of the infinite. . . . Still, in this war of persuasions, Christians struggle only by way of martyrdom, by surrendering their gift to others even in the moment of rejection. . . . This is the rhetorical beauty of Christ the stranger, calling the apostles, speaking to Mary in the garden, joining the disciples on the way to Emmaus, meeting his apostles again on the sea strand, over a shared meal: always offering himself anew, always displaying his presence as an unanticipated gift and unhoped-for reconciliation. This is the style of a martyr's expenditure, which is made in the hope of a return that it is powerless of itself to effect, but which is also made by a soul; committed to the grace of an infinite God who can always give souls to one another in the dispensation of his peace, in the shared scope of his infinite beauty.[104]

If peace is what marks the beauty of Christ, then is it obvious that martyrdom is necessarily what such peace demands? One need only turn to controversies within the Christian tradition on whether, for instance, killing is morally permissible, however tragic, despite the demand emanating from the agape of God's trinitarian life. In this instance, I have Augustine to Paul Ramsey, among others, in mind who hardly saw their views on just war as antithetical to the peace of Christ; in fact, they saw it as warranted by agape's demand to love one's neighbor, however paradoxical that may sound on the surface.[105] What else can Christians do in the face of human suffering at the hands of enemies wielding their guns and machetes with the intent to massacre?

The moral ambiguity of Christian peace, however, is indicative of a further ambiguity that goes to the heart of the central problematic in the reclamation of beauty for theological ethics. If we assume that Hart is right about the inherent nonviolence of beauty, then what are we to make of beauty's moral failures? Like Goizueta, Hart is more than cognizant of such failures, of the ambiguous moral success of beauty in the concrete.[106] Hart's response, however, moves in a slightly different direction than Goizueta's: instances of moral failure in the presence of beauty do not necessarily imply that beauty has "failed" to make persons good and just. Instead, we should marvel at the fact that moral failure—moral atrocities even—often takes place in the shadow of beauty, as if to remind us that goodness rather than moral failure is the final word or telos of being:

There is an unsettling prodigality about the beautiful, something wanton about the way it lavishes itself upon even the most atrocious of settings, its anodyne sweetness often seeming to make the most

> intolerable of circumstances bearable: a village ravaged by pestilence may lie in the shadow of a magnificent mountain's ridge; the marmorean repose of a child lately dead of meningitis might present a strikingly piquant tableau; Cambodian killing fields were often lushly flowered; Nazi commandants occasionally fell asleep to the strains of Bach, performed by ensembles of Jewish inmates; and no doubt the death camps were routinely suffused by the delicate hues of a twilit sky. Beauty seems to promise a reconciliation beyond the contradictions of the moment, one that perhaps places time's tragedies within a broader perspective of harmony and meaning, a balance between light and darkness; beauty appears to absolve being of its violences.[107]

Fair enough, but we would still need to account for the fact that so many atrocities have also been committed either in the name of beauty or in the so-called defense of beauty. Nazi officers did not simply perform their horrific acts while listening to classical music; they also massacred populations in their desire to "secure" a certain kind of classical music—to protect the "beauty" of German culture—from cultural pollution. This truth deserves unvarnished attention. Chapter 3 will examine this relationship between the arts and authoritarianism further and show how taking this problematic relationship seriously can refine (or redefine) what it means to say (or what we ought to mean when we say) that the arts are morally consequential. For now, however, it is important that we sit with for a while the uncomfortable reality that the moral power of the arts is not as powerful as it is often described or hoped to be. If beauty is in fact for justice rather than simply a distraction or mockery of justice, then what accounts for its seeming lack of moral power, its inability to dispose persons toward the right and the good? Posited differently, what are we to make of the fact that the agapeic telos of beauty is not necessarily actualized or evoked consistently if at all? (Or, what are we to make of the fact that beauty often fails spectacularly in actualizing agape in the world?)[108] Such inconsistent (or failed) actualization does not necessarily mean that beauty is theologically suspect, but the reality of inconsistent (or failed) actualization occasions (and demands) closer scrutiny of what it might mean to say that beauty is morally salient, that it has moral purchase on our daily lives. Is it not also the case that even those who may not have a right to beauty, as McCormick might put it, given perhaps their culturally impoverished social situations, still lead morally beautiful lives, maybe even exemplify the beautiful? Otherwise, only great artists would be moral exemplars, but to be sure, plenty of great artists have led morally suspect lives, while many who are not socially privileged or who are nonartists or simply lack artistic sensibilities, live morally extraordinary ones. If so, then what moral necessity does beauty serve other than as an aesthetic to the good, that is, as a means of elevating and calling attention to the persistence of goodness?

There is of course immense value in not losing sight of the inherent goodness of creation: that evil, as I noted above regarding Hart's theological aesthetics, is not the final word on being. As Patricia A. Lamoureux remarks, drawing from Balthasar, "we see the world, though 'seared with trade' and 'bleared, smeared with toil,' as beautiful when viewed in light of the Easter promise that newness and transformation are possible, despite the tragedy and conflict that too often permeate reality. It is only in light of such a vision that we can understand Fyodor Dostoevsky's comment that 'beauty will save the world.'"[109] The challenge, however, is discerning how beauty effects such redemption, since we also need to account for the fact that experiences of beauty lead to moral failure as much as they are transformative. Beauty—the beauty of the divine being—is the origin, intent, and destination of creation, but the claim is also that seeing such beauty in creation is morally self-actualizing. Beauty not only makes itself visible in creation; with beauty's perception, creation is also made beautiful in its rightful ordering of relationships. It is the latter claim that requires greater theological scrutiny unless it merely pertains to an affirmative statement of the eschatological ideal rather than a claim about the practical need and realistic prospects for aesthetic forms and experiences in the realization of the right and good in the concrete here and now.

If, as I noted at the top of this section, Hart's theological aesthetics reflects the general spirit of the contemporary turn to beauty in theological ethics (i.e., its broadening of moral agency to include moral vision and affectivity), his theological aesthetics also captures the essential problem that persists in this turn to beauty. It is one thing to map out a theological position on the normative power of beauty for the moral life. But it is surely another thing entirely to map out how beauty is morally powerful, how it forms our affectivity in such a way as to realize its moral vision in concrete human experience. We may have good theological reasons to elevate beauty and insist that its moral vision corrects our notions of moral agency to include the role of affect, the senses, its embodied character. But those theological reasons lose performative reliability without a more robust account of how our affectivity is trained in its moral vision, for affectivity is not in itself disposed or prone to the moral life that beauty might endorse; it can be bent or trained toward a variety of moral visions. In chapter 4, I will turn to the theology of Jonathan Edwards to parse out more specifically why affectivity can be susceptible to moral manipulation. Even joy and pleasure can be bent or even trained toward grotesque ends; delight is hardly the sole possession of beauty, as we will see from an Edwardsean perspective. For the time being, it is important to note why it is necessary to appreciate the need for such an account. Beauty presses us to a life of beauty, which is to say a life defined by empathic fusion where persons are loved in themselves as enfleshed persons (Goiziueta), or by embodied mutuality, participation, and creativity in contrast to hierarchical submission and obedience (Ross). But what is missing is how contemplating beauty, attuning ourselves to its many expressions, both natural and artifactual, and delighting in it and valuing its forms, trains or converts our seeing, looking, hearing, and feeling so that the impetus to act accordingly is actualized concretely. That absence is especially felt in Hart's insistence on the fundamental nonviolence of Christ's beauty, given that it exists in stark tension with the inconvenient truth that being in the presence of beauty—loving it, caring for it, wanting it—does not necessarily immunize us from a life of violence, even a life of evil.

As David Bromwich observes, "Morality and imagination have something to do with each other, and both have something to do with the human power of sympathy."[110] But, Bromwich notes further, pity, like sympathy, can "[serve] as a unique and trusted assistant" in justifying our selfishness rather than the opposite, which complicates claims to the morally transformative power of the human imagination. But, he maintains, "pity can be made agreeable to selflessness."[111] Imagination can thus be made critical to morality but only if we retrain our "manners or habits" of self-regard.[112] But the question is how. How can this be accomplished? Is it accomplishable? We will need to raise similar questions with respect to the turn to beauty in theological ethics. If beauty and ethics are both to have something to do with one another, then the emphasis on embodied affect that binds them will need to be recast beyond generalizations, that is, beyond normative claims that beauty mediates a particular vision of the good. This is not to contravene the position that beauty, as Goizueta asserts, is tied to justice in that it helps us to "'penetrate much deeper into the essence of the ethical [by giving] us as a norm the conduct of an exemplary life.'"[113] But that is surely an "at minimum" claim given that certainly for him beauty is more than simply a giver of norms but, more precisely, is transformative of human agency in conformation to those norms. How else to understand the mediating power of popular Catholicism, as he sees it?[114] Or, for Hart, how else to understand the move from beauty's nonviolence to its demand for martyrdom? But the gap that persists is how the affective experience, or embodied affect, of beauty leads to the motivation to act, since, again, it is hardly the case that such motivation is necessarily aesthetically self-generative. The longer that gap remains, the more sentimental the turn to beauty can appear and the more unsettling the question posed by the novelist Marilyn Robinson, "Why are some not able to 'see' all this glory?"[115]

Inasmuch as the turn to beauty in ethics is not inattentive to the morally ambiguous possibilities of beauty while insisting that, despite the ambiguities, beauty is morally transformative, we will need to ask whether such accounts of beauty's moral power are possible beyond theological affirmations that they are possible. How do we move from a theological affirmation of beauty's moral possibilities to a theological account of how our affective experiences in response to beauty bridge the gap between the potentiality to act to the actual "motivation to act" in line with that perception of beauty?[116]

NOTES

1. Ross, "Women, Beauty, and Justice," 81.
2. Examples include Brown, *Religious Aesthetics*; Viladesau, *Theological Aesthetics*; Dyrness, *Visual Faith*; Sherry, *Spirit and Beauty*; Farley, *Faith and Beauty*; and Barbeau and McGowin, *God and Wonder*.
3. Ross, "Women, Beauty, and Justice," 81.
4. Ross, 81. See also Ross, *For the Beauty of the Earth*, 28.
5. Ross, "Women, Beauty, and Justice," 84.
6. Ross, 85.
7. Ross, 86.
8. Ross, 83.
9. Ross, 89.
10. Ross, 92.
11. Ross, 90. See also Ross, *For the Beauty of the Earth*, chap. 3, where she also highlights the work of the African woman and 2004 Nobel Peace Prize winner Wangari Maathai as well as the art/craft work of Berber women in Morocco.
12. Ross, "Women, Beauty, and Justice," 90.
13. Ross, 90.
14. Ross, 91–92.
15. Ross, 91.
16. Following Goizueta's own practice, in only this chapter I use US Hispanic, Hispanic, and Latino/a interchangeably and refrain from using the identifier Latinx that is increasingly used in contemporary academic scholarship.
17. Goizueta, *Caminemos con Jesús*, 102.
18. Goizueta, 103–4. For more on the Hispanic celebration of the Holy Week triduum, particularly at the San Fernando Cathedral, see 32–37.
19. Goizueta, 105.
20. Goizueta, 104.
21. Goizueta, 105.
22. Goizueta, 104.
23. Goizueta, 82.

24. Goizueta, 85.
25. Goizueta, 85.
26. Goizueta, 85. See also Goizueta, "Rediscovering Praxis," 60: "If, in capitalism, the life of the worker becomes an object to be manipulated in the service of the commodity, in Marxism the life of the worker becomes an object to be manipulated—even by the worker himself—in the service of the future 'New Person'; 'his own life is an object for him.'"
27. Goizueta, *Caminemos con Jesús*, 88.
28. Goizueta, 111.
29. Goizueta, "Rediscovering Praxis," 60. For Goizueta, Marxism and capitalism provide ready examples of the triumph of poiesis in Western modernity. Though capitalism is typically understood as antithetical to Marxism, both presuppose the notion that "production is the prototypical human activity." As such, Goizueta suggests that the fundamental difference between the two amounts to no more than divergent opinions on the criteria of production or the ends of human activity. Thus, from the vantage point of Marxism or capitalism, "human life is viewed and valued as the means or instrument through which we produce a desirable product, whether that product is income and profit, food, or the classless society." Goizueta, *Caminemos con Jesús*, 85.
30. Goizueta, *Caminemos con Jesús*, 94.
31. Ross, "Aesthetics and Ethics," 142.
32. Ross, 141.
33. Ross, 142.
34. Goizueta, *Caminemos con Jesús*, 96.
35. Goizueta, 93.
36. Goizueta, 93–94.
37. Goizueta, 94.
38. Goizueta, 110.
39. Goizueta, 91, 92.
40. Goizueta, 110.
41. Goizueta, 107.
42. Flores, *The Aesthetics of Solidarity*, 141.
43. Flores, 136–41.
44. The notion of aesthetic praxis (or aesthetic solidarity) as preparation for justice is suggested in Flores's use of the term "promote" and other similar verbs. For instance, she states that aesthetic solidarity "operates . . . to promote justice," that "solidarity[,] . . . promoted by aesthetic engagement, is central to justice," and "aesthetic solidarity also is directed toward the pursuit of justice" (Flores, *The Aesthetics of Solidarity*, 142). I take her position to be essentially Goizueta's, especially given that she sees her account of aesthetic solidarity as building on Goizueta's account of aesthetic praxis. In the concluding chapter of her book, Flores cites the following passage from Goizueta in support of her position: "'A community is defined by such intersubjective relationships. A byproduct of authentic community is, thus, the birth and development of free and unique human persons.'" (142; see also Goizueta, *Caminemos con Jesús*, 75, 107). Goizueta seems to be suggesting that when there is aesthetic praxis (intersubjective relationships), then there is justice. Flores can be read as essentially defending such an if/then formulation when she comments that "authentic intersubjective community is thus a requirement of solidarity that affirm the dignity of human persons. This kind of relationship, promoted by aesthetic engagement, is central to justice" (Flores, 142). In chapter 5, I suggest that Flores

can also be read as operating with (though not in an explicit and systematized manner) a more nuanced relationship between aesthetics and justice.

45. Ross, "Women, Beauty, and Justice," 81.
46. Ross, "Aesthetics and Ethics," 132.
47. Alexander, *Saving Beauty*, chap. 1.
48. McCormick, *God's Beauty*, 11–21, 113–49.
49. McCormick, 77–88.
50. Ross, "Women, Beauty, and Justice," 86.
51. Ross, *For the Beauty of the Earth*, 25–31.
52. Goizueta gives this greater historical socioeconomic concreteness in mapping out what he calls a theological aesthetics of the borderland, that is, popular Catholicism as it has been practiced "in the history of Latino/a communities as borderland communities." Goizueta, *Christ Our Companion*, 126. Such a theological aesthetics elevates the theological theme and significance of living in and being from the in-between land of "Galilee" (128).
53. McCormick highlights what he calls four biblical visions of beauty: creation and the Sabbath, the Garden of Eden, the Promised Land, and the Reign of God. See McCormick, *God's Beauty*, chap. 1.
54. McCormick, 8.
55. McCormick, 41.
56. McCormick, 40, 41.
57. McCormick, 70–75.
58. Francis, *Laudato Si'*, para. 45: "In some places, rural and urban alike, the privatization of certain spaces has restricted people's access to places of particular beauty. In others, 'ecological' neighborhoods have been created which are closed to outsiders in order to ensure an artificial tranquility. Frequently, we find beautiful and carefully manicured green spaces in so-called 'safer' areas of cities, but not in the more hidden areas where the disposable of society live." It is interesting that so much of McCormick's positions on beauty and justice (in *God's Beauty*, published in 2012) are also taken up by Pope Francis in *Laudato Si'*, promulgated in 2015. As we noted above, McCormick, like Alexander, defends natural beauty as theologically, religiously, and morally revelatory. This position is also carried forward by Pope Francis. On this issue, Francis writes in *Laudato Si'*, para. 97: "The Lord was able to invite others to be attentive to the beauty that there is in the world because he himself was in constant touch with nature, lending it an attention full of fondness and wonder. As he made his way throughout the land, he often stopped to contemplate the beauty sown by his Father, and invited his disciples to perceive a divine message in things: 'Lift up your eyes, and see how the fields are already white for harvest' (Jn 4:35). 'The kingdom of God is like a grain of mustard seed which a man took and sowed in his field; it is the smallest of all seeds, but once it has grown, it is the greatest of plants' (Mt 13:31–32)."
59. On the importance of urban planning that is both aesthetically pleasing and morally elevating, see Francis, *Laudato Si'*, para. 150: "Given the interrelationship between living space and human behavior, those who design buildings, neighborhoods, public spaces and cities, ought to draw on the various disciplines which help us to understand people's thought processes, symbolic language and ways of acting. It is not enough to seek the beauty of design. More precious still is the service we offer to another kind of beauty: people's quality of life, their adaptation to the environment, encounter and mutual

assistance. Here too, we see how important it is that urban planning always takes into consideration the views of those who will live in these areas."

60. See, for instance, McCormick, *God's Beauty*, 46–47. He also turns to John O'Donahue to call attention to the Greek etymology of beauty, *kalein*, which alludes to the idea of calling, of being called to something beyond oneself (46).
61. McCormick, 47.
62. McCormick seems to concede as much in passing when he observes that "there is, of course, no guarantee that beauty will unself or decenter us in ways that render us just or compassionate" (*God's Beauty*, 48). But he insists that beauty is essential to a just life and society insofar as it provides "the contemplative and self-transcending rest" that is needed anyway: "a life without any openness to the transcendent or the neighbor is a deeply impoverished existence in which no one should be long enslaved" (48). Later I suggest that such a deeply qualified claim to beauty's moral power is indicative of a larger problem that besets the turn to beauty in theological ethics.
63. Alexander, *Saving Beauty*, 91.
64. Alexander, 91.
65. Alexander, 93.
66. Alexander, 95.
67. Alexander, 93.
68. Ross, "Aesthetics and Ethics," 142.
69. McCormick, *God's Beauty*, 116.
70. Ross, "Aesthetics and Ethics," 135.
71. McCormick, *God's Beauty*, 116, 117.
72. Ross, "Aesthetics and Ethics," 135.
73. Ross, 136.
74. Ross, 137; see also 143.
75. Ross, 139.
76. Ross, 141.
77. Goizueta, *Caminemos con Jesús*, 106.
78. Goizueta, 108.
79. Goizueta, 109.
80. Goizueta, 108, 91.
81. Goizueta, 92.
82. Goizueta, 109. Cf. Francis, *Laudato Si'*, para. 215: "By learning to see and appreciate beauty, we learn to reject self-interested pragmatism. If someone has not learned to stop and admire something beautiful, we should not be surprised if he or she treats everything as an object to be used and abused without scruple. If we want to bring about deep change, we need to realize that certain mindsets really do influence our behavior. Our efforts at education will be inadequate and ineffectual unless we strive to promote a new way of thinking about human beings, life, society and our relationship with nature. Otherwise, the paradigm of consumerism will continue to advance, with the help of the media and the highly effective workings of the market."
83. Goizueta, *Caminemos con Jesús*, 102.
84. Ross, "Aesthetics and Ethics," 142.
85. Goizueta, *Caminemos con Jesús*, 119.
86. Goizueta, 121–22.
87. Goizueta, 123.

88. Goizueta, 127.
89. Goizueta, 129.
90. Ross, "Aesthetics and Ethics," 132.
91. Ross, 144.
92. Ross, 145.
93. Ross, 145.
94. Ross, "Women, Beauty, and Justice," 93.
95. Ross, *For the Beauty of the Earth*, 76–77.
96. Ross, 77.
97. Ross, "Women, Beauty, and Justice," 92.
98. Ross, "Aesthetics and Ethics," 146.
99. Compare this to George Weigel's conception of statecraft, wherein violence, war in particular, is considered an essential, legitimate political tool in the service of peace. See Weigel, "Moral Clarity in a Time of War," esp. 377–88.
100. Hart, *Beauty of the Infinite*, 2.
101. Hart, 3.
102. Hart, 4.
103. Westphal, *In Praise of Heteronomy*, 215.
104. Hart, *Beauty of the Infinite*, 442–43.
105. See Paul Ramsey's defense of militant intervention as an agapeic duty: "The Western theory of the just war originated, not primarily from considerations of abstract or 'natural' justice, but from the interior ethics of Christian love, or what John XXIII termed 'social charity.'" Ramsey, *The Just War*, 142.
106. See, for instance, Hart, "A Sense of Style," 249. Here he notes how the "style of Christ" (his light and beauty) "is a difficult style to catch hold of, and not everyone cares to try." He has in mind Christians who endorse, on Christian theological and biblical grounds, what he considers to be morally dubious positions such as the death penalty. "Clearly, those who think it possible to be faithful to the figure of Christ as he appears in the gospels and also to argue in favor of the death penalty are, before all else, philistines. Their sensibilities are manifestly too barbarous and obtuse to see and appreciate the style of Christ at all, because it is simply too refined, subtle, and elegant for them, and certainly too negligent of commonsensible ethical expectations and the regrettable necessities those somethings entail; it is a style, rather, that expresses a form of life thoroughly absorbed in a far more essential and otherworldly loveliness."
107. Hart, *Beauty of the Infinite*, 16.
108. In "A Sense of Style," Hart returns to this question indirectly and simply rests in the hope "that what draws us to the good [i.e., the charity of Christ] is that it is also eternal beauty" (249). He underscores this hope by turning to John 8:1–11 and calling attention to Jesus's style in responding to the scribes and Pharisees who sought to stone a woman caught in the act of adultery. They end up leaving the woman alone, and Hart attributes Jesus's style of engagement as the motivating factor: "In dispersing the woman's accusers with a cool irony that leaves them haplessly silent, and in then granting her a forgiveness wholly unencumbered by any ponderous expressions of disapproving decency or piety, and without even any prescribed penance, Christ demonstrates how a single graceful gesture, performed with sufficient moral and aesthetic skill, can express all the dimensions of beauty and charity" (249). While we might surmise that Jesus's style played a role in swaying the scribes and Pharisees, John 8 gives little indication of what made Jesus's style

effective, that is, what made Jesus's "cool irony" morally persuasive, necessarily. One can also imagine Jesus's response "'He who is without sin among you, let him be the first to throw a stone at her'" (Jn 8:7, NRSV) eliciting a retort on what counts as sin, who counts as a sinner per the Law. The question, then, is what makes Jesus's aesthetic approach to the situation ultimately, as Hart puts it, compelling or beguiling so as to thwart or deflate the reasonableness of such a retort. This pertains to what I emphasize below as the persistent challenge of the question of how beauty does its moral work, which is different from whether it does moral work; it is the former and not the latter that remains insufficiently attended.

109. Lamoureux, "Introduction," 3.
110. Bromwich, *Moral Imagination*, 3.
111. Bromwich, 32.
112. Bromwich, 36.
113. Goizueta, *Caminemos con Jesús*, 94.
114. "In popular Catholicism," Goizueta writes, "the people's action is mediated by physical symbols, such as the bread that is shared and the flowers placed on Jesus' corpse, by physical gestures, such as kissing the crucifix or kneeling alongside Mary, by physical movement and processions, by singing songs and playing musical instruments." Goizueta, *Caminemos con Jesús*, 103. And these actions provide each participant a sense of self and self-worth (103), which in turn empowers them to act in the larger society and culture in ways that affirms and regards persons as ends rather than as means or instruments (128–30). The moral conversion effected by popular Catholicism is therefore not so much about achieving a new moral standard as it is a realization or empowerment of personhood. "One might go so far as to say that the remainder of the story becomes an account of Juan Diego's *conversion* from a technological or instrumental understanding of human action to an aesthetic understanding. In the beginning, his surrender to her beauty and the beauty of the birds' music had become the basis for his *empowerment* as a person" (109, emphasis added).
115. Yeager, "Suspended in Wonderment," 130.
116. Yeager, 130.

3

WHOSE ART? WHICH COMMUNITY?

We have encountered a number of iterations of the claim that the arts are morally consequential or that aesthetic practices are integral to the moral life, effecting moral transformation. But how should we account for this affirmation? Is it defensible, and if so how? It is insufficient, as I have suggested in the previous two chapters, to insist that art can lead to certain kinds of moral outcomes depending on its purported beauty or on the narrative it depicts or the kind of artwork it is (e.g., social novel or popular religious art). Such insistence does not adequately account for art's moral failures or successes or, in other words, its pluralism of outcomes. As Richard Posner maintains at least with literature, its "value cannot reside in its moral content because works 'often invite a variety of incompatible moral responses.'"[1] Beautiful art may indeed encourage or elicit acts of moral goodness, but it can also elicit immorality as well as nothing at all. A Victorian novel may engender a desire in its reader to embody the social mores it depicts or may elicit others to reject them as illiberal and morally repugnant. Others may read the novel and eventually forget having read it at all, going on about their daily lives unaffected, or may have no desire to read it to begin with, chafing at its purported importance, maybe thinking it boring. Such outcomes—the multiplicity of them—complicate any claim that art is morally salient, morally consequential. Can anyone know what will result from art? While some may regard art as morally valuable and be moved in one particular, perhaps intended, moral direction, art can also unintentionally move another in an entirely different direction. Why is art, then, morally consequential to some and morally ineffectual or irrelevant to others? Moreover, why do some give certain kinds of art moral regard and dismiss other kinds of art as morally irrelevant, and why do others disagree and think that a different kind of art is morally important? What accounts for such selectivity? In short, is the capacity of art to capture a person's moral imagination and to move them accordingly unpredictable and unexplainable? If it is, then we will need to confront the prospect that what we can reasonably affirm is only the hope that the arts are morally consequential. But at what point such hope amounts to wishful thinking may be the more unsettling prospect.

I do believe that we can do more than simply hope that the arts are morally consequential. How the arts are morally consequential, however, demands that we better account for the moral pluralism of the arts, that is, the reality that the arts engender multiple moral outcomes, some intentional, some not. Such pluralism does not undermine the moral prospects for the arts. Instead, that the arts often lead to multiple outcomes underscores the fact that the arts are action-oriented; they are not without effect on their participants. But the open question is why they move their participants along the multiple trajectories that they do and whether one kind of trajectory is more possible than another.

In this chapter, I begin the work of constructing a response to this question by turning to a number of theorists of aesthetics and their attempts to account for the relationship between aesthetics and ethics. Works by Elaine Scarry and Marcia Muelder Eaton will be primary, though they will serve mostly as base points for other theorists who will help to expand and put together the clues that Scarry and Eaton place before us. Starting with Scarry will be especially important, since her work on beauty and justice, as we saw in passing in chapter 2, is often cited as endorsing a strong account of art as morally consequential. But as I also intimated in chapter 2, Scarry's work is overly simplified by some of her interpreters; the way she links beauty and justice is not as linear as it is often taken to be.

Scarry as well as Eaton and additional theorists who will be considered in this chapter push a reassessment of the interactive dynamics between the arts and their audiences, asking what kind of "work" art can elicit and accomplish and to what extent we can consider the kinds of actions that it provokes to be morally consequential. More significantly, they push further the following question: What conditions enable the kind of "work" that art engenders to transfer over into the moral sphere? What I am particularly interested in is how each theorist under consideration reveals, at times explicitly and at other times by what they do not say, how we regard works of art matters as much as if not more than *that* we regard works of art. For instance, that some may prefer (or not) to live in communities brimming with artists, galleries, theaters, and museums or lament (or not) the absence of beautiful scenery, landscapes, or works of art is instructive of the kind of moral work art is capable of doing. In short, the moral efficaciousness of art—and thus its capacity to move persons in one direction or another—will depend on the kind of moral regard one brings to the perception of art.

Though each theorist this chapter considers inhabits nontheological disciplines, the aim in considering their works is to identify additional themes and questions that theological-ethical engagements in aesthetics and ethics have neglected. This will assist the larger task of refining a theological-ethical framework for thinking constructively about the relationship between aesthetics and ethics and, specifically, what it might mean to claim aesthetics as an integral source for Christian ethical reflection. The theological-ethical shape of this framework, which will be held together by a reassessment of the nature of the emotions in relation to the affections, will emerge more clearly in chapter 4 as it builds on the following distinction I hope to make in this chapter: works of art are not in themselves intrinsically morally consequential but are nonetheless morally consequential depending on what we mean by ethics. Accordingly, when claims are made that aesthetics is critically important to the moral life—that it can broaden our vision or morally school us—the force of such claims spring from their assumptions about what the moral life is and not necessarily about the inherent moral power of art per se.

LATERAL REGARD AND FORWARD MOMENTUM

The importance of what we assume about the moral life with respect to what we see in the arts (or would like to see in the arts) as morally salient or efficacious is not obvious. But unless we are sharply attuned to the hidden role of those assumptions, we will find it difficult to account for the various claims we make about the arts, that is, what they can do, why what they can do is morally consequential, and why we think certain kinds of art is morally consequential more so than others. For starters, consider Elaine Scarry, whose slim but influential volume *On Beauty and Being Just* sets out to rebut what she claims is a common political critique against the act of looking, reading, or, more generally, perceiving and being attentive to beautiful objects, including art.[2] The critique holds that such aesthetic acts of perception, "by preoccupying our attention, distracts attention from wrong social arrangements. It makes us inattentive, and therefore eventually indifferent, to the project of bringing about arrangements that are just."[3] Scarry's rebuttal to this critique relies on recasting aesthetic acts of perception as more dynamic than this critique allows. This critique assumes that perceiving art that is beautiful only benefits the one who is perceiving the artwork and not the artwork that is being perceived. In other words, aesthetic perception is essentially selfish. This is mistaken, according to Scarry.

Consider the effect of perceiving a beautiful artwork or how such an aesthetic act of perception "saves lives or directly confers the gift of life."[4] Scarry elaborates that perceiving something beautiful "quickens. It adrenalizes. It makes the heart beat faster. It makes life more vivid, animated, living, worth living."[5] Accordingly, one looks at a beautiful photograph, painting, or poem with such value as if one's quality of life would be significantly diminished without it, "as though one's life depended on it."[6] And insofar as we find the beautiful artwork valuable to us, we find the beautiful artwork itself, that it exists, valuable for its own sake. In this way we, the perceiver of the beautiful artwork, confer the gift of life to the object perceived. As Scarry puts it, objects "being perceived as beautiful [seem] to bring them to life or to make them life-like."[7]

When the perceiver accords value or confers the gift of life to the beautiful artwork perceived, the perceiver is led to accord "a fragility and consequent level of protection" to the beautiful artwork.[8] Such protection often takes two distinct forms. One form is what Scarry calls "lateral regard," a kind of aesthetic stewardship.[9] Lateral regard means that if I find, say, a vase beautiful, then I will more likely attempt to discern the beauty of other vases as well. Lateral regard therefore entails extending the recognition of fragility in one particular object to other like objects and wanting to protect them.[10] Such horizontal extension of fragility and protection is why Scarry thinks that, in part, we are drawn to the symmetry of artworks;[11] artworks that reflect a high level of equality and proportion are the kind of artworks that incite lateral regard more so than other artworks. (The idea here is that lateral regard would be symmetrical if we had to visualize it.)

The second way we accord fragility and protection to beautiful artworks is through aesthetic creation and re-creation, or what Scarry calls "forward momentum." Forward momentum conceptualizes the notion that "beauty brings copies of itself into being. It makes us draw it, take photographs of it, or describe it to other people. Sometimes it gives rise to exact replication and other times to resemblances and still other times to things whose connection to the original site of inspiration is unrecognizable."[12] At times, forward momentum is described as an end in itself, or the telos of aesthetic perception: within aesthetic perception is the capacity "to incite, even to require, the act of replication" or "unceasing begetting."[13] Or, "a visual event may reproduce itself in the realm of touch . . . which may in turn then reappear in a second visual event, the finished drawing."[14] Scarry's example of Dante's *La vita nuova* provides a more concrete instance of such an inevitable desire or push to create and re-create the objects of one's aesthetic perception:

> Thus the beauty of Beatrice in *La vita nuova* requires of Dante the writing of a sonnet, and the writing of that one sonnet prompts the writing of another: "After completing this last sonnet I was moved by a desire to write more poetry." The sonnets, in turn, place on Dante a new pressure, for as soon as his ear hears what he has made in meter, his hand wants to draw a sketch of it in prose: "This sonnet is divided into two parts . . ."; "This sonnet is divided into four parts."[15]

By now it should be clear that Scarry scarcely thinks that aesthetic acts of perception only benefit the one who perceives beautiful art; perception is equally if not more beneficial to the artwork that one perceives. This latter benefit is manifest through lateral regard and forward momentum, the two mutually reinforcing movements that looking (or any act of aesthetic perception) motivates. The aesthetic act of looking at a beautiful artwork can incite the desire to regard this particular artwork and other artworks deemed similarly beautiful as fragile and alive and thus worthy of protection (lateral regard). This act also incites the desire to replicate the object of one's perception, that is, to create and re-create the beauty one perceives through successive aesthetic acts, such as painting, sculpting, writing a poem, or just additional acts of looking (forward momentum). Scarry's account of lateral regard and forward momentum therefore calls attention to how acts of aesthetic perception stir an array of successive aesthetic actions that signal the perceiver's desire to sustain the beauty in her or his "perceptual field,"[16] which, according to Scarry, signals further the lessened interest in the perceiver's own self and greater interest in the value of the beautiful artwork. This "radical decentering," Scarry argues, reveals the critical importance of aesthetic perception for the life of justice,[17] for without such perception, one cannot appreciate "the perspective of all others," as justice requires.[18] Radical decentering, increasing awareness of others, and engendering a conviction of the others' value are how beauty or, more broadly, aesthetic perception, exerts pressure toward justice, calls us to justice,[19] or, as Scarry also describes, "acts as a lever for justice."[20]

Yet, the role of lateral regard and forward momentum in supporting justice is not as causally straightforward as Scarry makes it out to be. How she characterizes the moral status of lateral regard and forward momentum reveals how much she assumes with respect to the meaning of justice and how much of those assumptions are brought to bear on her moral claims about looking, reading, and listening. The following remarks are instructive:

> Beauty may be either natural or artifactual; justice . . . is therefore assisted by any perceptual event that so effortlessly incites in us the wish to create [e.g., via forward momentum]. Because beauty repeatedly brings us face-to-face with our own powers to create, we know where and how to locate those powers when a situation of injustice calls on us to create without itself guiding us, through pleasure, to our destination. The two distinguishable forms of creating beauty—perpetuating beauty that already exists; originating beauty that does not yet exist—have *equivalents* within the realm of justice.[21]

It is important to note that the claim of equivalence reinforces a larger claim that Scarry makes about how lateral regard and forward momentum and acts of justice are not analogous; they are, more precisely, the same. Consider her choice of description specifically with respect to lateral regard. Again, lateral regard pertains to how perceiving or finding an artwork beautiful compels one ("involuntarily") to seek out, discern, or perceive the beauty of other artworks.[22] We now need to add that for Scarry, the dynamic of lateral regard also amounts to distributing our regard for the value of beauty to other beautiful artworks in a manner that is fair, that is, as if we are making a "pact" with other beautiful artworks, agreeing to protect them, to value them.[23] Lateral regard therefore is a form of "fair distribution."[24]

Lateral regard as fair distribution is not an incidental characterization. This characterization allows us to see how lateral regard is compatible with features of justice, given that fairness "is already an abiding part of the way we every day think and speak about justice."[25] There is truth to this for sure; fairness is part of our common intuitions of justice. Scarry's assertion, however, is also a careless generalization. What "fair distribution" means is not always the same across human communities. It is also not the only way that justice can be (and has been) understood, but it is certainly one way of talking about justice that is distinctively Rawlsean, and Scarry invokes Rawls readily. One striking instance is when she claims that the convergence between beauty and justice is clear "if we look first at the connection between beauty as 'fairness' and justice as 'fairness,' using the widely accepted definition by John Rawls of fairness as a 'symmetry of everyone's relations to each other.'"[26]

It is of course debatable that fairness as Rawls defines it within his neo-Kantian constructivist framework is as widely accepted as Scarry claims it to be. (Correlatively, it is debatable that his definition of fairness ought to be taken as normative.)[27] Regardless, the larger point to underline here is that activities that arise from acts of aesthetic perception—lateral regard and forward momentum—are not simply aesthetic actions but instead are rendered morally important by virtue of the definition of justice Scarry carries. Almost as default, she takes for granted that Rawls's account of justice as fairness is normative and universally true. Consequently, the idea of justice as fairness should also appear in the spheres outside of ethics, including the sphere of aesthetics, lest the universal objectivity of justice as fairness be less than universal. As Scarry observes, again invoking Rawls, "beautiful things give rise to the notion of distribution, to a lifesaving reciprocity, to fairness not just in the sense of loveliness of aspect but in the sense of 'symmetry of everyone's relation to one another.'"[28] This level of convergence between beauty and justice (as fairness) is what prompts Scarry to claim that beauty and justice are not analogies but, as we noted, are instead equivalent concepts, with one standing in the place of the other when one is absent. "In periods when justice has been taken away . . . beautiful things" have always inspired or fueled the "aspiration" to justice as fairness.[29]

The power of Scarry's eloquence notwithstanding, is the claim of equivalence between lateral regard and forward momentum, on the one hand, and justice, on the other hand, convincing? Scarry's account of lateral regard as an aesthetic consequence of looking, reading, or listening is not unpersuasive: that we tend to want to preserve or care for objects we are drawn to, especially beautiful art objects (or those that we consider beautiful), is not experientially foreign to many of us, I submit. The sadness and horror over the burning of the Notre Dame cathedral in Paris and the botched restoration of works of art are perhaps indicative of the veracity of lateral regard.[30] Also with forward momentum, inasmuch as it beckons us, in a highly conceptualized way, to recall moments in which an experience of perceiving art, perhaps in a museum, gallery, or public space, was so captivating or intriguing that we could not help but take a closer look, stare more intently, read the curator's inscription next to it, or even take a picture of it with our phone. We might also recall being moved to undertake more adventurous forms of looking and study as a consequence. Consider the recollection of the art critic Holland Cotter: "After I saw a show of early Buddhist sculpture [at the Japan Society] in 1983, I went home, packed a bag and flew to Tokyo. I needed to go to where that art came from, and I spent a month visiting temples and monasteries across the country."[31] Experiences such as these hint at the kind of generative aesthetic capacity of art objects and how integral and commonplace the experience of repeated attention is to the perceptual experience of art. The concept of forward momentum identifies and draws our attention to this feature of aesthetic experience, allowing for more descriptive accounts of how we in fact interact with art objects in daily life. The perception of art is not a static event. Oftentimes, to perceive art—whether sculpture, photography, poetry, line drawings, or architecture—is to perceive it repeatedly; in other words, such aesthetic perception can elicit successive acts of aesthetic creation and re-creation.

But despite the experiential familiarity of lateral regard and forward momentum, is it as obvious, as Scarry suggests, that in these two aesthetic actions we can hear "John Rawls's formulation of what, since the time of Socrates, has been known as the 'duty to justice' argument: we have a duty, says Rawls, 'to support' just arrangements where they already exist and to help bring them into being where they are 'not yet established'"?[32] Scarry makes it clear that lateral regard and forward momentum direct us to justice—the "first leads to the second," as she puts it.[33] But we need to wonder if that line of causation is possible precisely because her particular notion of justice makes it plausible. Even if one were to concede that lateral regard and forward momentum are capable of schooling us in the meaning of justice, it seems far too convenient that they are the kind of aesthetic practices that are "equivalent" to the skills that befit questions of Rawlsean justice.

Street parades and playing fields as well as river races (Scarry singles out Thomas Eakins's paintings of sculling) all make present to our senses the meaning and urgency of justice as fairness, Scarry claims.[34] But the moral witness that such artworks and aesthetic experiences provide would seem dependent on a prior commitment to such a conception of justice.[35] It is worth noting that for Rawls, justice as fairness indicates the need for what he calls the "original position," or the hypothetical situation from which deliberation about what justice requires must begin. In this condition, all persons are under a "veil of ignorance" wherein their social position or status, their religious and racial identities, and so forth are hidden from view. Only then could we determine the principles of justice.[36] With that in mind, it is curious that Scarry would propose, among other things, that paintings of men rowing, white men rowing no less, can call us to justice as fairness even if, as Scarry takes the time to note, almost as if anticipating this misgiving, Eakins chose to paint rowers, such as the Biglin brothers, who "issued an open challenge to the 'gentlemen-only' rowing clubs of Britain" (figure 1).[37] While the beauty of these paintings' symmetry, proportion, and harmony may be worthy of admiration and study, can we necessarily parse in these features a sense of justice as precisely as Scarry defines it, unless that is the kind of justice we are hoping to see or have supported by these paintings in the first place?

FIGURE 1. *The Biglin Brothers Turning the Stake,* 1873. Thomas Eakins (American, 1844–1916). Public domain via the Cleveland Museum of Art, Open Access initiative, Hinman B. Hurlbut Collection 1984.1927, https://www.clevelandart.org/art/1984.1927.

ART, COMMUNITY, AND MORAL THEORIES

That Scarry links her account of lateral regard and forward momentum to justice in a Rawlsean key suggests that her claims about the moral salience of the arts say as much about her assumptions on the nature of the moral life as they do about what she thinks the arts can do. We can go a step further and say that her account of the moral salience of the arts is made possible because of the kind of assumptions she holds about the nature of the moral life. Is it not striking that the moral instruction emerging from lateral regard and forward momentum is so precisely attuned to and supportive of Rawlsean justice as fairness? We see a similar pattern of thought, but more explicitly and intentionally, in Marcia Muelder Eaton's claim that aesthetic and moral judgments are complementary.

For Eaton, the arts are integral to moral judgment but only because they have the power to cultivate in us the kind of skills that make moral judgments possible. As Eaton states, citing Marcia Cavell, "In moral judgments, 'We don't so much justify our judgments as explain them. . . .' We point to details, give new emphasis to them, and show new patterns and relationships between them. Moral sensitivity develops in particular contexts. We have to pay attention to the tone with which something is said, as well as to the content, and to the relations between the speakers, or to meanings of other words spoken earlier or later."[38] Such moral sensitivities are not unlike the sensitivities of either a good art critic or the kind of skills belonging to novelists, dancers, painters. "When [an artist] attends to relationships and patterns of expression, one relates and arranges specific things. Attention to fit and implications challenges one to attend closely to a variety of elements, and challenges one to develop powers of perception, reflection, and imagination."[39] For Eaton, such work of artistic, aesthetic attention is exactly what is entailed in the work of ethics. "The study of ethics brings to the foreground features of the human situation that must be attended to and the connections between them. Art does this as well, and it does it by requiring many of the skills necessary for 'reading' the features foregrounded."[40] In addition to R. M. Hare, Eaton claims Michel Foucault, Charles Altieri, R. W. Hepburn, David Wiggins, Hilary Putnam, Iris Murdoch, and Martha Nussbaum, among many other theorists, as constituting the spectrum of claims that see aesthetic skills and moral skills as parallel and convergent.[41] In short, the point is to see that the construction of individual lives (or the moral skills requisite for such construction) is not unlike the aesthetic skills needed for the construction of a story or some other work of art.

In calling attention to the likeness between aesthetic and moral judgments, one of Eaton's aims is to refute arguments that prioritize aesthetics over ethics and claims that suggest that without aesthetics, ethics is hampered. On this, she has in mind the following kinds of perspectives that insist on a tight "causal connection" between aesthetic and ethical experiences:

> People who really participate in real art are morally improved. Urban designers from Thomas Jefferson to Jane Jacobs have argued that beautiful cities make for better citizens. When the Baltimore Aquarium opened a new Caribbean Reef exhibit, the curator said she believes that when people see how beautiful the ocean ecosystems are, they will be more likely to take action to protect these environments. Indeed, many ecologists do report that the beauties of nature initially drew them to their specializations.[42]

We have seen theological-ethical versions of these claims throughout chapters 1 and 2 as well as earlier in this chapter with our assessment of Scarry. While Eaton is not unsympathetic to such claims, for she too believes that aesthetics is consequential for ethics, she does not think that the importance of aesthetics for ethics is one of direct causation, or a direct line from aesthetics to ethics, but instead is one of interdependence.

Eaton's invocation of interdependence can be misleading. For Eaton, interdependence underscores, as we saw above, how moral judgment requires a certain kind of "appropriate style and content," which is not unlike "aesthetic skills."[43] On this view, aesthetic judgment and moral judgment are similar. But if they are similar, could this mean that aesthetic skills can be morally transferable and thus that aesthetics can "lead to" ethics (so, learning to be good in art can be a kind of moral training as well)? In this regard, interdependence would seem to simply circle us back to the kind of causative relationship between aesthetics and ethics that Eaton finds questionable.

It is important to note, however, that while moral and aesthetic judgments are similar or parallel—in other words, there is a descriptive likeness between the two—Eaton's claim of interdependence points to similarity in a different sense. Aesthetic and moral judgments are similar because they are interdependent, by which Eaton means more specifically that when we make claims about aesthetics, they are in fact claims about ethics. In this respect, while ethics may not be dependent on aesthetics as the strong causative accounts suggest in the passage cited above, what is the case is some degree of the converse. As Eaton observes,

> Even if it were true that people for whom aesthetic activity plays a significant role in their lives were more ethical than others, the priority of the aesthetic would still not be established. Advocating city beautification via claims about the moral benefits *presupposes* ethical preferences. Saying that more fountains and neater streets will make better neighbors *presupposes* a theory of what makes citizens "better." Just as claiming that eating more salmon makes one healthier *depends on* a particular conception of health, valuing beauty as a means to goodness *presupposes* a concept of moral goodness. Theories of artistic genius that attribute special ethical insights to art makers, even if true, also *presuppose* a concept of what it means to be ethical.[44]

Theories about what aesthetics can do for ethics presuppose or, more strongly, depend on a particular conception of ethics. For Eaton, then, to claim that aesthetic and moral judgments are similar is not simply a descriptive observation but one that indicates what she thinks is morally valuable. What is morally valuable is the capacity to "see alternative actions and life choices" as integral to moral judgment.[45] That is "one reason people [including Eaton] value art. . . . [I]t invites openness to consideration of various courses of actions, various choices of the sort of person reasonable people may want to be. . . . Art . . . helps us to remove our blinders."[46] That art is valued in this way and is perceived to aid in the importance of such a conception of moral judgment speaks to the interdependence of art and ethics, but it is an interdependence that is rooted in and emanates from a particular account of ethics. For Eaton, that account seems to be one in which the capacity to evaluate ends and choose one or another is favored over an account in which the self is situated within a particular universe of ends and sees their task as cultivating their social attachments. The former account of ethics, the one Eaton favors (what we might call a liberal account, not unlike the Kantian trajectory to which John Rawls belongs, aligns with her view of art as providing moral options rather than a school for moral formation (what we might call a more communitarian account of ethics).

Whether Eaton assumes a kind of liberal conception of the self rather than a kind of communitarian conception is not the precise point here. That she assumes or promotes some particular vision of the self is the essential insight, and it reinforces her broader point that claims to aesthetic and ethical convergence rely on a particular moral posture. "Considering alternatives is a necessary part of mature ethical deliberation," she argues.[47] Such a conception of ethical deliberation foregrounds the moral value of art. Such foregrounding is also operative in the accounts of aesthetics and ethics we saw from Susan Ross and Roberto Goizueta in chapter 2, though as we also discussed, they, whether intentionally or not, waiver between, on the one hand, presenting their accounts as anchored by a particular account of moral agency and action in their view of what art can do and, on the other hand, simply regard aesthetics as more descriptive of the nature of moral agency and action than other ethical paradigms. Eaton is more explicit in her theorizing: if art is morally valuable, then such a view of its moral importance is made possible by a particular view of what is morally important; one's moral assumptions ultimately call the shots.[48]

Consider further what Eaton claims is the capacity for art to generate and sustain community. Sometimes, she argues, aesthetic appreciation, the activity of noticing a particular artwork and finding pleasure in it, is a private, individualistic affair. "Obviously individuals can all by themselves savor objects and events aesthetically—enjoy a shade of blue or consider the intrinsic properties of a lily of the field or the sound of a slit-gong (the long, hollow percussion instruments used by some peoples of New Guinea)."[49] But Eaton notes that private appreciation can also lead to communal appreciation. To explicate her claim, she refers us to what she thinks is a common scenario, challenging us to test its validity against our own experiences of aesthetic appreciation: "Much everyday activity of human beings exhibits the [following] same structure. On a beach with strangers, someone picks up a shell and alerts general attention by saying, 'Wow, look at this! Isn't it beautiful?'"

Private appreciation or enjoyment can often lead to the sort of appreciation that desires its communication to other persons. Such communication is motivated by an interest in the interests of others, their well-being. And it is concern for their well-being that can potentially lead to the formation of community:

> To return to the example of folks on the beach, one imagines acquaintances and strangers responding to the speaker's call for attention to the beauty of the shell. Some come closer, ask to hold it for themselves, or inquire whether there are many others like it in the area. For however fleeting a time, a focused group exists. The focus will be maintained if, for instance, some contemplators decide to go shelling together or to establish a shell museum. Focus will have to be maintained even longer if what is undertaken is the building of an earthen mound, a pyramid, or a cathedral. But maintained and sustained, a focused group turns into a community.[50]

Private aesthetic appreciation can engender conversation and thus deliberation among a diverse group of participants. Such conversation and deliberation can lead to the formation of a focused group that, if maintained, can be a prelude to a more enduring, sustainable form of community. A focused group in Eaton's view is a nascent form of community; in a focused group, its members "sense a connection" to each other as they become involved in "joint activity."[51] Private aesthetic appreciation can lead to the joint activity of communal aesthetic appreciation, thereby creating a sense of connection between persons. Perceiving a particular work of art or a beautiful object may provoke descriptive and evaluative commentary about the object in question, which may provoke further the desire to share that commentary in part because one thinks that it will be beneficial to another's well-being. Why else would I remark on the beauty of a seashell or the architecture of a cathedral to another person unless I thought that it is important for them to share in the appreciation of this object, just as it is important to me?

For Eaton, the descriptive and evaluative commentary that arises from aesthetic appreciation does not merely involve talking or direct speech but can also involve both artistic creation and aesthetic gestures, such as gazing and pointing, or what she refers to as acts of contemplation. Both artistic creation and aesthetic contemplation are communicative in nature. "When one creates art," according to Eaton, "one does it in the awareness of others and with the intention that they will respond to the fact that someone created it with that intention." With respect to forms of contemplation, Eaton claims that we gaze and point in response to particular artworks "in the belief that they will bring others to respond to certain intrinsic properties." Both the creation of art objects and the various forms of aesthetic contemplation provoke, echoing Scarry's notion of forward momentum, "further acts of creation that, in turn, encourage more occasions for awareness and contemplation." And according to Eaton, artistic creation and aesthetics acts of contemplation can reflect or "instill a sense of responsibility" inasmuch as both activities are engaged "in part for the good of others."[52] More specifically, we make a statement about some artwork so that others can also participate in our perception of it in the hope that they too will recognize and share in our sense of value for the artwork in question.

According to Sally M. Promey, communication to others is exactly what we do when we engage in the activity of "display." Display encompasses the creation of not only art but also "the numerous modes of visual communication" that are either exhibited or performed.[53] What is significant for our purpose here is Promey's argument that intrinsic to display is a sense of the public, "the verbal form 'to display' includes 'to make public' (and, with just a bit of extrapolation, to make or create publics) among its synonyms." Granted, "display also sometimes carries with it connotations of ostentation, superficiality, or falseness,"[54] but the essential point is that all these connotations, as part of display, are public-oriented, which is to say modes of relating to others. As a mode of relating, display assumes the recognition of another's existence and is something essentially communicative. "More specifically, display generates a discursive space, a social and political arena, where cultural negotiations about identities both individual and collective take place."[55]

But not all forms of display can generate conversation, a discursive space, in the manner just described. "Some art forms and artworks contribute more than others" in eliciting and sustaining a response from someone. Accordingly, Eaton is willing to acknowledge such a thing as bad art: "Inferior or sentimental art allows for laziness—or anaesthetized rather than heightened, aestheticized attention."[56] At the same time, however, she hesitates to specify what sort of art objects can best or more effectively engender and sustain conversation and deliberation among persons. She will only go so far as to say that art or, to use Promey's language, forms of display with certain "intrinsic properties" will challenge and reward "repeated attention" but will demure in identifying what such properties might be or resist offering exemplary examples of art objects with such properties.[57] Be that as it may, there is such a thing as good art, and good art can generate relatedness and conversation, an invitation to deliberate about the specific intrinsic properties perceived. This may be the case with pop art, K-pop, and hip-hop and maybe even a Jackson

Pollock painting, a Broadway play, Mozart's arias, a Julia Margaret Cameron photograph, the kinds of sculpture that adorn the steps of local town halls, the art deco Chrysler Building, the horizontal lines of a midcentury modernist house, and perhaps even Mount Rushmore. But whatever the art form or art object, they are good if it contributes to sustaining community if and when it engages individuals in conversation. "The more and the longer that a particular artwork inspires me to invite others to engage in similar perception and reflection, the more and the longer I and those others will tend to maintain our interrelationship."

Yet, Eaton sounds a warning: "There is no guarantee, of course, that the existence of great art alone will make for a more sustainable community."[58] Still, she insists that it can contribute to the formation of sustainable community because, she thinks, private aesthetic contemplation is atypical. What is more typical is collective contemplation: "Human beings *by nature*," Eaton argues, "engage in descriptive and evaluative commentary. When they do, it is rarely just to hear themselves talk. . . . Again, this is not done simply for individual gratification. Such speech and action is done in awareness of others and often in the belief that others will benefit."[59] It is noteworthy that Eaton's belief in art's capacity to sustain community pivots on a particular account of human nature; rather than saying that "X" is what art does because it is intrinsic to the very nature of art, she claims that "X" is what art does because "X" is intrinsic to what it means to be human; anthropology precedes aesthetics in this context.

But since there is no one way of being human, Eaton suggests that what we think art can do for us will vary. So, take the following assertion: "My claim is that art makes a special kind of contribution to one necessary feature of sustainable communities: in a sustainable community, individual members are aware of other members and take some responsibility for their well-being."[60] Yet, Eaton is reluctant, as she is with respect to what counts as good art, to say that this claim is a universal one or to specify the claim in a manner that is universally applicable. She claims a desire "to avoid imperialism that comes with making universal judgments about what in general is sustaining about art." Her chastened stance is born from the recognition that "individual communities have special needs."[61] And in order to know what art can do to sustain individual communities, we need a better sense of what these communities' identities are and the specific needs to sustain those identities.

Eaton admits that she has struggled with "who 'I' am [or who she is], let alone who 'we' are."[62] In addition to being a white female Minnesotan, among other attributes, she identifies herself "as someone who strives to be a member of the group Cass Sunstein has called 'enlightened citizens of a free democracy.'" And as one who identifies with such a conception of democratic community, she asks, "What does this 'we' need from art in order to sustain ourselves?" Her response:

> In my own attempts to answer the question of what "we" need from art in "our" efforts to sustain communities and subcommunities, I rely heavily on ideas presented about a century ago by Leo Tolstoy. He defined art as the communication in a medium of feelings so sincerely felt and skillfully presented by the artist that members of the audience who experience the work come to feel the same way. The upshot is that artists and audience members are united in a spiritual unity or, as I would put it, are aware of and have a sense of responsibility for the well-being of the commons. The unabashedly moral character of this view is present in all of the concepts in the phrase "enlightened citizens of a free democracy."[63]

Eaton is not skeptical about the moral potentiality of art; she believes that art can support community. But we need to be more precise. What sort of community is art meant to fashion?[64] What sort of community do we want art to fashion? What sort of community do we hope that art can contribute to fashioning? Eaton believes that art can support her community because her community believes in the moral value of art, a value that is shaped by her community's specific vision of democratic life. Thus, for Eaton the value of art is assumed given her communal membership, and why art is considered something to be valued is informed by that membership. For Eaton and presumably other persons who regard themselves as committed to her brand of democratic life, it is a question not of whether art can support community but rather what such persons want out of art, what they are hoping to gain from it. These questions for Eaton can only be answered by attending to who they are, what kind of community they see themselves belonging to, or what kind of community and therefore persons they hope to be. As one who identifies with if not aspires to enlightened democratic citizenship, Eaton thinks that art that unites persons in a kind of spiritual unity is needed. Such a need includes being on the lookout for and attuning one's attention to art that challenges assumptions and communicates diverse perspectives rather than, say, art that simply commemorates or that accentuates and amplifies convention, a dominant point of view, or the status quo:

> Two of the most frequently assigned fictional works in America's high schools are *To Kill a Mockingbird* and *The Color Purple*. This must be

> because teachers believe that they encourage and challenge students and because they are worthy of their attention. There is a difference between reading a book and *reading* a book. *Reading* is engaging in aesthetic activity of the sort that contributes to the development of skills necessary for becoming an enlightened citizen—critical analysis and moral imaginativeness, to name just two. But not just anything can be *read* in such a way. One can read but not *read* a Harlequin romance. These are books, but not books that demand much of the reader. Enlightened citizens of a free democracy need precisely the things that good art demands.[65]

For Eaton, it is not that enlightened democratic citizenship benefits from the mere existence of Harper Lee's and Alice Walker's novels; it is not simply good enough to be around such works of art. Art festivals, galleries, and displays are not inherently humanizing; violence can erupt just as equally as expressions of solidarity in such venues.[66] Enlightened democratic community benefits when persons read, listen, or look in a certain way with a certain set of commitments. Moreover, such a community benefits when there exists real opportunities for as many of its members to access, regardless of means, the arts and to be given the chance to read, listen, or look in that particular way.[67] In other words, a community of enlightened democratic citizens is sustained when its members recognize (and are actively encouraged to recognize) that being open to works of art that challenge, upend, and enlarge points of view are indeed beneficial for such community. Art is capable of moral work inasmuch as it does its work on behalf of a particular community and that moral work is successful if persons approach art—reads it, looks at it, listens to it, enjoys it—with a particular posture toward it, being open to its potential to school them in the attitudes and habits necessary for a certain kind of citizenship.

Art can do a lot of things: it can help us to express certain feelings and punctuate particular ideas or thoughts. Art can help us to appreciate the elegance of form, or the technicalities of brushstroke, color, and so forth. Art can help us to be more attentive to detail and readily discern patterns or can distract us and help us find respite. And some kinds of art or art forms can do certain things better than other kinds of art. But some of these functions will be prized over others, and some art forms will be preferred over others, while some functions and specific art forms will be considered morally relevant and others less so, and this will be the case as a reflection of what a particular community believes it needs from the arts and how it values the arts. Thus, an artwork's value is not inherent but is socially or

FIGURE 2. Photograph taken by Amanda Choi on September 18, 2021. Art once displayed in public spaces in the borough of New Providence, New Jersey, found discarded adjacent to its municipal recycling lot.

communally constitutive. Consequently, art can be considered expired and having exceeded its value, or it can be elevated and promoted as indispensable (figure 2). Furthermore, it should not be assumed that a community will necessarily desire, prefer, elevate, and provide access to the kind of art that will ultimately sustain its well-being. "Art can destroy as well as build" inasmuch as communities can be mistaken on what they need.[68] (In this regard, can a community sustain itself when, for instance, it desires and creates art that depicts war and its atrocities as entertainment?)[69] But Eaton's argument is simply to point out that if we think art is morally important, why or how we think art is morally important cannot be had apart from a larger recognition of our attachments to a community that regards art in a particular way.

We can take art and gentrification as a pertinent case study on the communal situatedness of art. Art may sustain communities by anchoring neighborhood and economic revitalization efforts, but the question we should be asking is, which communities are we speaking of here? What the college-educated, tech-savvy, higher-income, so-called creative class may see with

FIGURE 3. Photograph taken on August 2, 2019, by author. The lower Manhattan outpost of Brooklyn Flea's famed Smorgasburg food stalls are set against the backdrop of a mural at the redeveloped World Trade Center site in New York City, adjacent to the World Trade Center 9/11 Memorial and Museum. The mural complements the kind of social space and experience that makes Smorgasburg a wildly popular attraction to so-called hipsters as well as foreign tourists and higher-skilled workers in industries such as finance, social media, and technology. Other parts of New York City, especially Brooklyn, are experiencing a similar confluence of art, food, and gentrification.

respect to art may not necessarily align with how other communities, especially socioeconomically marginalized immigrant communities and communities of color, regard and value art. To one community, art engenders creativity, supports entrepreneurship, and punctuates a dynamic urban experience, but to another community their art is a harbinger and sustainer of gentrification and displacement of longtime residents of lesser means. It is not that art is inherently gentrifying, but its moral importance will depend on the who and how of art: who is making the art and how is it being valued (figure 3). Indigent communities may regard art as valuable as much as nonindigent communities, but what they want and need from the arts often diverge.[70] Art may indeed be morally valuable, but what that means requires attending to how a particular community envisions that value.

INSTITUTIONS OF ART AND MORAL PLURALISM

Eaton crystallizes a thesis that began to emerge with our engagement of Scarry. Even if aesthetic experiences and moral experiences are distinguishable, this does not mean they are separable. As Eaton remarks, "most experiences do not come neatly parceled that way."[71] The inseparability of aesthetics and moral experiences does not necessarily mean they are one and the same but rather that whatever we hope to see in aesthetics with respect to ethics—that is, whatever moral power we think art can have, effect, or exercise—it cannot be delineated neatly from the larger social frame from which we approach art.

So, for instance, when one is asked to respond to a painting in view, one might comment on specific aspects of its form: its brushstroke, colors, perspective, and so on. "I like the dominance of the color red in this painting" or "I like the picture of the bike in the painting," one might respond initially. But our perception of the painting will certainly be different "when we are given certain bits of information."[72] The paint used is blood, and the picture of the bike is one that, in actuality, was stolen from an Asian American toddler in Sunset Park, Brooklyn. (Eaton uses the example of an artwork that utilizes color produced by dying goldfish.)[73] Depending on how we might feel about the use of blood for paint (and our general views about violence) and whether we think it is acceptable to have a bike stolen for artistic purposes and whether we feel a sense of discomfort, maybe even outrage, that an artist could do such a thing especially to a child of color even for the sake of art, we may feel the need to revise our initial assessment of the painting. "This suggests," according to Eaton, "that aesthetic response is a result of aggregate rather than separate perceptions."[74] This aggregation can include more than just what we know about the technicalities of the painting (what genre it belongs to, how we might classify its style, who the artist is, the artist's history, training, etc.) but also the kind of social and moral sensibilities we bring to our aesthetic perceptions.

All in all, our aesthetic perceptions are informed by a wide array of experiences, including moral ones. We can insist that the way we look at art should not include the influence of such experiences, as modernists or formalists do, which would explain why they are only willing to talk about art in terms of form.[75] Such restrictions only reinforce the larger point that how we perceive art, value it, and conceive of it as purposeful or useful is tied to what we bring to this perception and especially what we think we ought to bring to this perception. Perception of art is never aesthetically pure, if there is ever such a possibility. How we respond to art, or the range of our responses, changes depending on the values we bring to it and how those values color what we know about specific artworks. Consequently, one's moral sensibilities, once we know more details about an artwork, may very well alter the assessment of it, including its importance and usefulness. While a mural depicting a scene from a slice of American history hanging in a college's vestibule may have not struck a troubling chord at first, upon knowing more about it in light of one's commitments to diversity, equity, and inclusion, one might feel the need to question its continued display.[76] The same might go for a statue of a nondescript Confederate soldier in the middle of another southern US university's campus.[77] And, as more of Flannery O'Connor's racism comes to light, perhaps her literary canon deserves a critical reassessment.[78] As Eaton summarizes, with more information "we look for positive features that we did not look for before—instances of an intriguing use of perspective or application of an interesting color theory or expression of democratic values—or, negatively, we notice how boring the composition is or we scrutinize it for and find traces of sexism, fascism, or sadism, for instance."[79]

Nicholas Wolterstorff makes the point that aesthetic and moral perceptions are tightly woven together in a similar way but with a stronger emphasis on how art moves us to action. In other words, for Wolterstorff, how we create as well as respond to art is in large part a function of the kind of aims that are brought to it. Works of art "are objects and instruments of action whereby we carry out our intentions with respect to the world, our fellows, ourselves, and our gods."[80] In addition, Wolterstoff states, "Works of art equip us for action. And the range of actions for which they equip us is very nearly as broad as the range of human action itself. The purposes of art are the purposes of life."[81] Take, for instance, a person who insists on responding to art in only an introspective way and resisting a nonaesthetic response to it, thereby focusing only on its form or the artist's technique and relativizing the significance of the artwork's subject matter. Such insistence reflects giving "preferential status to one action—that of *focusing* on the work." Wolterstorff then concludes, "He is not recommending that we put the work of art to *no* use. He is recommending that we give preference to the use of serving as object of *contemplation*."[82]

This example is meant to intentionally bring to mind the general trajectory of modernist or formalist approaches to art, and Wolterstorff turns to them as a way of calling attention to what he calls a society's "institution of art." A society's institution of art refers to the "characteristic arrangements and patterns of action whereby works of art are produced in that society, whereby they are made available for the use of members of that society, and whereby members of that society are enabled to make use of them."[83] Such characteristic arrangements and patterns amount to the values and understandings that shape society's regard for art, its production, purpose, and use. Formalism's prevalence, he argues, coincides with the rise and entrenchment of what he refers to as society's institution of high art, wherein the act of aesthetic contemplation of art is given preponderant weight. Thus, any talk about art as serving or being relevant to spheres of life outside aesthetic contemplation is often stymied or regarded as polluting the purity of art:

> You and I, along with the rest of those who think and write about the arts, are participants in our society's institution of high art. And the basic reason we all endemically overlook the fact that the intended public uses of art are multitudinous, thinking instead that music is for listening to, painting for looking at, and poetry for reading, is that we are so deeply immersed in our own institution of high art, where indeed almost all art *is* art for contemplation, that we find it virtually impossible to rise up far enough to get a perspective on the landscape surrounding, where not only is art for contemplation to be seen but very much else besides. . . . [W]e have been bewitched by participating in our own institution of high art.[84]

I will return to the issue of formalism and its championing of aesthetic contemplation (through the works of Cilve Bell and Peter de Bolla, among others) in chapter 4 to assess how its understanding of contemplation and, specifically, aesthetic emotion masks the integral role that moral concerns play in aesthetic concerns. But for the present, it is important to point out that while Wolterstorff laments our bewitchment with the formalist institution of high art and thus the primacy of aesthetic contemplation, he is not suggesting that how the arts occur in our society (its creation, use, perception, and reception) can occur apart from institutions of art. Instead, he is claiming that the institution of high art that formalism represents limits what we think art is and can do, which conceals the fact that art throughout human history has been more than simply for the sake of contemplation. "Art in general is not thus divorced from life, and never has been. Yet when we in our society think about the arts we persistently think of them thus."[85]

Wolterstorff observes astutely that even for formalism, art is meant to do something; for formalism, art is meant to move us to contemplate itself, its so-called aesthetic qualities. He is also surely right that such a view of art is pervasive in contemporary society. But at the same time, that is only one of several competing approaches to the arts. In any given society, it may be the case that one institution of art is ascendant, but this does not necessarily mean that a society thus holds a monolithic view of art and what its purposes are. Even within a particular institution of art, Wolterstorff remarks, there are competing traditions (or what we might call subinstitutions) of what art means or should mean. This is even true for formalism, with its diverse schools of thought on the nature of art.[86]

We are thus called back to the thesis that we distilled from Eaton: when claims are made about the moral importance of art, specifically in their capacity to engender and reinforce skills pertinent to the life of "enlightened citizens of a free democracy," such claims are about how a particular "we" sees the value of art, particularly the moral value of art. This does not mean that this is the only "we" and thus the only way of valuing art with respect to its role and importance for democratic life. Democratic communities come in various shades and stripes.[87] It is just that Eaton thinks her vision of democratic life is the right one. In addition, democratic communities are, of course, not the only forms of governance, and just as there is a diversity of communities, there will be a diversity of views on the worth and maybe even worthlessness of art. Such a position, one broadly suggested by Eaton—and intimated more precisely by Wolterstorff in his claim that one's view of art is a consequence of one's particular cultural, social, and economic habituation—anticipates a pluralistic conception of art's moral salience: art will always result in a diversity of moral outcomes.

ART AS A RELATIVE MORAL GOOD

Another way of thinking about art's unavoidable moral pluralism is to think about art as morally flexible: that art's moral effect or work is dependent on the person or persons who engage the arts and the moral interests, concerns, or intentionality that they bring to that engagement. This is not to say that art in itself—or, in a manner of speaking, on its own—is powerless to act on those who perceive it or is unable to move persons toward some sort of action. Recall Scarry's claim, as we saw earlier, that art and specifically beautiful art—or at least that which we perceive or consider as beautiful—moves us forward and laterally in acts of aesthetic stewardship and acts of aesthetic creation and re-creation. Looking or reading often begets successive acts of looking, reading, writing, drawing, sculpting, and so forth. Or, looking or reading often engenders the desire to look at or read other similarly captivating artworks. In other words, acts of aesthetic appreciation can inspire all sorts of successive acts that aim to extend whatever pleasure, enjoyment, or curiosity the initial experience of appreciation may have sparked. But can we count such "lateral regard" and "forward momentum" as contributory to the moral life, to the life of justice in particular, unless they are accompanied by or framed within a corresponding sense of what justice means and the kind of practices and skills that best serve the realization of such an account of justice? Without such framing, how lateral regard and forward momentum, as Scarry describes them, contribute to the knowledge and actualization of justice is difficult to explain, since it is not unreasonable that both aesthetic movements can also slide into a kind of narcissism. Scarry claims that forward momentum can serve as a school for justice, specifically the notion of justice as fairness. But how that can happen without a level of intentionality to that effect is unclear. What is to prevent the act of aesthetic creation and re-creation from spiraling into a form of aesthetic self-absorption rather than a sense of, as Scarry argues, caring for beautiful objects as if they are "alive"? How, for instance, does loving to paint over and over again the beauty of palm fronds constitute a training ground for justice?[88] What moves or transfers such love to the realm of justice? Is it not entirely possible for such a love to be motivated by either a kind of artistic obsession or, less intensely, simple aesthetic appreciation? Thus, it is a leap to suggest that art is inherently supportive of justice, as Scarry proposes. We do better to instead heed what Eaton ultimately concedes: that whatever it is we see in the arts as supporting relationship, mutuality, and dialogue is reflective of how a particular community of persons conceives of such bonds and practices and what is needed to advance their conception of them.

Eaton's concession warns against uncritical generalizations about the status of art as a moral good. Take as a case in point the claim that art is antiauthoritarian. While it may indeed be true that art, as Eve Ewing proposes, can challenge authoritarianism, the veracity of such a claim cannot be universally so. More specifically, we can certainly point to numerous historical instances in which authoritarians felt threatened by art.

> As Hitler understood, artists play a distinctive role in challenging authoritarianism. . . . Authoritarian leaders throughout history have intuited this fact and have acted accordingly. The Stalinist government of the 1930s required art to meet strict criteria of style and content to ensure that it exclusively served the purposes of state leadership. In his memoir, the composer and pianist Dmitri Shostakovich writes that the Stalinist government systematically executed all of the Soviet Union's Ukrainian folk poets. When Augusto Pinochet took power in Chile in 1973, muralists were arrested, tortured and exiled. Soon after the coup, the singer and theater artist Victor Jara was killed, his body riddled with bullets and displayed publicly as a warning to others.[89]

But it cannot be that authoritarians have typically rejected art because art is intrinsically subversive of structures of power or state leadership.[90] Even Ewing admits, albeit in passing and as if beside the point, the inconvenient truth that Hitler extolled representational forms of art, rather than abstract art, with a special interest in "heroic" images and "pastoral landscapes of the German countryside."[91] Hitler's attraction to and identification with one of the leading European operatic composers, Richard Wagner, especially his opera *Rienzi,* is well documented.[92] Thus, it is certainly not the case that authoritarian leaders have rejected art; what is the case instead is that only specific art forms and artworks are seen as morally laudable by virtue of what those artworks and forms are purported as facilitating, assisting, and enabling. This is why Frankfurt School social theorists such as Walter Benjamin and Theodor Adorno were cool to art's moral possibilities in their recognition that "aesthetic technologies can be used not merely to falsify popular will but to whip it into a frenzy." Fascists, for instance, "convert[ed] political violence into artistic expression." Authoritarians, more generally, have long recognized that the aestheticization of violence could be of value for their own political designs and values.[93] For Adorno, what he calls the "culture industry," the instrumental rationality of profit, capital, and commodification, accomplishes the same by producing art—popular art or "mass culture"—that reinforces "interchangeable sameness" and "conformity."[94] The alternative for Adorno is a form of autonomous art, or the need to elevate or reclaim a kind of art "produced 'privately' and not on demand for a particular consumer (church, state, patron)."[95] In short, "Art can also be a tool in the hands of those in power who act to create shared perceptions" even if, "as Marx warned, those perceptions constitute a false consciousness."[96] If art is to have a moral effect, then we need to specify the kind of art that we think will catalyze that effect.

For Hitler, abstract art was degenerate inasmuch as the people making such art and those who supported its production and enjoyment were "Jewish people, Communists, or those suspected of being one or the other." With that in mind, it is important to specify that if authoritarians are suspicious of art, it is the art of those who are on the social peripheries and the kind of countercultural art that reflects their marginalization that are suspect. "Like the proverbial court jesters who can openly mock the king in his own court, artists who occupy marginalized social positions can use their art to challenge structures of power in ways that would otherwise be dangerous or impossible," states Ewing. So, it is not any kind of art that is antiauthoritarian. When it comes to resisting authoritarianism or, at least, staving off authoritarian tendencies, what Ewing has in her sights is the need to support art that occupies spaces outside the racial, religious, and gender mainstream: Muslim, LGBTQ, and hip-hop art, just to name a few.[97]

If we can trace a long history of authoritarian suspicion of certain kinds of art, then such selectivity can also be traced in the equally long history of democratic advocacy for the arts. As Russ Castronovo points out, Scarry is one of the more prominent contemporary expressions of this advocacy.[98] We can count Eaton as well, given her explicit admission as one who aspires toward enlightened democratic citizenship. Their forebears include W. E. B. Du Bois, who "invoked painters—Picasso and Matisse—as an experience in perspective that would rewrite the political DNA of citizens." Jane Addams was another who regarded "aesthetic forms from poetry to film" as critical to "her attempts to refashion the modern city after the classical city-state."[99] The photographer and urban reformer Jacob Riis was yet another well-known advocate for the democratic importance of the arts, belonging to the broader City Beautiful movement of the late 1800s and early 1900s in the United States.[100] During that period, the belief in the integral linkage between art and democracy found its way into and pervaded the mission of higher education, according to Castronovo: "in course syllabi, outlines for university extension courses, doctoral dissertations, and textbooks in philosophy, art, rhetoric, and literature . . . aesthetics became institutionalized as an academic subject charged with the mission of creating and maintaining a democratic culture."[101] However, the aim of this aesthetic pedagogy for democracy, as Castronovo demonstrates further, was to emphasize a specific kind of art, art that "transcended specific content" and called attention to "formal principles and timeless properties that governed human sensation."[102] Thus, much of the curricular focus was on aesthetic "harmony, symmetry, proportion, balance, unity, simplicity, and purity of form," which would serve as the aesthetic basis for "a civic pedagogy designed to remake individuals into disinterested, dispassionate citizens with an eye for social order and equilibrium."[103] A book published in 1890 and used in a University of Michigan course exemplified this focus on form over content. As Castronovo notes, this book by Fred N. Scott, titled *Aesthetics*, proposed that aesthetics instruction

> should . . . encourag[e] social and political behavior guided by order, unity, and symmetry. By seeking satisfaction in formal properties that encase affect and action, the citizen as aesthetic subject internally adjusts him- or herself to criteria that . . . are also the hallmark of state-sponsored liberalism. . . . As different sections of this book illustrate, this gentle program is what makes democracy beautiful: petty thieves intuit ethical standards from encounters with well-proportioned

> artworks; anarchists have no desire to dynamite cities that have become beautiful; disaffected populists come to appreciate the wonders of trans-Pacific trade by thinking about the totality of form.[104]

It is worth noting that this line of thinking on art and democracy—specifically its emphasis on the humanizing power of aesthetic form—would be taken up in more specific and stark ways by the New Criticism movement that would emerge after World War II. New Criticism produced art that employed form divorced from historical or biographical content based on the view that such a focus on form would mediate feelings and actions away from moral deformity and toward capacious postures toward others.[105]

Historical instances of authoritarian suspicions and democratic championing of the arts underscore the extent to which claims about the moral value of the arts are typically about the moral value of a certain kind of art, a certain style of art, or a specific feature of art. Or, they are claims, as they are for John Dewey, about the moral value of looking at art in a certain way or with a certain attitude about what art "genuinely" is (i.e., a particular theory about art). At first, one might read Dewey as conceptualizing art pluralistically, that is, neither inherently democratic nor authoritarian. "For Dewey, 'the work of aesthetic art satisfies many ends, none of which is laid down in advance.'"[106] The diversity of human experience confirms such a view of art. One's regard for some "object" (a vase, a picture) as a work of art will depend on one's "ordinary experience," and just as ordinary experience is not uniform, universal, or timeless, the same is true in regard to what we think art is and does.[107] "Art is prefigured in the very processes of living. . . . Thus it varies the arts in ways without ends."[108] But Dewey's larger aim emerges when he claims that we ought to regard art in this multitudinous way. "Art experienced in this manner makes subjects restless, unwilling to accept customary and stultifying social patterns as either pleasurable or desirable. Art spurs 'the first stirrings of dissatisfaction,' inciting interrogations of convention, precept, and established order," which is befitting of democratic life.[109] But this is so assuming one holds a theory of art that encourages if not demands that we experience art in such a manner. It is not art in itself that is democratic, but it can be if that is how one theorizes and approaches it.[110]

Authoritarians are hardly iconoclasts or cultural philistines, and liberals are not necessarily the opposite. Rather, authoritarians, like defenders of liberal values, are more concerned with regarding the arts and kinds of artworks in a certain way, and authoritarians and liberals are typically at variance on these matters of regard. And even if, as we saw with Ewing above, authoritarians feel threatened by art produced by persons on the margins, that is, those outside the authoritarian's (twisted) sense of the "normal," there is no guarantee that defenders of democracy would necessarily embrace as morally beneficial the art that authoritarians might reject, especially if history is to serve any kind of guide on the matter. Again, as Castronovo underlines, the American tradition of arts advocacy on behalf of democratic citizenship was less interested in who made art and the content of the artwork and more interested in the ways in which aesthetic form—symmetry, proportion, harmony, etc.—would shape the intentions, emotions, desires, and habits of persons toward liberal values. When form is prized over subject matter, then the question of which kind of art is more or less conducive to antiauthoritarian values becomes murkier.[111] Furthermore, we do well to keep in mind that the history of democratic advocacy for the arts was not wholly nonviolent. Even Riis, referenced above, thought that "beauty is not fitted for survival among all ethnic groups."[112] "The German has an advantage over his Celtic neighbor in his strong love of flowers. . . . His garden goes with him wherever he goes," wrote Riis. Thus, in German tenements in New York City in the Lower East Side, the work of "police clubs" was less severe based on the premise that in communities that were not as aesthetically inclined as the German ones there would be the need for greater "police-beats" and "force patrols" to stave off rioters.[113] In sum, the symmetry and unity of aesthetic form not only served as a balm for illiberalism but also set the grounds from which the paternalism of force could be employed to maintain democratic life.[114]

ART AND MORAL DISAGREEMENT

Art is therefore neither morally edifying nor corrosive, at least not in some intrinsic way. This is not to say that art is morally inconsequential. However, whatever moral claims are made about the arts, they will vary from person to person or community to community depending on the moral interests and attitudes that such claims are meant to serve and express. Divergence and therefore disagreement on what kind of art is morally valuable and why should not be surprising. And not only disagreement about what kind of art is morally salient (e.g., painting versus theater, abstract versus representational art) but also disagreement over the same kind of art and even a particular work of art should be expected. For Riis, the beauty of a flower garden and the regularity, proportion, and symmetry of art were taken to have socializing force toward democratic reform, uplifting indigent immigrants into a "civic-minded body." Others looked to the same aesthetic sensibilities as the necessary escapism for the indigent, lest their "urban despair might erupt into revolutionary action."[115] Riis's view assumed that the poor could be transformed, though perhaps the Irish less so than German immigrants, as we saw above, whereas his detractors were less optimistic and thought that it was more beneficial for democracy for the poor to be "bound to civic authority."[116] Either way, this difference reflected a more fundamental underlying disagreement over the meaning of community, the nature of the moral subject, and the parameters of citizenship. It was this underlying political and moral disagreement that demarcated their contrasting views on the moral salience of art, on what moral work art can do and what kind of art is most capable of such work.

Such sharp lines of disagreement abound in modern life. In Norway, for instance, heated exchanges over the public display of Pablo Picasso's concrete mural *The Fisherman* (created with the Norwegian artist Carl Nesjar) fall along the lines of competing political and social priorities. For some, its removal from a government building called Y-Block, even while undergoing renovations, is a "crime" against Norwegian identity. For others, its removal from the building, which was the site of the 2011 bombing by the right-wing Norwegian Anders Behring Breivik, is more a matter of maintaining a safe working environment.[117] This is only one work of art, but views on whether it should be displayed and if so in what particular place are multiple, moving along competing senses of social value, national identity, and political priorities.

Whether art is morally salient and how it is salient may depend more on the moral frameworks that persons bring to their consideration of art than on some belief in the inherent moral power of art. This proposition is more about approach than content. Art can depict a variety of things; it can depict violence, "the dark underside of the human condition," or it can depict "sentimental pictures of loving well-fed, healthy families."[118] But whether one or the other— or maybe both— is morally salient and how one (or both) is morally salient will depend on how we approach and interpret it. That will depend further on our moral situatedness, the community with which we identify, and what this community's values are. And that particularity informs what we should pay attention to and how we should be paying attention as well as ultimately what we should do after paying attention (or because we have paid attention).

Yuriko Saito proposes that "there are correct and incorrect interpretations of art" and

> that we have a moral obligation to try to experience works of art correctly, to attempt to do more than simply get as much aesthetic pleasure as possible from an object or event. . . . Doing otherwise, she insists, shows a selfish, self-centered, close-minded attitude, "an *unwillingness* to put aside our own agenda, whether it an ethnocentric or present-minded perspective of the pursuit for easy pleasure and entertainment." One *ought* . . . to respect each work, *give it a chance to* open our eyes and mind.[119]

FIGURE 4. Flight 93 National Memorial. In the background, a view of the Wall of Names and Memorial Plaza from the vantage point of the Visitor Shelter. Public domain photograph via US Park Service, https://www.nps.gov/media/photo/gallery-item.htm?pg=4001156&id=C497B1CA-155D-451F-67921A3F3E77B214&gid=C48E80C8-155D-451F-67B5959A640D6969.

That Saito thinks that we must be willing to pay attention to art, to allow it to affect us, underscores a larger moral frame that shapes her perception of art, its importance. Because we believe it is important, we ought to give it a chance to do its important work on us. Not unlike Saito, Eaton believes that art can expose corruption, vice, and social injustice.[120] But can mere exposure be morally efficacious, that is, engender moral outrage? What should we make of instances in which exposure engenders the kind of moral response that perhaps deviates from the intention to call awareness to social injustice and human tragedy? Consider the Flight 93 National Memorial that commemorates the victims of the hijacked passenger plane that crashed in Shanksville, Pennsylvania, on September 11, 2001. The victims are memorialized through a series of walls on which their names are engraved (figure 4). But how should we appreciate or interpret these walls? As remembrances of the victims, of their heroic actions on Flight 93 against the Al-Qaeda terrorist hijackers? Or as a call to discourage immigration by building walls along US territorial boundaries, especially between the United States and Mexico?[121] Again, Eaton believes that art can call our attention to moral wrongs. What may matter as much if not more, however, is a sense that fighting injustice is a priority to begin with. Correlatively, what may matter as much if not more is a prior openness or willingness to be exposed and challenged by art and its depictions. Art may very well open our eyes and mind, as Saito proposes, but that work may be possible only if we are open to the prospect of having our eyes and minds challenged by art from the start. Otherwise, corrupt persons may not care for the art they are looking at, which may even end up serving to justify and rationalize their corruption.[122]

ART AND MORAL CHANGE

Riis was a social reformer who believed ardently in the power of art to ethically reform, and his public staging of magic lantern shows provides a cautionary tale. His aim was to transform the general public, both upper and working classes, both capital and labor, into a civil, democratic collective. What resulted from the lantern shows, however, was "anything but civil."[123] While the art shows certainly drew "audiences of well-heeled citizens," they also "gather[ed] rowdies to public parks, intriguing store merchants but also exciting crowds teetering on the end of working-class unrest."[124] In these instances, "aesthetic education double[d] as popular agitation," reinforcing not only civil society but also attracting a mere crowd of persons or, worse, a mob.[125] And Riis seemed to have expected as much in eventually hiring, for at least one magic lantern show, what were in effect armed security guards, "stout men" . . . [with] good hickory clubs," to enforce public decorum and subdue the various groups of persons butting against each other, fueled by various class antagonisms, verging on riotous behavior.[126] "The slippage from projecting pleasing images to wielding 'good hickory clubs' illustrates the easy interchangeability between art and violence, between beauty and punishment."[127] That interchangeability is illustrated further in a showing in Elmira, New York, during the summer of 1877. At this magic lantern show Riis skipped the security guards, though the governor of New York's deployment of "bayoneted soldiers" took their place and stood guard to quell the crowds that formed and the violence that erupted between the merchants, store owners, and striking railroad workers who were drawn to the show. The example of Riis's magic lantern show is not to suggest that the disagreement and discord engendered by art are always or necessarily accompanied by violence. But the divergent, disorderly results of his show in towns such as Elmira are indicative of the dangerous side of art, its potentiality to divide rather than unite and support deliberation toward the goal of mutual understanding.[128]

A more contemporary example proves equally instructive on this point. In the spring of 2019, the town of Newnan, Georgia, forty miles southwest of Atlanta, displayed throughout the sides of the town's buildings "17 large-scale banner portraits, images of ordinary people who make up Newnan."

These banners were a part of the "Seeing Newnan" initiative.[129] Included in these banners were portraits of an African American woman resident, a white resident who worked at the local mill, a waitress of Mexican descent, and two sisters who were local high school students and whose parents immigrated to Newnan from Pakistan. Both sisters are Muslim, and they are wearing hijabs in their portrait.

In displaying these portraits, taken by the photographer Mary Beth Meehan, the intent, according to its organizers, was to show how the town had changed demographically into a diverse community. This transition was seldom recognized, according to Robert Hancock, one of the sponsors of the art project. "'We were in these little bubbles. I thought this project could pierce the bubbles. . . . People needed to open their eyes and see what a beautiful, diverse place we live in,' he said."[130] He is also quoted as saying, "'Hopefully it will make people think—gosh, there are 40,000 people here in Newnan. I don't really know anybody, do I? We all know less than 1 percent.'"[131] But the reaction to the portraits had the opposite effect, especially the portraits of the two Muslim sisters. "'I feel like Islam is a threat to the American way of life. . . . There should be no positive portrayals of it,'" said one person.[132] Another "said there were not enough Muslims in Newnan for the [sisters] to be included in the art installation in the first place."

While residents of Newnan disagreed over the banners, their disagreement was not necessarily about the moral value of art per se; there is little indication that arguments erupted over whether art should be banished from their town's public spaces. The ensuing disagreements, however, circled around their communal attachments and preferences or, more specifically, their competing visions of the good, or what kind of social life ought to be protected, elevated, or pursued. As one resident made clear in his response, what he objected to was the feeling that the portraits aimed to push him to accept a form of life that he found morally objectionable: "'I do not feel like the two women in the photo are radical or dangerous,' he said. 'I just do not think Newnan should be pushed to embrace Islam.'"[133] Much of the objections surrounded the portraits of the Muslim sisters and not as much around the portraits of Newnan's white residents.

Do these objections imply that art cannot change minds, alter the way we see one another, the way we see the world? Does it imply that art only taps into our preconceptions and tends to reinforce them instead of rupturing them? At the very least, it is important that we acknowledge the very real capacity of art to engender conversation that is rancorous, discordant, and often divisive. With art, you never know what you're going to get, and in fact you might get the exact opposite of what you're hoping for. In other words, "Aesthetics are not always pretty or predictable." The employment of art to engender communal conversation and understanding typically leads to "multiple public bodies" that stand in contrast to one another and even, more problematically, oppose and disavow one another.[134] That is one lesson to draw from Newnan as well as Elmira, and it complicates the variety of claims that art can change minds, alter vision, or transform our moral imaginations. If art can change minds and, more specifically, engender mutual recognition and understanding between persons, we will need to wonder whether such change is accomplishable by art alone or whether it will depend on minds changing first. Given that so much of how we regard art is tied to the kind of community or "public body" that we identify with, minds changing first may indeed be the key.

NOTES

1. Eaton, *Merit, Aesthetic and Ethical,* 155, citing Posner, "Against Ethical Criticism," 11.
2. Scarry, *On Beauty and Being Just,* 58. This critique is accompanied by a second political critique, Scarry argues. "The second argument holds that when we stare at something beautiful, make it an object of sustained regard, our act is destructive to the object. . . . The complaint has given rise to a generalized discrediting of the act of 'looking,' which is charged with 'reifying' the very object that appears to be the subject of admiration" (58). In the following, I will focus on the first political critique only because how she responds to it will make clear why she thinks the second political critique is mistaken.
3. Scarry, *On Beauty and Being Just,* 58. Although Scarry says little about the sources or the leading proponents of this political critique, we can detect a similarity to Immanuel Kant's distrust of beauty as that which possesses a power that overwhelms perceivers' attention so much so that they are unable to draw their gaze away from beauty and presumably their own infatuation with beauty. Perceivers are thus unable to direct their gaze toward more significant matters, such as justice. From this perspective, beauty operates on a one-way model of power. On Kant's critique of beauty, see Steiner, *Venus in Exile,* chaps. 1 and 2.
4. Scarry, *On Beauty and Being Just,* 23.
5. Scarry, 24–25. See also Steiner, *The Scandal of Pleasure.* Steiner refers to the beauty of art as "a realm of thought experiments that quicken, sharpen, and sweeten our being in the world" (8).
6. Scarry, *On Beauty and Being Just,* 30.
7. Scarry, 68.
8. Scarry, 89. Far from distracting our attention and reifying the beautiful object, "noticing its beauty increases the possibility that it will be carefully handled" (65). We do not only recognize it as beautiful, but because it is beautiful, we value it as if possessing life. "The almost-aliveness of a beautiful object makes its abrasive handling unthinkable," Scarry says. "The mind recoils—as from a wound cut into living flesh—from the possibility that the surface of Jan Brueghel the Elder's painting *Flower Stems in a Clay Vase* should

be cut, torn, or roughly touched. Its surface has been accorded the gift of life: this can have nothing to do with the subject, the live flowers, for—look at them, jonquils, roses, fritillaria, tulips, irises, peonies, hyacinths, lily—they were already cut even as the painter painted them into their place inside the vase; and the same mental recoil would be felt if the surface that were roughly touched depicted only a pair of discarded shoes or one of Turner's groundless mists or Klee's colors. The surface of the canvas has become, in the standard protection we accord it, *semisentient*. Stone statues of gods, too, in the moment of being revered, come to life, as in Rilke's poems where the mouth of Apollo trembles and the eyebrows of Buddha lift" (69). Consequently, we seek to secure and cultivate such objects' existence. "Beauty seems to place requirements on us for attending to the aliveness or (in the case of objects) quasi-aliveness of our world, and for entering into its protection" (90).

9. Scarry, *On Beauty and Being Just*, 114.
10. Scarry, 66–69.
11. Scarry, 93–109.
12. Scarry, 3.
13. Scarry, 3, 5.
14. Scarry, 4.
15. Scarry, 5. Scarry cites Mark Musa's translation of Dante's *La vita nuova*, xv, xvi, 29, 30. Scarry offers other instances of forward momentum, such as Pater's account of how Verrocchio impacted the young Leonardo da Vinci. See Scarry, *On Beauty and Being Just*, 3–4. Later in the text she writes, "Hymn and palinode . . . reside inside most daily acts of encountering something beautiful. One walks down a street and suddenly sees a redbud tree—its tiny heart-shaped leaves climbing out all along its branches. . . . It is as though one has just been beached, lifted out of one ontological state into another that is fragile and must be held onto lest one lose hold of the branch and fall back into the ocean. Like Odysseus, one feels inadequate to it, lurches awkwardly around it, saying odd things to the small leaves, wishing to sing to them a hymn or, finding oneself unable, wishing in apology to make a palinode. Perhaps like Dante watching Beatrice, one could make a sonnet and then a prose poem explaining the sonnet; or, like Leonardo looking at a violet, one could make a sketch, then another, then another; or like Lady Autumn, listening with amazement to a stanza Keats has just sung her, one could sit there patiently staring moment after moment, hour by hour" (31–32).
16. Scarry, *On Beauty and Being Just*, 7.
17. Scarry, 114.
18. Castronovo, *Beautiful Democracy*, 28.
19. Scarry, *On Beauty and Being Just*, 109.
20. Scarry, 100.
21. Scarry, 115 (emphasis added).
22. Scarry, 91.
23. "'Fair' is connected to the verbs 'vegen' (Dutch) and 'fegen' (German) meaning 'to adorn,' 'to decorate,' and 'to sweep.' . . . But 'fegen' is in turn connected to the verb 'fay,' the transitive and intransitive verb meaning 'to join,' 'to fit,' 'to unite,' 'to pact.' 'Pact' in turn—the making of a covenant or treaty or agreement—is from the same root as 'pax, pacis,' the word for peace." Scarry, 92.
24. Scarry, 91.
25. Scarry, 91.

26. Scarry, 93. Scarry does not provide a reference for this line from Rawls. However, it can be found in Rawls, *A Theory of Justice*, 11. Though Rawls does not characterize his concept of fairness as belonging to a particular aesthetic, it is not out of the question. For an insightful discussion on the aesthetic shape of Rawl's justice as fairness, see Flores, *The Aesthetics of Solidarity*, 51–60.
27. One of the leading critiques of Rawls is, for instance, Sandel, *Liberalism and the Limits of Justice*.
28. Scarry, *On Beauty and Being Just*, 95.
29. Scarry, 97, 99.
30. McAuley, "As Flames Engulfed Notre Dame, a Fire Brigade Chaplain Helped Save the Treasures Inside"; and Khazan, "Spanish Woman Botches 'Ecce Homo' Painting in an Attempt to Restore It."
31. Cotter, "Portraits in Zen, from Celestial to Comic."
32. Scarry, *On Beauty and Being Just*, 115.
33. Scarry, 99.
34. Scarry, 106–7.
35. Willie James Jennings intimates as much when reflecting on whether Scarry is right that art can "open us to seeing suffering and pain." Jennings wonders whether art can do that on its own or whether it needs to be anchored by a particular commitment to justice that prioritizes the "poor and destitute," or those afflicted by "the powers." His conclusion: "Unfortunately, Scarry's hope lacks the truth that can only be established with the prophetic. Only if we understand who and what God wants us to see, only as we see whose bodies are in pain and being broken as we see other things can paying attention lead us from the operations of death and toward life." Jennings, "Embodying the Artistic Spirit and the Prophetic Arts," 262.
36. See Rawls, *A Theory of Justice*, 11–13.
37. Scarry, *On Beauty and Being Just*, 106.
38. Eaton, *Merit, Aesthetic and Ethical*, 92. See also Cavell, "Taste and Moral Sense," 275.
39. Eaton, *Merit, Aesthetic and Ethical*, 92.
40. Eaton, 154.
41. Eaton, 91–92. Eaton cites the following example from R. M. Hare: "The leader of a Himalayan expedition has the choice of either leading the final assault on the mountain itself, or staying behind at the last camp and giving another member of his party the opportunity; yet it is easy to suppose that no argument concerned with the interests of the parties will settle the question—for the interests may be precisely balanced. The questions that arise are likely to be concerned, not with the interests of the parties, but with ideals of what a man should *be*. Is it better to be the sort of man who, in the face of great obstacles and dangers, gets to the top of the nth highest mountain in the world; or the sort of man who uses his position of authority to give a friend this opportunity instead of claiming it for himself? These questions are very like aesthetic ones. It is as if a man were regarding his own life and character as a work of art, and asking how it should best be completed." Hare, *Freedom and Responsibility*, 150, as cited in Eaton, *Merit, Aesthetic and Ethical*, 92. Eaton sharpens Hare's aesthetic characterization of moral deliberation by describing Nussbaum's position in the following way: "The study of ethics brings to the foreground features of the human situation that must be attended to and the connections between them. Art does this as well, and it does it by requiring many of the skills necessary for 'reading' the features foregrounded. Just as moral rules can be taken not

as laws that determine whether acts are right or wrong but as guidelines for identifying salient features of moral actions, so artworks can be construed not as telling us what is right or wrong but with identifying salient features. They do this not just by presenting subject matter that possesses those salient features but also possessing themselves properties that one must perceive—and that often one must work to uncover" (154).

42. Eaton, *Merit, Aesthetic and Ethical,* 83.
43. Eaton, 90.
44. Eaton, 83–84 (emphases added).
45. Eaton, 156.
46. Eaton, 155.
47. Eaton, 155.
48. To some extent, I would say that Flores's account of aesthetics and solidarity is more aligned with Eaton than Ross and Goizueta at least with respect to making explicit the foregrounding of moral assumptions. If aesthetics is integral to solidarity, genuine solidarity (versus consumptive solidarity) can only be a reality if we are intentional in seeking out aesthetic experiences that are "characterized by relationships of mutuality, equality, and participation that foster human dignity." Flores, *The Aesthetics of Solidarity,* 141. So, for Flores not any kind of aesthetic experience will be impactful, only those that have a particular moral character. Such a measure or assessment of aesthetic experience can only be had if one is committed to the value of a particular moral framework.
49. Eaton, 201.
50. Eaton, 201–2.
51. Eaton, 200.
52. Eaton, 202.
53. Promey, "The Public Display of Religion," 35–36.
54. Promey, 35.
55. Promey, 38.
56. Eaton, *Merit, Aesthetic and Ethical,* 204.
57. Eaton, 203
58. Eaton, 208.
59. Eaton, 201 (emphasis added).
60. Eaton, 199.
61. Eaton, 207.
62. Eaton, 207.
63. Eaton, 207–8.
64. This is the kind of question that Russ Castronovo notes is often not asked by those who propose the importance of aesthetics for political community. See Castronovo, *Beautiful Democracy,* 28. It is one that Eaton acknowledges and attempts to address in discerning her identity and its implications for art.
65. Eaton, 208. Eaton suggests that science fiction is essential to the kind of enlightened democratic citizenship she aspires. "Artworks can not only ask us to examine our lives and our relationships within communities but also make us consider the very limits of what might be possible for life itself. Many works of science fiction, I think, do this by causing us to ask, for example, to what extent we are ready to grant rationality and other aspects of humanity to entities" (157).
66. See, for instance, Duhart, "What Is Art All Night?"

67. For instance, when jazz trumpeter Wynton Marsalis proposes that expanding access to the arts, especially jazz and classical music, is the key to unleashing the arts' possibilities in sustaining the kind of community that New York City is or should be. See Marsalis, "Wynton Marsalis on Arts in the After-Times (Future NYC)."
68. Eaton, *Merit, Aesthetic and Ethical*, 205.
69. This is a question that is raised in Rubsam, "The Cinema of Atrocity."
70. See, for instance, Florida, *The Urban Crisis*, 37–38. See also Moskowitz, *How to Kill a City*, 16, 20. Moskowitz's reference to marketing material for Colony 1209, a building in New York City constructed in 2014 in the predominantly Latinx but rapidly gentrifying Brooklyn neighborhood of Bushwick, is telling. The sales brochure states, "Here you'll find a group of likeminded settlers, mixing the customs of their original homeland with those of one of NYC's most historic neighborhoods to create art, community, and a new lifestyle. Let's Homestead, Bushwick-style" (36). For another specific case study adjacent to New York City, see Rojas, "A Revival Comes to Newark, but Some Worry It's 'Not for Us.'"
71. Eaton, *Merit, Aesthetic and Ethical*, 97.
72. Eaton, 96.
73. Eaton, 95.
74. Eaton, 96.
75. Clive Bell's landmark book *Art*, originally published in 1914, is an exemplar of this point of view. We will consider this way of regarding art more specifically in chapter 4.
76. This refers to the controversy at the University of Kentucky over the 1934 wall-length mural by Ann Rice O'Hanlon, which "is covered with vignettes that are intended to illustrate Kentucky's history. At the center of the mural is an image of enslaved people tending to tobacco plants, and at the bottom, there is a Native American man holding a tomahawk and peering out from behind a tree at a white woman as if poised for attack." See Jacobs, "Students' Calls to Remove a Mural Were Answered."
77. See Svrluga, "As Colleges Grapple with Racist Legacies, a Monument at Ole Miss Will Finally Go." For a more sustained exploration of Confederate statues and monuments and the various ideologies, convictions, and religious narratives that are central to their various regard, see Newson, *Cut in Stone*.
78. See Elie, "Everything That Rises."
79. Eaton, *Merit, Aesthetic and Ethical*, 96.
80. Wolterstorff, *Art in Action*, 3.
81. Wolterstorff, 4.
82. Wolterstorff, 3.
83. Wolterstorff, 21.
84. Wolterstorff, 24.
85. Wolterstorff, 27.
86. Wolterstorff, 45.
87. See Dahl, *On Democracy*, 100–18.
88. Scarry, *On Beauty and Being Just*, 33–46, where she calls attention to the repeating motif of palms in the Nice paintings of Henri Matisse.
89. Ewing, "Why Authoritarians Attack the Arts."
90. Of art's subversiveness she writes, "Art creates pathways for subversion, for political understanding and solidarity among coalition builders. Art teaches us that lives other than our own have value" (Ewing, "Why Authoritarians Attack the Arts").

91. Ewing, "Why Authoritarians Attack the Arts." This was the case with Soviet communism too. See Nemoianu, "Hating and Loving Aesthetic Formalism," 53–54.
92. Horowitz, "The Specter of Hitler in the Music of Wagner." For more historical context on Wagner's use by the Nazis, see, for instance, Rose, *Wagner*; and Weiner, *Richard Wagner and the Anti-Semitic Imagination.*
93. Castronovo, *Beautiful Democracy*, 8.
94. Adorno, *The Culture Industry*, 98, 103–4.
95. Bernstein, "Introduction," 10.
96. Eaton, *Merit, Aesthetic and Ethical*, 206.
97. "We need the arts because they make us full human beings. But we also need the arts as a protective factor against authoritarianism. In saving the arts, we save ourselves from a society where creative production is permissible only insofar as it serves the instruments of power." Ewing, "Why Authoritarians Attack the Arts."
98. Castronovo explicitly singles out Scarry as a contemporary successor of the arts for democracy movement that took hold in the late 1800s and early 1900s in the United States. See Castronovo, *Beautiful Democracy*, 27.
99. Castronovo, *Beautiful Democracy*, 7.
100. Castronovo, 33–34. See also Riis, "The Tenement House Blight."
101. Castronovo, *Beautiful Democracy*, 11.
102. Castronovo, 12, 13.
103. Castronovo, 12.
104. Castronovo, 14–15.
105. Castronovo, 17–18. Castronovo cites Ransom, "Forms and Citizens," 45. On the New Critics, see Berman, *From the New Criticism to Deconstruction.*
106. Dewey, "Art as Experience," as cited by Castronovo, *Beautiful Democracy*, 56.
107. Dewey, "Art as Experience," 297–98. We will return to his notion of ordinary experience and art briefly at the start of chapter 4.
108. Dewey, 303, 304.
109. Castronovo, *Beautiful Democracy*, 56.
110. The importance of theory with respect to what we can expect from art is underscored in his example of plants: "It is quite possible to enjoy flowers in their colored form and delicate fragrance without knowing anything about plants theoretically. But if one sets out to understand the flowering of plants, he is committed to finding out something about the interactions of soil, air, water and sunlight that condition the growth of plants." Dewey, "Art as Experience," 297.
111. To make matters even more complicated, there were times when, for instance, fascists and communists extolled nonrepresentational art such as formalism rather than rejecting it as degenerate. As Nemoianu notes, "Fascist authorities were inconsistent: on occasion they made justifications or excuses for 'great authors' of the past. Moreover, these authorities, like their Communist relatives at different points in time, sometimes condoned formalism as the lesser evil when allusional or allegorical opposition tended to emerge." Nemoianu, "Hating and Loving Aesthetic Formalism," 54.
112. Castronovo, *Beautiful Democracy*, 41.
113. Castronovo, *Beautiful Democracy*, 41, citing Riis, *How the Other Half Lives*, 124–26.
114. Castronovo, *Beautiful Democracy*, 41.
115. Castronovo, 34, 43.
116. Castronovo, 45.

117. Rodgers, "Picasso Mural Torn from Building after Years of Dispute."
118. Eaton, *Merit, Aesthetic and Ethical*, 206.
119. Eaton, 207 (emphases added), citing Saito, "The Aesthetics of Unscenic Nature," 103.
120. Eaton, *Merit, Aesthetic and Ethical*, 207.
121. Wagner, "Trump Says He Found Inspiration for Border Wall at Memorial for Flight 93 Victims." "President Trump said he found inspiration for his long-promised wall on the U.S.-Mexico border during a visit to the Flight 93 National Memorial in Pennsylvania, which honors the lives of 40 people killed in the Sept. 11, 2001, terrorist attacks. 'They built this gorgeous wall where the plane went down in Pennsylvania, Shanksville. And I was there. I made the speech,' Trump told Hill. TV. 'And it's sort of beautiful, what they did is incredible. They have a series of walls, I'm saying, it's like perfect. So, so, we are pushing very hard.'"
122. Edelman, *From Art to Politics*, 102.
123. Castronovo, *Beautiful Democracy*, 52.
124. Castronovo, 60.
125. Castronovo, 54.
126. Castronovo, 52.
127. Castronovo, 53.
128. "Aesthetic resources designed to instruct and elevate subjects posed dangers to ethical citizenship" (Castronovo, 60). Elsewhere Castronovo writes, "Lessons of aesthetics are not schematic, which is precisely why they are dangerous" (64). Such is the lesson of Elmira. "Riis's problem at Elmira was that he expected images to establish sensus communis, a common understanding in which individuals, though divided by different interests with respect to capital and labor, could overcome class antagonisms by effectively imagining themselves in the place of others. In his view, strikes erupted precisely because of a lack of common understanding between employer and employee: if they could only see their 'common interests,' then 'the man who does the work and the man who hires it done so that he may have time to attend to his own' would recognize each other as 'workmen'" (54).
129. Burch, "How 17 Outsize Portraits Rattled a Small Southern Town." For all portraits, see Meehan, "Seeing Newnan."
130. Burch, "How 17 Outsize Portraits Rattled a Small Southern Town."
131. Campbell, "Seeing Newnan."
132. Burch, "How 17 Outsize Portraits Rattled a Small Southern Town."
133. Burch.
134. Castronovo, *Beautiful Democracy*, 60.

4

IS ART ABOUT THE EMOTIONS OR THE AFFECTIONS?

In the opening of the first volume of *Ethics from a Theocentric Perspective,* James M. Gustafson notes that theological reflection is "guided by certain perceptions of both historical and highly contemporary circumstances in society, culture, and religion."[1] Our perceptions of such circumstances are not necessarily coherent, neatly delineated, or systematic and can be confused, disoriented, or unformed. He then goes on to explicate this point about perception through an aesthetic lens. If our perceptions about the world are not always coherent and consistent, then our perceptions can lead to "mixed impressions: sometimes more the cacophony of Gunther Schuller or John Cage than with the harmonious completions of melody that one enjoys in Brahms, Beethoven, and Schubert." Gustafson presses the point further through examples of visual art: "It sometimes leaves one with the impressions of the mature Jackson Pollock rather than with the subtle but formed totality of Monet, not to mention the integration [of] his tremendous figures that Michelangelo provides in the Sistine Chapel ceiling." Gustafson concludes by asserting that the cacophony of the pianist Cage and the painter Pollock are themselves the products of particular perceptions of the world: "No doubt even the modern movements in art, foreign as they seem to an earlier Western tradition, are informed by a perspective. It may be a technical perspective on what constitutes a musical idea and its expression, or it may be something as deep and perhaps implicit as attempting to resonate with a general view of the world, or the spirit of the times."

But if the creation of artworks emerges from particular perceptions of the world, then what about how they are received? In other words, is the reception as much as the creation of art tied to particular perceptions of the world? In another passing comment, Gustafson suggests that it is;

otherwise, distinctions between religious and aesthetic, for example, would be meaningless:

> Various persons listen to performances of Bach's *St. Matthew Passion*, or Haydn's oratorio *The Creation*. From the point of view of religious interest, each celebrates, both in the text and in the music, central themes in the Christian religious heritage. In each case text and music refer to events that are interpreted to have deep religious significance. . . . It is difficult from the perspective of religious piety to distinguish the aesthetic from the religious aspects both of the compositions and of the experience of hearing them. Yet surely each can be viewed as basically an aesthetic object, and the experience of many listeners is primary, if not exclusively, an aesthetic one. From an aesthetic perspective it is purely a matter of convention that the *Passion* is performed during Lent; it could just as well be performed during Advent. From the perspective of Christian piety it would be as odd, if not shocking, to hear the *Passion* during Advent as it would be to hear Bach's *Christmas Oratorio* during Holy Week. While distinctions can be made between aesthetic and religious aspects of objects of experience, and of the human experience of objects, they are distinctions made in part in relation to individual and group perceptions.[2]

Gustafson's reflections on aesthetics are few in his *Ethics from a Theocentric Perspective*; in fact, the passages cited above constitute his more complete paragraphs referencing aesthetics in that multivolume tome. But in these handful of lines, Gustafson shows not only the utility of aesthetics in underlining or illustrating a point,[3] but perhaps more important for our discussion, he shows the extent to which the creation of art and one's engagement with it are tied to context.[4] Not only the content but also the form of artworks emerge out of particular perceptions, interests, or views of the world, as well as the acts of looking, reading, and listening.

Like Gustafson, Ralph Ellison assumes that art is a function of context or perspective.[5] But Ellison goes several steps further by claiming that certain kinds of interests ought to drive art, especially for Black artists who, like any other American, have a stake in democratic forms of life. This claim leads Ellison to advocate for a certain kind of lyric poetry and ultimately a certain kind of novel as integral to the advancement of democracy. The novel is a critical democratic enterprise because "the novel has always been bound up with the idea of nationhood. What are we? Who are we? What has the experience of the particular group been? How did it become this way? What is it that stopped us from attaining the ideal?"[6] The novel therefore is more than "a matter of entertaining, but is a way of confronting reality, the nature of the soul and the nature of society."[7] And when a novel penetrates the "tragic realities of human existence," that is when the novel's moral power shines, when "we have a deeper appreciation for song and for the lyric mode."[8]

In Gustafson's case, art is what it is not because it exists in its own insulated sphere of value but instead because it expresses particular perceptions of the world. In Ellison's case, this is the foundation for a normative claim about art and its moral importance: art that makes a moral difference is art that speaks to or comes out of the lived experiences of an author's community. More precisely, novels that are rooted in the author's own lived experiences and perspectives are the ones that Ellison claims matter to him and what readers, more generally, should want out of novels. For Ellison, the novels that matter, or the ones that ought to matter, are ones that tell the truth about the author's "own sense of life[,] . . . his sense of the good life[,] . . . his sense of the moral dilemma of the nation."[9] "These questions and their answers are the novelist's responsibilities," which are vital to pressing forward the American project that Ellison claims is "an undiscovered country." If novels do not matter to us in this way, that is, if readers wind up being unmoved by what they are reading or end up reading or doing something else, it is because, according to Ellison, novelists have shirked their responsibilities: "if we find that we read sociology and history more than we read novels, it is not our fault as readers. It is the fault of the novelist because he has failed his obligation to tell the truth, to describe with eloquence and imagination as it appears from wherever he finds his being." He adds, "It is a terrible thing to sit in a room with a typewriter and dream, and to tell the truth by telling effective lies, but this seems to be what many novelists opt for."[10]

Ellison's account of the novel calls attention to at least three arguments that I have pursued thus far and a fourth I aim to develop further in this chapter. First, Ellison may be too sanguine to think that readers will be more interested in novels if they are only given novels that illumine and interrogate the tragic character of human life. This is the kind of instrumental temptation or tendency that I have endeavored to articulate, unpack, and argue against in preceding chapters, especially in chapters 1 and 2 in my survey of recent theological-ethical turns to art. But Ellison's additional insistence that novelists, American novelists especially, should focus on diving deeply into the details of their own American experience underscores the second kind of argument that I have also endeavored to make thus far, as we saw in chapter 3: that art can fashion a particular kind of community if it attends to what this kind of community needs (i.e., to what it needs to see or perceive about itself and the world) in order to be that kind of community. Ellison is desirous for a certain kind of American community, for a particular brand of democratic life, and he sees the novel—not just any kind of novel but rather one that emerges out of a wrestling with an author's own experiences of living as an American—as critical to realizing that desire. This explains his exhortation (though in the guise of criticism and blame) to especially Black authors to write novels of a particular sort, that is, novels that are not simply products of their imagination (which would move into the area of fantasy, he suggests) but instead are of an imagination that is informed by the struggles of the communities to which they belong.[11]

For Ellison, the novel can promote democracy if it is a certain kind of novel, one that is conscious of what a democratic community needs for its flourishing. More generally, this suggests that the novel is capable of substantive moral work on the condition that it is written with a particular telos in mind. But this proposition also presumes that the community to which the novel is intended also shares this telos. This reflects the third kind of argument that I have at least alluded to, also in chapter 3, which, more explicitly, is that art can and will do its moral work if its audience is willing to receive it on the consensus that it is worth their critical attention. Ellison is occupied primarily by the kind of moral work the novel can accomplish and believes that the novel can promote democracy if it is a certain kind of novel and if persons are receptive to such novels, or, at the very least, to the possible import of them for life together as free individuals. Persons can be receptive to novels in that way if, Ellison insists, novels delve into the truth of our lived experiences in American society. The impact that the essays by Ralph Waldo Emerson, Walt Whitman, and Henri Thoreau had on American life is, for Ellison, a historical validation of this argument. Their essays "fulfilled a need," according to Ellison, precisely at a moment when Americans needed to be reminded that "they were not Europeans" but instead were a people who "existed in a society and a country which was not very tightly structured and in which no one . . . could set a limit upon individual possibility, certainly not at the level of the imagination." While some dismiss their essays "as being a little too much on the optimistic side, I remind myself that there was a need for [their] optimism . . . at that time especially," Ellison remarks.[12]

However, if art's moral power is a function of the needs of the community in which it is created, displayed, and enjoyed, then to what extent is art capable of impacting the moral imagination and agency of persons independent of their actual interests, values, and predilections? In other words, what moral import does art have when the needs of a community change and the art that it encounters does not attend to those changed needs, interests, and values? To put it differently, what happens to a community's art when such change takes place? Can its art still speak to its audience, effect moral action, even moral change? Or does art that does not resonate with such change (which is out of sync with the experiences of its community) become irrelevant or anachronistic? It is because communities change, their experiences are transformed, that certain kinds of artists and artworks emerge, and this is no less true in the American context, Ellison claims: "Of course the first writers of any stature in the United States were . . . the Emersons, Whitmans and Thoreaus. . . . The Melvilles and Hawthornes, however, were part of our early nineteenth century; by midcentury this country had reached a certain crisis so profound that we fought a civil war, one of the bloodiest in history. It was then that America produced Henry James, Mark Twain and Stephen Crane." But in each of these instances, basic democratic commitments and ideals endured, and these writers wrote to the American polity with those commitments and ideals in mind and thus "asked them to interrogate" themselves and to concern themselves with "the most subtle type of moral consciousness."[13] But what if moral receptivity to such themes is diminished or, more radically, absent altogether? What then of art's capacity—the Emersons, Melvilles, Hawthornes, Twains—to call us to persevere and continuously recommit to the project of American democracy?

The worry underlining this question points to a fourth argument of this book, which is an implication of the first three, and it is expressed more explicitly and carried forward in a rather unsettling manner by the art critic Philip Kennicott in his reflection on the power or, more precisely, lack of power of what we might call conflict or disaster photography.[14] In a 2019 essay, he reacts with horror to a series of photographs that received wide media attention (in both legacy news outlets and social media).[15] The first is a photo of "Salvadoran migrant Oscar Alberto Martinez Ramirez and his toddler daughter, Valeria," who "died Sunday [June 23, 2019] after being swept away by a strong current while the family was trying to cross the Rio Grande into the United States." The photo depicts the "toddler in red shorts and tiny shoes, tucked inside her father's dark T-shirt, seemingly at rest as if napping with her dad on a hot afternoon." The second photo is similar; it recalls "Alan Kurdi, a 3-year-old Syrian Kurdish boy whose body washed up on a beach in Turkey in 2015." Both photos, in terms of their focus on the death of children, is similar to "a haunting photograph of a young Haitian girl at prayer but in fact crushed by the weight of falling concrete during the horrific earthquake of 2010. The child looks as if he or she is doing something fundamentally childlike—napping, playing, praying—that elicits one response (warmth and sentimentality), which is then immediately subverted by a darker, sadder truth."

All three images, according to Kennicott, are powerful in the juxtaposition of childhood innocence and the cruelty of "human or natural forces."[16] For that reason, he claims further, these photos' "power to elicit social sympathy and political change"—addressing the war in Syria, the immigration crises in both the United States and Europe, and the poverty and political instability in Haiti—explain the extent to which they were shared repeatedly and widely on social media and cable television networks. And yet, Kennicott wonders why these photos did not ultimately have the power of "breaking through" the conscience of the wider public, especially in the United States, to take political action on these problems, to be less indifferent, and to "make the effort to understand who these people are, how they died, how they probably suffered and how we would feel in their place."

Kennicott's own reaction to these images is plainly one of horror. He is equally horrified by their ineffectuality in moving the public to respond to each event, to address them, better understand the forces at play in each conflict or event of suffering, and seek their resolution. His analysis of such inaction leans on the American public's "nationalism," or the increasing mood to focus on its own plight rather than moving its interests outward toward the plight of those outside its own borders.[17] So, he writes, "But when nationalism has successfully dehumanized the other, there is no breaking through, and people who imagine that a photographic message must assuredly be so powerful that it will touch all hearts are forced to grapple with a more confounding truth: Not all consciences operate alike, not everyone is susceptible to what seems a basic, even rudimentary level of empathy."[18] If the photographs are to function as "an exercise of conscience," then what is required, he proposes, are "time, effort and openness." This is moral work, which is to say committed, intentional choices and actions on the part of the looker or viewer to allow the photos to matter to them in a way that elicits empathy for the photos' subjects. Otherwise, it is more than conceivable that one may indeed respond unsympathetically with the following kind of attitude—"'People shouldn't cross borders without permission'"—and from this attitude to the following judgment: "The drowning becomes a kind of punishment. . . . Bad things happen to those who break the rules." Kennicott thus concludes that "the power of a photograph like this depends on the time we devote to it and our basic sense of who these people are."

That last clause—"depends on the time we devote to it and our basic sense of who these people are"—deserves emphasis, for it reflects the kind of moral perception or vision that we must bring to these photos, or the kind of moral perception or vision that we are willing to accept through these photos, if we hope to have them settle into our minds and agitate us toward sustained action.

In short, the moral power of the photos is dependent on the kind of persons the viewers of the photos are in the first place. Are we willing or not to be transformed by the photos; are we willing to be vulnerable, to perceive them in a way that would move us empathetically, or are we only willing to perceive them in a way that "reaffirms an existing sense of the world"? The title of Kennicott's essay is all too apt in this respect: "We used to think photos like this could change the world. What needs to change is who we are."[19]

The importance of moral perception, or the kind of moral perception that delimits our aesthetic practice of reading, listening, or looking, calls attention to the kind of persons we are and how who we are matters to what art is morally capable of doing. Who is doing the looking, reading, and listening is a question that is critical to the question of what art can do in the sphere of ethics, that is, its moral purposes, uses, functions, or ends. But in saying so, in calling attention to this linkage between the who and the how of art, the implication is not that art is only "moral" or morally relevant when persons approach it with a particular moral perception but rather that art is morally relevant from the very start inasmuch as the reception of art cannot be neatly divorced from a particular moral perception. If one is not moved by art, it is not because art is morally irrelevant but rather that the moral perception that one brings to art is of the sort that insulates the artwork from moral consideration. This is to some extent the realization that Kennicott comes to learn in struggling with the seeming moral impotence of photos capturing episodes of human misery and tragedy: they seem to possess the power to capture our attention, but apart from motivating likes and shares on social media, their moral effect is typically fleeting.

Kennicott's realization forces us to wrestle with an inconvenient truth about art and ethics: the moral power of the arts (inasmuch as it has moral power) is dependent on the social positionality of the person or persons who engage the arts (i.e., the kind of moral perceptions that we—viewers, readers, listeners, and creators of art—bring to art because of our social, economic, political, and cultural positions or communal contexts and formations); apart from this, art has no intrinsic moral power. But to the extent that this inconvenient truth is a realization—it is a truth he is forced to draw only after coming to grips with how these photos have been received with deafening inaction instead of moral urgency, outrage, and resolve—Kennicott's essay also raises the question of why the pivotal role of moral perception is often neglected in our (misguided) assumptions about what art is and can do. Why is it that we often hope for so much from the arts, especially with respect to ethics, but in practice they often fail to come through? As was noted at the very outset of this book, if we believe in the moral relevance of art as much as our contemporary academic (theological-ethical) discourse of it seems to reflect, then it would seem more than reasonable to embark on a wholesale transformation of how we teach ethics and form moral sensibilities by advancing arts education more so than traditional ethics curricula. But that we have not perhaps is an implicit acknowledgment that art is hardly sufficient. As Kennicott suggests, our hopes for the arts as a morally transformative power require attending to the kind of people we are if those hopes are to bear fruit. And who we are (and how that informs or orients us toward the arts) matters as much if not more than the kind of art that we think will effectively elicit moral action. Otherwise, we should be able to count on certain kinds of artworks and certain kinds of depictions (such as those of human suffering) to move persons in definite directions, but, in reality, we cannot count on them to do that kind of work. Again, as Kennicott realizes, the kind of moral work we want art to do will depend on the kind of people we are. But why, then, is the linkage between what the arts can do and the kind of persons we are underestimated, maybe even unacknowledged?

In this chapter, I want to give closer attention to this issue of dependency and address the question of its prevailing disregard within society by assessing the sustainability of the modernist notion of aesthetic emotions and proposing the importance of the affections as a corrective. As we saw in chapter 3 (and briefly in the introduction), the legacy of modernism (or aesthetic formalism) on popular cultural understandings of what art is and is for are vast and profound. Nicholas Wolterstorff attributes the rise and influence of modernist institutions of art—their privileging of contemplation as the primary aim of art—for solidifying a wider cultural attitude that the arts exist in a distinct sphere of their own (hence the widely held regard for museums, galleries, concert halls, and theaters as the primary spaces to encounter and enjoy art). This is not an unreasonable attitude to have against the backdrop of competing views that tend to make art an epiphenomenon of social realities by regarding it as no more than a function of politics or economics or cultural whims and trends. Yet, it is equally limiting to insulate art from the broader purposes of life, that is, from human intentionality, attitudes, and perceptions. The modernist notion of aesthetic contemplation as the height of aesthetic experience maintains or perpetuates this insulation, according to Wolterstorff, severing our awareness of how the social contextualization of art is key to understanding what art is and how it shapes, informs, and functions in daily human life. But we also need to call greater and specific attention to how modernist conceptions of aesthetic emotion (and not just aesthetic contemplation) further masks the extent to which artworks are what they are (or do what they do or not) depending on particular perceptions that are brought to bear on them.

For many modernists, the primary distinction of art is its emotive character, its capacity to appeal to and elicit human emotion. This privileging of the emotions enables modernists to conceive of art as a sphere of its own. However, the emotions, as I argue in this chapter, cannot be so easily separated from our perceptions of the world as modernists would have us think. I argue further that the implications of this modernist mistake—the insistence that certain kinds of emotional responses or states are inherent to the nature or definition of art—is one that comes to the fore when we are attuned to the ways in which the Christian tradition has distinguished the emotions from the affections. We find a notable instance of this distinction playing out in Thomas Aquinas's moral anthropology; it also plays out in striking, consequential ways in Jonathan Edwards's moral thought. My aim in this chapter is not to provide a comprehensive explication of their accounts on the emotions and affections and underlying theological anthropology and doctrine of God but instead to only provide an account of how they distinguish emotions from affections and the kinds of implications we can draw from that distinction for our assessment of modernist aesthetics and ultimately the potential and limits of the arts' capacity to effect moral change.[20] Especially with respect to Edwards, his theology is well known as an aesthetical one, where beauty and the language of symmetry, proportion, and consent are central and replete throughout his vast corpus and theological vision. But the aim of this chapter, or this book for that matter, is not a systematic mapping and mining of his theological aesthetics as such, though I will appeal to general features and trajectories of it briefly in chapter 5. My primary aim here is to draw attention to an aspect of Edwards's thought that is not typically treated in interpretations of his aesthetics—the distinction between the emotions and affections and, as we shall see, his application of that distinction in his assessment of revivalism—on the premise that this dimension of his theology expands and sharpens the applicability of his thought especially in the arena of contemporary art-ethics discourse.

Edwards's and Thomas's distinction between emotions and affections—especially Edwards's revision of Thomas's delineation of them—has a threefold import for our present discussion. First, it will amplify the critical role of perception in how and what we know about the world and call sharp attention to the role of perception in human emotional life. When modernism's claims are refracted through a theological framework that accounts for emotions as different from affections, the position that emotions can solely be "aesthetic" will necessarily be problematic. While modernists prefer to think that art, properly understood, elicits emotional responses about itself, what is often missed is the extent to which such emotional responses are tied to a particular relationship—affective relationship—that persons have with art, which disposes them to have such emotional responses. The comingling of affection language and emotion language aids to obscure this interdependence: that our emotional—and, correlatively, aesthetic responses—are dependent on antecedent commitments, values, and orientations.

The significance of this dependence can be summarized as such: the very nature of art (what art is, and what it can or cannot do) cannot be understood apart from who we are as creators as well as admirers and consumers of art. This claim to an extent resonates with what John Dewey, as we saw in passing in chapter 3, claims is the constitutive importance of "actual life-experience" in whether and how one regards something as art.[21] That there could be such a resonance should not surprise given Edwards's legacy in the development of the American pragmatist tradition, of which Dewey belongs.[22] So, if for Edwards our affective relationality is key to our aesthetic and thus emotional responses, Dewey might specify such relationality and its importance more sociologically as "part of the significant life of organized community."[23] Consider, for instance, as Dewey does, the Parthenon. If it is a great work of art and specifically if the ancient Greeks thought of it as a great work of art, how would we understand it as such apart from excavating the lives of the Athenian citizens who created and admired it? For Dewey, knowing who they were entails knowing their needs, their desires, and what brought them joy. Thus, Dewey concludes, "In order to understand the meaning of artistic products, we have to forget them for a time, to turn aside from them and have recourse to the ordinary forces and conditions of experience that we do not usually regard as esthetic."[24] To some extent, this is not far from the kind of notion that I am trying to capture through my claim that for Edwards our affective relationality is key to our aesthetic-emotional responses. Accordingly, Edwards, like Dewey, can be taken to align with the view that art in itself does not determine or set the terms of its own perception as art but instead must cooperate with and ultimately depend on the viewer's antecedent experiences.

While the notion that affective relationality is key to our emotional and thus aesthetic responses can be counted as both Edwardsean and Deweyan, Dewey complicates this shared notion through his at times ambiguous use of the term "emotion." This ambiguity underscores the value in leaning on and elevating Edwards's way of separating out the language of the emotions from the affections, as I shall do in this chapter. Such distinctions bring into sharp focus how and why our aesthetic-emotional responses are constitutive of our moral perceptions or orientations. Dewey can be regarded as implying as much when he claims that "emotions [in contrast to 'automatic reflexes' of, say, a 'disturbed infant'] are qualities . . . of a complex experience that moves and changes. . . . Experience is emotion but there are no separate things called emotions."[25] For Dewey, emotions are dependent on the particular life experiences of persons; they "belong to the self that is concerned in the movement of events toward an issue that is desired or disliked." But despite this dependence, Dewey will go on to say that emotion is "the moving and cementing force" of experience. "It thus provides unity in and through the varied parts of experience." The role that Dewey ascribes to emotions in these latter two quotations would seem to undercut the earlier assertion that emotions are dependent affairs or phenomena, that emotions, because of a person's experiences, are what they are rather than the other way around. But to refer to the emotions as "the moving and cementing force" of experience, whether intentionally (and perhaps clumsily) or not, provides modernism the opportunity to insist that there is such a thing as aesthetic emotions divorced or independent of "actual life-experience." Such a position is untenable, as I will endeavor to show in this chapter, and part of this effort will be to map out how modernism's conceptual frame lacks the capacity to avoid its own contradictions, that is, to avoid the notion that art, for it to be recognized as such, requires its audience to in fact approach art in a particular way; it requires, in other words, antecedent commitments about the value of art, what counts as art, and how to approach it "properly." In short, modernism's own ways of defending aesthetic emotion are self-defeating. And it is Edwards's way of untangling emotions from affections that proves why such a defense of aesthetic emotion will necessarily be so.

Second, this assessment of modernism—the problematic of conceiving of emotions emerging and contained within an independent aesthetic sphere—goes beyond modernism and applies to the general turn to the arts in theological ethics. As we saw earlier particularly in chapter 2, a number of theological ethicists rely on the arts to underscore the holistic nature of moral knowing, specifically the role the emotions play in moral judgment and action. While modernism is interested primarily in turning to the emotions to secure for the arts their own sphere of relevance, theological ethics is more interested in pointing to the relationship between art and emotions to broaden the arts' relevance to spheres of life outside itself, namely to ethics, to the nature of moral reasoning and agency. Regardless of the diverging aims, the consequences, oddly enough, converge in that both do not adequately recognize the import of the distinction between emotion and affection. If art does something, whatever it does (appeal to the emotions especially), it does so because of one's affective relationship to it. That is why, particularly in theological ethics in its turns to both literature and beauty, it struggles to account for the moral successes and failures of art, that is, the reality of art's moral pluralism.

Third, Thomas's and Edwards's way of distinguishing emotions and affections—and, to emphasize once more, Edwards's amendment of Thomas's understanding of their relationship—will raise the question of the extent to which a person's perception, or way of perceiving the world, can be changed by art. If what art can and cannot do is inextricably linked to one's perceptions (to one's affectivity), then to what extent is change of perception possible through a relationship or engagement with art, that is, through looking, reading, or listening? (In other words, what can art actually do with respect to ethics? What can it do to engender and sustain moral action or effect moral transformation and change?) Circling back to Kennicott's realization of the moral limits of conflict and disaster photography (photos of human suffering and tragedy), the argument I will ultimately advance in this chapter is that perceptual or affective change through art will be restricted. Thus, how we think about the transformative possibilities of art will need to be reassessed within a broader account of what is needed to form good persons. For art to realize its moral power, persons will need to be formed to be receptive to the transformative possibilities of art. But this will require that persons engage the hard (or harder) work of being formed by an array of nonaesthetic practices. This in some respects means that ethics will need to be the priority over aesthetics if, paradoxically, we want to give art the chance of being a morally transformative experience. I will attend to this paradox—or the question of what kind of moral work is required for art to morally matter—with greater scrutiny in chapter 5, but for now I turn to modernism's efforts to link art to the emotions and a theological account of the affections that indicates how such an effort is misguided.

THE MODERNIST MISTAKE: AESTHETIC EMOTION AND THE MISUSE OF THE AFFECTIONS

Modernist conceptions of art, or aesthetic formalism, have been a predominant force in shaping how we think about both art in contemporary life and objects of wide criticism. To elevate art to the status of pressing significance in the company of sociopolitical and economic issues, modernism rests on an universalizable account of what art is irrespective of its time and circumstance. If questions of justice, what it is and how it should be instantiated in society, are part and parcel of the human experience, so too is the question of art: what it is, why it exists, and why it is a phenomenon constitutive of every culture. Noticing and appreciating its ubiquity, then, requires identifying the salient features of an object that merits its designation as art objectively. One important pushback on these modernist aims is not necessarily that art is less significant than economics, politics, or ethical concerns but rather that the formalist's definition of art narrows too strictly what counts or does not count as art. A striking example is feminist critiques of formalism that demonstrate not only how gender affects the creation of art but also how it is received by its audience.[26] Formalists tend to discount certain works as nonart if they are not created by a solitary, so-called artistic genius (as Kant envisioned).[27] An art object is received as such when such genius is recognized especially in the expression of a specific form in the art object. But feminist critiques point out that this assumes that formalist engagement of the arts is strictly noncontextualized, which is questionable given numerous instances of art produced by women that are often regarded less favorably than art produced by men.[28] Is such difference simply an indication that women have traditionally been unable to produce art whereas men have been more capable, for whatever reason? Or is it indicative of the role of gender and, more specifically, gender bias in the production and reception of art? Feminist aesthetic criticism leans on the latter.

This kind of criticism highlights insightfully the problematic separation between art and everyday experiences maintained by aesthetic formalists and reveals the subjectivity in art more so than an objective standard to art. In other words, the category of art encompasses a wider spectrum of objects and experiences than modernists are willing to allow. In regard to this push to broaden modernist aesthetics and reenfranchise art produced by women as well as persons outside the Anglo-European context, it should be specified that the modernist's desire for an objective, universalizable account of art (one that ultimately narrows what counts as art) is itself a contextualized approach to art. To put it differently, if modernists are mistaken in their attempts to identify a universalizable account of art, which ultimately results in an arbitrary narrowing of what art is, then this error has a corollary: that our perceptions of art, that is, our perceptions of what counts as art and why art is meaningful or worthy of serious attention, is not simply a function of looking, listening, or reading. Instead, more complexly, the status of something as art—being able to tell that it is art and worthy of our attention as such—depends on being formed (or being disposed or oriented) to look or listen or read in a particular way.[29]

Modernism's reductive account of aesthetic emotions—or the emotions elicited by art as art or "genuine" art—provides a partial but significant explanation for what I earlier referred to as the modernist mistake, that is, their insistence that the regard for an object as art does not "[depend] on factors that exist outside of it," such as the perceiver's personal and collective identities, social affiliations and values, and even biases of various sorts (racial, gender, political).[30] Below, I provide a more detailed sense of how the modernist concept of aesthetic emotions perpetuates this mistake, and I shall do so by highlighting the arguments of select modernist thinkers. These arguments, I propose, are in many respects inconsistent, by which I mean that despite their intentions, they underscore the difficulty of maintaining the separation between art and "factors that exist outside of it," a difficulty that is acknowledged, albeit implicitly, in the very arguments that modernists make in defense of such separation. To a large extent, their inability to acknowledge and address more explicitly the inherent difficulty of separating or insulating art from larger social, cultural, and moral concerns and interests is, I propose, exacerbated by their misuse of the terms "emotions" and "affections." The distinction between the two terms will be elaborated further in the proceeding section through Thomistic and ultimately Edwardsean lenses, where I will also indicate the implications of this distinction for the question of art and moral action and change.

Aesthetic Emotions: Under Which Conditions Do Aesthetic Emotions Arise?

For modernists, as Todd Cronan describes, it is art's capacity to move its beholder emotively that defines the essence of art, or what art is and should be. A premise of this argument is that artworks can produce emotive responses "regardless of who the viewers are[,] . . . when they are[,] . . . [and] what their attitudes toward the work are."[31] More radical versions of this notion have been taken up by postmodern accounts of art in their insistence on the sensorial immediacy of art if what one is viewing (or listening to, touching, and so forth) is indeed art.[32] "The value of the work—what makes it 'top quality'—lies in the degree of effect it has on the subject who views it."[33] Interpretation of the work of art is less important than determining the "efficacy" of the work of art whether it directly agitates or moves the viewers' body, especially their "emotional state."[34] Such emotive states are sometimes described as a "violent encounter" or "traumatic."[35] However it is described, the basic point is that art "[interrupts] the normal function of the beholder's nervous and perceptual systems," and as such, the viewers' assumptions are "undermined; the beholder is de-formed."[36] Such effects on our emotional state of being are made possible by the "formal qualities" of art—"qualities inherent in line and color"—rather than artistic representation and intentionality of the artist.[37]

Such a sentiment is exemplified by Clive Bell, an art critic of the famed Bloomsbury Group whose influence extended to the work of artists including Paul Gauguin, Henri Matisse, Salvadore Dalí, Georges Braque, and Jackson Pollock.[38] As Bell famously wrote, "The starting-point for all systems of aesthetics must be the personal experience of a peculiar emotion. The objects that provoke this emotion we call works of art. All sensitive people agree that there is a peculiar emotion provoked by works of art. I do not mean, of course, that all works provoke the same emotion. On the contrary, every work produces a different emotion. But all these emotions are recognizably the same in kind. . . ."[39] The emotion produced by art is what Bell calls "aesthetic emotion," and it is this kind of emotion that he claims further is evoked by an "essential quality in a work of art," what he also calls "pure form."[40] "The contemplation of pure form leads to a state of extraordinary exaltation and complete detachment from the concerns of life."[41] This is an emotional state that is peculiar to art and no other arena of human experience: "Art transports us from the world of man's activity to a world of aesthetic exaltation. For a moment we are shut off from human interests; our anticipations and memories are arrested; we are lifted above the stream of life."[42]

For Bell, there is a good deal at stake in this definition of art. At the very least, it helps to delineate the different experiences we have with a wide array of objects; our emotional experiences of some objects count as aesthetic experiences and thus as being attentive to the art element of those objects, to the presence of pure form. This delineation is important for Bell, since it preserves art, which is to say that it avoids the absurdity that all things are or can potentially be counted as art because they elicit emotional responses in us. So, is watching a bird flying in a dazzling way, while possibly provoking an emotional response, an aesthetic event, or is such an avian event an instance of something else? It is not quite art, in Bell's judgment, since art's pure form, he claims, is more artifactual than a natural creation.[43] Bell acknowledges the possibility that this determination is an arguable point, but what interests him primarily is upholding art as having an integrity of its own and that integrity is tied to being definable in a distinctive way: an object's pure form elicits its own kind of emotions. Bell does not deny that objects of all sorts can evoke an emotional response. But to say then that all objects that do so count as art renders the idea of art meaningless. It is the dilution of the term "art" that concerns Bell primarily. While an object can evoke in us an emotional response, this emotional response is an aesthetic response (and thus a recognition of and response to art) if it is a response to a particular quality perceived in the object, to the object's pure form.

Yet, is the delineation of emotions as aesthetic and as some nonaesthetic as tidy as Bell makes it out to be? Perhaps a different way of posing the question is this: To what extent is the pure or significant form of an artwork capable of moving us aesthetically? Does the form itself move us emotively? That is, is the provocation of emotion by form a power intrinsic to the form itself? At first, Bell insists that such a question is beside the point: "'Why are we so profoundly moved by forms related in a particular way?' The question is extremely interesting, but irrelevant to aesthetics. . . . For a discussion of aesthetics, it need be agreed only that forms arranged and combined according to certain unknown and mysterious laws do move us in a particular way, and that it is the business of an artist so to combine and arrange them that they shall move us."[44] But in another instance, Bell is willing to entertain the question substantively. Especially curious is his emphasis on the importance of seeing artworks, their expression of pure form, in a certain way, "as ends in themselves." More specifically, he asks rhetorically, "for objects seen as ends in themselves, do we not feel a profounder and a more thrilling emotion than ever we felt for them as means?"[45] Bell thinks that seeing something as pure form, and to see it as an end in itself, is an occurrence that all persons at some point or another have experienced without prompting, learning, and consciously doing so. In another rhetorical question, Bell posits, "All of us, I imagine, do, from time to time, get a vision of material objects as pure forms. We see things as ends in themselves. . . . Who has not, once at least in his life, had a sudden vision of landscape as pure form? For once, instead of seeing it as fields and cottages, he has felt it as lines and colours. In that moment has he not won from material beauty a thrill indistinguishable from that which art gives?"[46]

But to what extent is this true? Is it true that all of us have at some point felt the force of pure form, whether in a landscape or an art object, spontaneously, without effort on our part? Bell's claim is speculative at best. Additionally, consider what Bell claims elsewhere, the kind of information that one must bring to an object to be noticed and, correlatively, felt as art. He states that knowing that an artwork consists of a combination of forms that "expresses an emotion that the artist has felt" is determinative of how we regard the artwork. What is important is knowing that the artwork is produced by an artist with the intent of combining forms to express a particular emotion. To demonstrate the point, he turns to the question of why one may not be moved emotionally by a replica of a painting even if the original may have elicited specific emotions. "A literal copy . . . leaves us cold; its forms are not significant"; what is missing in a copy is "the emotion which empowers artists to create significant form."[47] In other words, what is absent is "the actual lines and colours and spaces in a work of art caused by something in the mind of the artist which is not present in the mind of the imitator."[48] If we are moved by the original work of art and not by its copy, it is because we know that the original "is always the work of one who is possessed by this mysterious emotion." If a copy is to move us like its original (if it is to have any possibility of doing so), then we need to know that it was created by someone who is not simply a "trained observer" but one who engaged the process of replication with the feeling of the original artist.[49]

It bears noting that Bell seems to backpedal slightly when he claims that to be moved by an object's pure form one need not "bother about the feelings of the artist"; instead, "feel[ing] the aesthetic significance of the artist's forms suffices."[50] In other words, we do not need to know what emotion the artist is attempting to convey through aesthetic form in order to experience an emotion upon looking at the artist's work of art. However, what we do need to know is that the work of art is an attempt by its creator to "create significant form."[51] It is this knowledge therefore that one needs in order for an object to possibly make an appeal to us as art, to possibly move us emotionally by virtue of its form, that is, how its lines, color, depth, dimension, and so on are combined and reimagined. This is why Bell thinks that it is necessary to know something about what the artist is trying to aim for, that is, the kind of aesthetic problem she is trying to solve in her projects, such as how to express herself "within a square or a circle or a cube, to balance certain harmonies, or reconcile certain dissonances, to achieve certain rhythms, or to conquer certain difficulties of mediums."[52] Knowing this allows us to delineate between what is art and what is not. So, if the artist produces something primarily to, for instance, convey information rather than trying to "create significant form," then the artist is not producing art per se. And once we are able to delineate between art and nonart, Bell suggests that we will be better positioned to experience emotionally art for its aesthetic value rather than its other possible uses. This is what the "vulgar" miss, according to Bell, for they think that what we should be looking for in art is whether the artist is making "something lifelike," but the emotional experience that may arise from art intended to be lifelike is not an aesthetic experience.[53] When we feel something for an artwork because of our regard for how it combines and arranges various aesthetic forms or techniques, only then can we say that we are aesthetically experiencing it as a genuine work of art. The contrast that Bell draws between the so-called vulgar and nonvulgar spectator reinforces a feature of his account of art that he does not explicitly acknowledge but is nevertheless a central feature of his account: that art appears as art—that we can emotionally experience art as art—only when we bring specific information to the object, when we intentionally look for certain things in it on the premise that certain features of the artwork count while others do not.[54]

Aesthetic Emotions and the Necessity of Aesthetic Training

In suggesting that it is important to know what artists' intentions are in their artwork—the kind of aesthetic problem they are grappling with, as Bell puts it—Bell, wittingly or not, underscores a problem endemic to modernism's focus on the relationship between an artwork's capacity to elicit an emotive response and its status as art. For modernism, an artwork and its meaning reside in the power of its formal qualities such as the way its lines and colors are expressed and whether those qualities—its aesthetic forms—elicit an emotive response in its beholder, the one who reads, listens, or looks. Consequently, as Cronan observes, the question of an artwork's meaning, its status as art, ends up shifting to its audience and, more precisely, to the centrality of the beholder's emotive reactions to the form of an artwork as the primary determinant of the artistic meaning and significance of the artwork. And to some large extent this is no accidental shift: modernism's emphasis on the power of an artwork's form to elicit a sensory, emotional response is intended to bypass controversy and the prospects of interminable disagreements on what art is and what an artwork means in favor of what the artwork does to the viewer's "body," the kind of emotions it elicits.[55] In practice, however, modernism ends up exacerbating disagreement about art but on the very level that it thinks such disagreement is avoided, that is, on the level of the emotive response to the artwork. Which emotions or whose emotions count or ought to be considered the right aesthetic response? Can we determine which emotive responses are characteristically aesthetic? Are some emotive responses more appropriate to art, or are certain kinds of emotions more appropriate to a specific artwork? Or, do aesthetic forms elicit certain emotions more so than other emotions? Is this sort of adjudication possible?

Some modernists argue that these are irrelevant or nonsensical questions, given the very nature of emotions. Emotions are private and not shareable. Thus, whatever emotive responses there are to art, they are different for each person, and "those differences need not be reconciled." "What would it be like to disagree about affect? *Can* there be disagreement, or just registration and calibration of the difference between irreducible sensations?"[56] For Cronan, if there cannot be disagreement (if disagreement is precluded as a matter of course), then we run into the additional problem of what we might call equivalence, that everything and anything can become art, which upends the differentiation of emotions, specifically aesthetic emotions from nonaesthetic ones. What an artwork or aesthetic experience is itself becomes completely personal and arbitrary. This, as I explain further later on in this chapter, is a potential dilemma that theological-ethical turns to the arts, to its capacity to tap the emotional dimensions of knowing, also runs into. In the context of equivalence, art becomes an object, and any object can become art, since the determining factor in what makes something art is how one feels about it, whether we are moved emotively by it. If how I feel when I see something, or what my emotive experience of it is, determines whether it is art or something else, then the "ontological difference between the work of art and the world 'outside' it" breaks down. And "once the work of art loses its 'art' status and becomes like an object, it also becomes available to beholder response in the way that any object does."[57] As we saw above, this is one problem that Bell endeavors to avoid by suggesting that not all artworks elicit the kind of emotions that are appropriate to art. Not all emotive responses are aesthetic, except for those that are elicited by virtue of knowing (and perhaps a trained knowing, an intellectual "habit," to refer to a word he uses) something about artists, that their works are not simply duplications of other artworks and that their intentions are to resolve a particular aesthetic problem. Such knowledge is critical to identifying objects that count as art and thus to experiencing them emotively for their value as art.

Cronan too emphasizes the need for attending to an artist's intentions: what differentiates an artwork from other objects, he argues, is the intentionality of the artist that is embodied in the artwork. Where Cronan diverges from Bell is on the kind of intentionality that is needed. Cronan thinks one needs to seek out artists' actual intent underlying their work, whereas Bell is only interested in knowing that artists, whatever their motivations, are seeking to get their audience to experience something in particular through the expression of form in the artwork. Whatever the difference, the point that is crucial to underscore is that intentionality delineates the difference between an object and an art object. As Cronan states, "one does not bring intentions to bear on the experience of objects in the way one does with artworks."[58] "Intentions [of the artist] make works of art different from other objects in the world where intentions do not matter or do not figure centrally."[59] For modernism, an artwork's art status is a function of how its forms elicit an emotive response irrespective of the artist's actual intentions. That for Cronan is too consequential, a too high a price to pay for the sake of avoiding disagreement about art, about its meaning and what it is as art. For him, retrieving the importance of the artist's actual intention in how we view and interpret art and, correlatively, demoting the modernist emphasis on the centrality of the emotive response to art are critical. Without such a retrieval and demotion, he thinks that discourse about art and the broader act of experiencing art can only be subjective and individualistic and never be a collective, shared experience.[60] The very idea of art would then become meaningless. Only by paying attention more earnestly to an artist's real intention can we know how we ought to feel about an artwork.[61] And this kind of paying attention only happens by learning how to see art as art. Cronan proposes that part of that aesthetic education or formation must be centered on acquiring the skills of discerning the artist's actual intention. Only then can we know how to experience an artwork, the kind of feelings that are pertinent to the artwork in question.[62]

Feeling something for an artwork and feeling correctly—in Bell's case, feeling in light of, for instance, a visual artwork's combination of forms, its use of color, lines, brushstroke, depth perception, and dimension—requires approaching an artwork in a particular way, with the desire to experience it as art, which suggests that art is not, in a manner of speaking, self-interpreting or cannot on its own generate an emotional response. Correlatively, one cannot simply look at something and recognize it as art (or not) and thus feel accordingly. Instead, one has to approach an object with at least a prior sense of what art is (or what one thinks art is) and work at feeling something in relation to that definition. Whether Bell defines art correctly—as expressions of pure form—is to some extent beside the point. He does not deny that there are other definitions or forms of art, such as historical art, descriptive art, lifelike art, and so forth. But it is the commitment to a particular definition of art that is the salient point to notice in Bell's account of art, even if he does not necessarily notice it himself. For Bell, when we feel something for art because of what we know about its aesthetic forms (that the artist is striving to combine or arrange forms in certain ways), that feeling is to be distinguished from how we might feel about the artwork based on a different perception of it (we think of it as entertainment, as decoration, as a historical artifact, and so on). Bell simply assumes that art will be experienced emotionally in a particular way when its audience actively or intentionally regards something—its "arrangements and combinations of form"[63]—apart from personal satisfaction, without the expectation of conveying useful information or as an opportunity to welcome or communicate a particular idea or thought. Instead, one must be committed to seeing an object as pure form.[64] In other words, it requires structured effort, or new habits of looking, reading, and listening.

What we bring to a particular work of art helps to explain why we might feel a certain way about it. We experience a range of emotions with respect to art because we come to it with different perceptions about what it is. Otherwise, we could not make good sense of why art engenders particular feelings and why certain feelings should count as aesthetic and others as nonaesthetic. What feelings emerge in reaction to art are not self-categorizing; their delineation is made possible because of the priorities and interests we bring to our regard for art. For Bell, feeling something for an artwork based on a focus on its form is a distinct practice, one that contrasts with feeling something for an artwork for another reason. In other words, Bell moves on the premise that features of an artwork that are distinctively aesthetic are those that pertain to form, but what reason is there to think that these features are distinctively aesthetic and others are not? Why is an artwork that seeks to represent life accurately less aesthetically worthy than one that simply focuses on pushing the boundaries of how line, color, and dimension can be combined and expressed? Both kinds of art can be emotionally impactful, but determining which emotional experience is aesthetic is indicative of the viewers' wider interests and commitments that are brought to bear on that experience. What one thinks of as aesthetically relevant, then, is reflective of what a particular "community that shares cultural traditions" considers "worthy of attention"; it is this consideration that "is a necessary and sufficient condition of aesthetic experience."[65] What counts as an aesthetic experience, therefore, is never static.[66]

Aesthetic Emotions as Affections Reconsidered

Bell assumes, without acknowledging so explicitly, that we can experience an artwork as art—that is, have an emotional experience of artwork as art—if we know what to look for. (This undergirds the modernist stress on the importance of creating and maintaining the kinds of conditions that facilitate looking, listening, and reading. In other words, perceptual environments matter to how we perceive aesthetically, hence the relevance of museums and galleries as optimal spaces for "display," concert halls and the like for appreciating music as music, and so forth.) This assumes further that emotive responses to artwork require effort; it is something one works toward. I am less interested in how much effort and the kind of work that is required, at least for now (more on this in chapter 5), and more interested in being conceptually and descriptively sensitive to how our feeling about an artwork requires a certain kind of effort or, perhaps another way of putting it, requires being disposed to it with a particular telos in mind. What we might feel when looking as well as listening and reading is engendered by or is a function of particular commitments and attachments. This insight is easy to overlook when emotions and affections are comingled uncritically.

Consider Peter de Bolla, who not unlike Bell thinks that the emotive response that art engenders is indicative of the aesthetic value of the art object.[67] One's emotive response becomes the basis on which "evaluation of artworks becomes possible: if my response to a particular work is uniform, monotonous, weakly felt, or trivial I feel confident in assigning to it a lower aesthetic value than to one that elicits a varied, sustained, polyphonic, or deeply felt response."[68] In other words, the quality of the emotive response equates with the aesthetic value of an artwork. Given the importance of the emotive response for the aesthetic value of an object, de Bolla thinks that it is less important to ask what an artwork means, represents, or is trying to say.[69] These are the wrong questions to ask, he says, since they do not get to what makes art and its experience what it is: aesthetic. The more important question is "'How does it make me feel, what does it make me feel?'" This brings de Bolla squarely within the modernist tradition and its displacement of the problem of an artwork's meaning with the emphasis on the centrality of an artwork's capacity to elicit a sensory reaction.

As we saw earlier, for many modernist (as well as their postmodern successors), what we feel in the presence of art is not subject to debate, or at least shareable and communicable. Art generates emotive responses that are different, and difference is private and uncontestable. For de Bolla, however, one's emotive response to art is not simply "an inarticulate or inarticulable feeling; still less to an unreflective or 'emotive' response."[70] There is, he proposes, a "lexicon of emotion" when it comes to our emotive responses to art. This lexicon, however, does not come to us spontaneously or intuitively but instead requires learning. As he remarks,

> Can one person be equally at home with romantic poetry, baroque keyboard music, and abstract painting? Without wishing to be in the least hubristic, I think it is important to note that the perception of artworks does not necessarily come easy, as if all one has to do is open one's eyes in order to see. It may take many years of patient practice to grasp some works fully, whereas others may require specific kinds of knowledge before one can begin to attune oneself to their art.[71]

This notion of the need for training, de Bolla claims further, is something that is facilitated by the artwork itself. So, art elicits in us an emotive response, a certain feeling, and that feeling grounds if not inspires, motivates, and sustains an "aesthetic education" about what that feeling says about the artwork in question.[72] Only when we focus on the emotional response to an artwork are we experiencing it as art. This is what he means when he writes "that the extent of that training, or what it might consist in, is to a great extent indicated by the work itself."[73] "What I see is seen under the auspices of what the image presents to sight, what it lets me see."[74]

De Bolla is surely right that art can elicit emotive responses in us, sometimes intensely.[75] And his account of how our emotive responses to it can generate successive emotional attachments to the artwork is also noncontroversial. We saw examples of this in the previous chapter in relation to Elaine Scarry's notion of art's "forward momentum" and Eaton's observations of how art can engender something akin to a "focus group," at least temporarily. However, in thinking about emotive responses to art in this way, de Bolla places too much emphasis on the extent to which aesthetic training or education is something that is generated by a prior experience of artwork and gives little to no attention to the extent to which emotive experiences of artwork are themselves generated by a prerequisite: a prior aesthetic education or training, which informs our emotive reactions to art. The latter possibility seems to be cut off in de Bolla's many insistences that it is our emotive responses to particular works of art that teach us how to value the artwork before us: "Part of my argument about the value of artworks, of how we come to value some more than others, is based on the observation that the artwork itself guides us in how to approach it: the image, to some extent, teaches us how to look, the music how to listen, the poem how to read."[76] And yet de Bolla, wittingly or not, intimates the importance of a kind of aesthetic education or training antecedent to looking, listening, and reading; more specifically, he suggests that a prior commitment to being in relationship with art in a particular way is critical to looking, listening, and reading in an aesthetically relevant manner. For instance, de Bolla claims that being in the presence of art, by which he means allowing the art to reveal itself to us as itself rather than its audience bringing meaning to it, requires learning to accept that art can in fact reveal itself if we allow it to. As he writes with respect to Barnett Newman's *Vir Heroicus Sublimis,* an abstract expressionist painting that features a field of bold red on canvas:

> It seems to me that one has to *learn to accept* this pressure of presence, which is to say that it does not, at least initially, feel 'natural' or even warranted. . . . An initial sense of discomfort is not uncommon when in the presence of great works of art, and this is partly caused by the very insistent will to presence announced by such works. One way, perhaps the only way, of *learning to accept* 'the pressure of presence'

> is repeatedly to encounter the sense of discomfort associated with great works. When that happens—when discomfort is transfigured into something less irksome—what I am calling this 'will to presence' leads me both away from myself and, at the same time, toward a greater sense of fullness, self-presence.[77]

For de Bolla, the kind of training that is needed to be "present" to art is itself agitated and demanded by the kind of feeling one initially has when viewing art; one might feel at first discomfited, for instance. But we can also ask whether this training can be seen as necessary simply on the basis of that initial feeling. Perhaps upon feeling such discomfort one feels put off by the artwork and is consequently less inclined to give it the time of day. In this instance, what reason is there to give it a second or third chance or repeated looks unless one is instructed and committed to do so despite how one feels about?

That de Bolla ignores the importance of a preceding commitment to being open to the potential revelatoriness of art as art is not surprising given his uncritical association of emotion with affection. For instance, he will claim that "all we ever know of the artwork as *art* . . . is . . . the affective response, [which] indicates that we are in the presence of an artwork." The materiality of the artwork "is only brought to our awareness through the process of an affective experience." And "our affective experience gives us the sensation of becoming intimate with the work of art, closing the distance between it and ourselves."[78] While I have underscored the importance de Bolla places on the emotive response to art and how that emotive response elicits a desire to know more about the artwork in question, I have intentionally bracketed how he describes that emotive response as affective. By now, however, it should be clear that in associating such an emotional response as affective, he is underscoring how art affects its audience; it affects us by eliciting a certain bodily sensation.[79] Art affects us, which is to say it imparts knowledge about itself to us and thus elicits a bodily sensation. (This is why he will claim that an affective response is not just a simple feeling but is also "between emotive sensation and cognition"; our emotive response to art is tied up with the kind of knowledge it imparts to us about itself.)[80] This is similar to how Cronan employs the term "affective." When he describes modernism as taking the "affective turn," he means to underscore modernism's various accounts of how art affects its audience, its focus on the movement from art to the viewer, on how "color and line produce bodily responses that function and mean [*sic*] independent of the artist's agency," and for that matter the viewer's agency too.[81] In short, modernism is "affective formalism" because of its focus on what art does to the one who looks, listens, reads.

But this account of the affections or, more specifically, the equating of emotions with affections assumes that affectivity works primarily as a function of reception, which is to say that one's affectivity is a consequence of being acted upon. It is on account of art acting upon us that we are imparted with a particular perception about it, which is manifest in an emotive response to it. But could it not also be the case that how we feel about something is also a function of how we affect what is perceived or is on account of us acting on it or what we bring to its perception? This is more than a semantic sleight of hand, since it calls attention to the importance of disposition with respect to art. How we are disposed to art may matter as much if not more to how we respond emotively to art than what the artwork actually is (e.g., the quality of its lines and color, its form, what it is depicting, etc.). And our disposition, and thus our approach and attitudes toward art, will be determinative of whether we respond to art at all.

My proposal, to some extent, is intimated in de Bolla's claim that the encounter with art is of a twofold trajectory: "one moving in the direction of the viewer . . . [and] the other in the direction of the [art] object." Both movements "bear upon any affective response to visual art [and beyond] and have effects at the material level of . . . *aesthetic* experience."[82] Yet, while the second movement is the kind of affectivity I am concerned with—the ways in which our emotive responses to art is on account of how we move toward art or our preceding disposition to it—this second movement for de Bolla is itself (and can only be) a consequence of the first movement which is foundational; it is the capacity of art itself to move into the interior life of its viewer that occasions a feeling that becomes "so intense that we almost identify ourselves with the work, or colonize it, appropriate it." But why should we assume that our movement toward artworks (or our emotive response to it, to be more specific) is primarily initiated and ultimately sustained by the artwork itself or that the artwork itself is capable of drawing its audience to itself? Is that not asking too much of artworks or ascribing a level of power that art could not possibly have? Is there a descriptive and normative case to be made for the movement to work in the opposite direction and necessarily so, that is, to account for our response to art as constitutive of our desire to respond to it independent of the artwork's purported ability to move us in a particular way?

THE PRIORITY OF THE AFFECTIONS OVER THE EMOTIONS: A THEOLOGICAL INTERVENTION

Thus far, we have seen that modernist approaches to art are entangled in a contradiction. While that contradiction formally claims that art is a sphere of its own insofar as it alone can elicit specific emotions or feelings about itself (art is self-referential, in a manner of speaking), in practice it cannot dispense with the need for its audience—its viewers, listeners, and readers—to learn or know what to look for or pay attention to in order for art to be recognized and experienced as such. The need for aesthetic training or education, however, goes unacknowledged as a prerequisite, and if it is acknowledged this is only implicitly so or as if it is fully consistent (though it is not) with its formal claims about art's autonomy.

If modernism struggles uncomfortably and clumsily over the extent to which art's capacity to elicit an emotive response is dependent on how we approach it, this neglect is exacerbated in part by its additional inattention to the difference between affections and emotions. Separating out the language of affections from the language of the emotions, as I have begun to broach above, calls more specific attention to the possibility that how we respond to art or even respond to it at all is linked to antecedent commitments about the value of art, what kinds of art is worth one's time and consideration, and what features, properties, or aspects of art should be areas of primary attention. From the perspective of Jonathan Edwards, this linkage cannot be just a possibility but must instead be the case, or so I will endeavor to show next.

As an eighteenth-century Puritan thinker, Edwards lived and wrote well before the ascendency of modernism and was unfamiliar with its accounts of art. He nonetheless anticipates its quandaries in his account of the affections. For Edwards, the affections are distinguishable from the emotions in a manner that is not unlike Thomas Aquinas's delineation of the two, though Edwards deviates from Thomas in important ways. Noticing these deviations is critical; they point to a distinctive way of thinking about emotions and their cognitive status—or, in actuality, their relative noncognitive status—and thus the need to be leery of accounts of art that do not explicitly or sufficiently attend to the role an artwork's audience plays in what an artwork can effectuate. In short, when we think about art from an Edwardsean point of view, we are confronted with the very nonmodernist view that whatever art engenders in its viewers, it is not necessarily because of some property of the artwork itself (whether its form or content) but instead because of its audience's affective relationship to art. Therefore, emotions (or specific emotive responses) are not the purview of the arts, since it is our affective relationship to the arts that informs the kind of emotions we have as a response to them.

While the primary implication of Edwards's account of the affections (as distinct from the emotions) is to cast doubt on the viability of aesthetic emotions (or emotions that are distinctively aesthetic or specifically in response to art), this implication also makes clear why our epistemological and performative expectations of art must be limited. Art may indeed be a morally transformative power. But if it can inform and change our moral viewpoints and inspire and move us to moral action, it can do so not because art has some intrinsic property that is morally capable or powerful in that way. Instead, as Edwards's account of the affections and emotions underscores, it can do so depending on the kind of moral attitudes or persuasions we have. And to acquire such attitudes or persuasions requires the kind of work that is fundamentally nonaesthetical.

Thomistic Definitions

In his *Ethics from a Theocentric Perspective,* Gustafson writes of the term "affectivity" that it "includes 'senses,' attitudes, dispositions, and more particular *affections or emotions*."[83] "As I use the term," he writes further, "it [affections] refers to emotion."[84] The association of affection with emotion is certainly not unique to Gustafson, as we saw earlier with respect to modernist discourse on art and emotions, though the way he associates both terms, particularly through his interpretation of Edwards,[85] has certainly been influential in discussions on the emotions in contemporary religious and theological ethics.[86]

Intuitively, Gustafson's approach to affection and emotion as interchangeable terms makes sense and almost seems descriptively necessary. At what point can one say that an experience of anger, for instance, is an affection and not an emotion? Can one only be emotively angry and not affectively angry? Does it even make sense to ask that sort of question? Approaching the affections as emotions offers one way of underscoring and circumventing the kind of conceptual tangles one might fall into when trying to make clean distinctions between the two terms. Gustafson seems to be well aware of such pitfalls in *Can Ethics Be Christian?* "Feelings, emotions, affections, sensibilities—these are so uncertain in terms of their references that it might be well not to use the words. . . . One must constantly remember that [those terms] are in experience intimately related."[87] But how intimately related are they, and are they so closely associated that affection and emotion are essentially a distinction without a difference?

As I signaled briefly earlier especially in reference to de Bolla's uncritical comingling of the two terms, it is a distinction that makes a substantial difference, and how Edwards understands and utilizes that distinction reveals further what is at stake in discerning and maintaining the affections as something distinct from the emotions. Yet, inasmuch as Gustafson's own comingling of affections and emotions draws from Edwards's way of talking about the affections, demonstrating the usefulness of Edwards for our present discussion will require a degree of reconstructive work. This reconstruction requires noticing and appreciating the extent to which Edwards's language of the affections mirrors Thomas's language of the affections, which he differentiates from the emotions, while also noticing how Edwards diverges from Thomas. Such a comparative analysis would have given Gustafson sufficient pause to reconsider the necessity of carefully delineating the emotions from the affections. A brief sketch of Thomas's account of the affections and emotions will be helpful in clarifying key features of Edwards's account of the same. The implications of these features for the question of aesthetic emotions (i.e., the viability of the concept of emotions that are specifically aesthetic) and, relatedly, the question of the morally transformative possibilities of art will be mapped out subsequently.

At first glance, Aquinas's language of the passions of the soul as emotions seems to obscure more than clarify the relationship between emotions and affections.[88] In Question 22 of *Summa Theologica* II, Aquinas asserts that "it is evident that the passions of the soul are the same as affections. But affections manifestly belong to the appetitive, and not to the apprehensive part. Therefore passions are in the appetitive rather than in the apprehensive part."[89] Note how he interchanges affections and passions: the affections are appetitive, and the passions are appetitive too; therefore, the passions "are the same as" affections.[90]

As appetitive motions, affections and passions (or emotions) are the same, which is to say that both are powers to tend toward an object in relation to a notion of goodness. But the sameness of the affections and passions becomes more complicated when Aquinas later notes that "passion is more properly in the act of the *sensitive* appetite, than in that of the intellectual appetite."[91] In line with that delineation, Aquinas observes that the intellectual appetite, or the will, "consider[s] the common notion of good" in its capacity to "apprehend the universal" and thus moves toward or away from a particular object in relation to that sense of the universal good.[92] In contrast, the passions, as motions of the sensory appetite, "crave" the goodness that is particular to a specific object.[93] In other words, it is the sensory appetite or the passions that orient us to or away from a particular object beyond an intellectual grasp; the passions enable a grasping of an object in such a way that "the object also gets a hold of us" in one way or another.[94]

That "the passions of the soul are the same as affections" only in reference to their appetitive natures is in keeping with Aquinas's delineation of at least two kinds of love. As he asserts, "love differs according to the difference of appetites."[95] There is the movement of love that arises from the sensitive appetite (irascible and concupiscible), wherein love in this sense is a passion, or emotion.[96] Then there is the movement of love that arises from the intellectual appetite, what Aquinas refers to as intellectual love, since "it is in the will."[97] In Question 82 of *Summa Theologica* I, Aquinas employs the term "affections" to describe such an intellectual love. "Love, concupiscence, and the like can be understood in two ways. Sometimes they are taken as passions—arising, that is, with a certain commotion of the soul. And thus they are commonly understood, and in this sense they are only in the sensitive appetite. They may, however, be taken in another way, as far as they are simple *affections* without passion or commotion of the soul, and thus they are acts of the will."[98] Important to note at this point is that by construing the passions as motions of the sensory appetite, passions are "of the body" or, as he puts it, "found where there is corporeal transmutation."[99] Thus, one might say that a passion involves embodied motion, has a bodily, physiological correlate and expression. "For instance, *anger* is said to be a *kindling of the blood about the heart*."[100] To be oriented to an object emotively (or by the sensitive appetite) is to be so moved where one's skin tingles, forehead sweats, stomach turns, knees weaken, or heart beats excitedly, depending on the emotion. Affections, however, express themselves in a "disembodied" manner. Aquinas suggests as much when he states that "now there is no need for corporeal transmutation in the act of the intellectual appetite: because this appetite is not exercised by means of a corporeal organ."[101] It is interesting on this account that he says "when love and joy and the like are ascribed to God or the angels, or to man in respect of his intellectual appetite, they signify simple acts of the will *having like effects*, but without passion."[102] There is this "resemblance" because unlike human beings, the angels (and God) have no bodies, whereas human beings are soul-body composites.[103]

The corporeal character of the passions solidifies its distinction from the affections. But this difference does not mean that there is no connection or intertwining of the affections and passions. Even though they are similar in terms of their appetitive natures, given that the passions are of the body and the affections are simple acts of the will, in theory it would seem that the connection between affections and emotions is not intrinsic; love and joy, for instance, are in either the sensory appetite or the intellectual appetite.[104] But is an affective act of love conceivable as passionless? How can an act of the will that expresses itself in love or joy not be corporally, emotively felt? Perhaps for that reason Aquinas chooses to refer to loving and joyful expressions of the will as affections, suggesting that such acts of the will, while different from the passions formally speaking, are not wholly unrelated to the passions, at least in one sense, when simple acts of the will, depending on their intensity, "affects" the passions. Such an occurrence Aquinas refers to as one of "redundance": "when the higher part of the soul is intensely moved to anything, the lower part also follows that movement; and thus the passion that results in consequence, in the sensitive appetite, is a sign of the intensity of the will, and so indicates greater moral goodness."[105] In another instance, Aquinas refers to this kind of redundance as the "intensely moved" will "overflow[ing] into the sensitive appetite in so far as the lower powers follow the movement of the higher."[106] This can make sense experientially. In making, perhaps, an assertive, conviction-filled choice that we believe promotes our flourishing, "our experience of being perfected in relation to an intelligible good will be accompanied by noticeable bodily changes, such as a heightening of our energy level, a lessening of our awareness of physical discomfort, or a relaxation response."[107] In that way, one can say that the affections, such as love and joy, although they are "intellectual," are also the "same" as the passions insofar as the passions may intensify the affectivity of simple acts of the will.

To account for the affections and emotions in terms of redundance or overflow underscores, as Diana Fritz Cates puts it, their "indirect" connection.[108] That there is at least an indirect connection makes sense in light of Aquinas's insistence on the soul-body composition of the human person; due to that unity, the body and, correlatively, the emotions can hardly be considered ancillary to human life. But in maintaining an indirect connection, Aquinas allows for, I believe, a kind of autonomy to the emotions, but autonomy not in the sense that our emotions are something completely beyond our control. In saying that our emotions have relative autonomy, I mean to convey how Aquinas allows for the movements of the sensitive appetite to be controlled or moderated by the will and ultimately the intellect, as well as the converse, that is, the capacity of the emotions to inform and influence the will and intellect positively or negatively.[109] In either case, emotions as something different from affections provide Thomas a way of conceiving the emotions as a critical source of moral deliberation and judgment.

Edwardsean Modifications: Convergences and Divergences with Aquinas

Aquinas's delineation of the affections and emotions (as passions) is resonant in Edwards's thought, though the indirect connection between the affections and emotions will be less so for Edwards. That tighter connection does not vitiate the kind of essential distinction between affections and emotions that I believe Edwards, like Aquinas, assumes, but it does indicate how Edwards does not approach the emotions with the kind of relative autonomy that Aquinas does.

To be more specific, while the Thomistic language of appetite is not typical in Edwardsean moral psychology, it is not entirely absent in Edwards's approach to the affections either. Consider Edwards's assertion in *Religious Affections* that affections are "more vigorous and sensible exercises of the inclination and will of the soul."[110] I take Edwards's insistence on will and inclination as similar to Aquinas's approach to the will as an intellectual appetite. Human agency is not simply a function of choice, but being able to choose is, as Edwards says, "governed" by one's likes and dislikes, or the extent to which one is either "inclined or disinclined to what is in view."[111] Thus, like Aquinas, the will is object-oriented and pertains to our capacity to move toward or away (a matter of inclination) from an object based on our understanding or, more precisely, perception of it.[112] Insofar as one's exercise of will and inclination is rooted in the perceptual understanding of, as Edwards puts it, the soul or the mind, one's willing and inclining, as John E. Smith describes, expresses or gives insight into the basic character, disposition, or orientation of one's life.[113] Affections indicate the state of one's will and inclination, the "liveliness and sensibleness of [their] exercise." Without "the vigorous and sensible exercise of the inclination and will of the soul," argues Edwards, human activity would cease. "Such is man's nature, that he is very inactive, any otherwise than he is influenced by some affection, either love or hatred, desire, hope, fear or some other. These affections we see to be the springs that set men agoing, in all the affairs of life, and engage them in all their pursuits: these are the things that put men forward and carry 'em along, in all their worldly business."[114]

If Edwards, like Aquinas, generally locates the affections in the will (and its inclinations), then does Edwards, like Aquinas, locate the emotions elsewhere, namely in the body? A negative response to the question is not unreasonable given that Edwards takes affectivity to be what he calls sensible knowledge or "heart" knowledge. For Edwards, the meaning and importance of sensible knowledge is underscored if not revealed from the side of redemption.[115] As C. C. Goen notes, "Edwards . . . saw man as a sinner who needs to be remade—an event which is possible only as God grants him a 'new sense of the heart,' a holy affection at the very center of his being which radiates its transforming power through the whole man."[116] As radiating through the entirety of one's being, what divine grace effectuates is something different from speculative knowledge. "He that is spiritually enlightened" says Edwards, does not "merely rationally believe that God is glorious, but he has a sense of the gloriousness of God in his heart. There is not only a rational belief that God is holy, and that holiness is a good thing; but there is a sense of the loveliness of God's holiness."[117] The nature of conversion solidifies the qualitative difference between speculative knowledge (or notional knowledge as Edwards also calls it), which is a kind of abstract or bookish knowledge, and sensible knowledge, which is to have "pleasure and delight in the presence of the idea of [some thing]."[118] So, just as "there is a difference between having a rational judgment that honey is sweet, and having a sense of its sweetness," so too is there a difference between knowing about God and having a converted, "sanctified" knowledge of God.[119] Accordingly, as Smith remarks, the distinction between sensible and speculative (or notional) knowledge is meant to convey the reality "that *feeling and sense* make up the more profound level in human experience."[120] But would that not suggest that for Edwards emotions are located in the same "place" as the affections, that is, in the will and not the body?

The question is not as straightforward as it may seem, however, if we recall that we have been taking the corporeal motions of the passions to mean emotions in Aquinas. To do the same with Edwards is a bit trickier. Edwards only refers to passions in one paragraph of *Religious Affections*.[121] For now, however, it is important that we do not mistake Aquinas's passions for Edwards's reference to the passions and, in turn, not equate Edwards's comment on the passions as somehow pertaining to the emotions, at least not directly or simply.

So, then, for Edwards, where are the emotions located? Are they the same as the affections and therefore of the will and inclination, or are they different, and consequently, do they pertain to something other than will and inclination? Consider first that Edwards on occasion will refer to "affections of body" and "affections of soul." This distinction appears in one of his discussions on whether the saints in heaven are capable of experiencing affections (in this case, religious affections). Saints in heaven, he claims, "be not united to flesh and blood, and have no animal fluids to be moved." But that does not mean they cannot experience affections of the soul such as love and joy. When it comes to the saints in heaven, "We are not speaking of the affections of body, but the affections of soul, the chief of which are love and joy."[122] What might the affections of body be if they are not affections of soul, of will and inclination, and thus of the mind? That the affections can be experienced in the body is suggestive of Aquinas's notion that the passions or emotions are of the body. Edwards's later reference to "emotion of the mind" furthers this suggestion, and as such we can take affections and emotions that refer to the mind as properly "affections" and those that refer to the body as properly "emotions."[123]

Like Aquinas, then, we can say that for Edwards, emotions are different from affections and involve changes in the body; they are "constitutions of the body," of bodily sensation. Note that for Edwards, the movements of the body or "motions of the blood and animal spirits" are strictly different in their nature from the vigorous exercise of the will and inclination (affections).[124] As Edwards states, "it is not the body, but the mind only, that is the proper seat of the affections." This is so because the body is not capable of thinking, and since affections reflect the soul's perceptual understanding of an object, which is the basis of the soul's inclination or disinclination to that object, the affections cannot be of the body, only the emotions.[125]

It is at this point that we can start to detect the first divergence between Aquinas and Edwards. It is a subtle but significant divergence. For Edwards, the affections are neither located in the body nor dependent on the movements of the body; this is similar to Aquinas. And echoing Aquinas's notion of redundance between affections and emotions (that the will when intensely moved can spill over to the emotions in such a way that the emotions then buttress the movement of the will), Edwards notes in passing throughout *Religious Affections* that "the constitution of the body, and the motion of its fluids, may promote the exercise of the affections" insofar as such motion is an effect of or a reaction to the affections in the first place. As he remarks, the body's "reaction [to love and joy] . . . may make some circumstantial difference in the sensation of the mind."[126] This is so due to "laws of the union of soul and body."[127]

Those same laws, however, also establish the necessary and not simply reactive "alterations of the motions of [the body's] fluids, and especially of the animal spirits" by the affections.[128] As necessary, the relationship between the affections and the emotions is far more than the indirect connections between the affective expressions of the intellectual appetites and the emotive movements of the sensitive appetites in Aquinas, as noted earlier. Consider the following passage from Edwards:

> All affections whatsoever, have in some respect or degree, an effect on the body. As was observed before, such is our nature, and such are the laws of union of soul and body, that the mind can have no lively or vigorous exercise, without some effect upon the body. So subject is the body to the mind, and so much do its fluids, especially the animal spirits, attend the motions and exercises of the mind, that there can't be so much as an intense thought, without an effect upon them. Yea, 'tis questionable, whether an embodied soul ever so much as thinks one thought, or has any exercise at all, but that there is some corresponding motion or alteration of motion, in some degree, of the fluids, in some part of the body. But universal experience shows, that

> the exercise of the affections, have in a special manner a tendency, to some sensible effect upon the body, we may then well suppose, the greater those affections be, and the more vigorous their exercise (other circumstances being equal) the greater will be the effect on the body. Hence it is not to be wondered at, that very great and strong exercises of the affections, should have great effects on the body.[129]

A similar passage appears almost at the outset of *Religious Affections*.[130] But the version above has a couple of notable specifications that are less prominent in the earlier passage.

First, the claim that affections have a necessary effect on the body is not a backtracking from the earlier claim that the affections are of the mind and the emotions are of the body. Instead, it is Edwards's way of taking the unity of body and soul seriously in a manner that is consistent with lived experience. Note his insistence "But universal experience shows . . ." It is also to take the unity of body and soul seriously in line with scripture: "The Psalmist," for instance, "speaking of vehement religious affections he had, speaks of an effect in his flesh or body, besides what was in his soul, expressly distinguishing one from the other, one and again, Ps. 84:2: 'My soul longeth, yea even fainteth for the courts of the Lord, my heart and my flesh crieth out for the living God.'"[131] Second, Edwards is clear that there are different states or degrees of affections, and corresponding to those various degrees, in keeping with the unity of body and soul, different degrees of bodily effects follow: the greater the affections, the greater the bodily, emotive commotion. For Edwards, this gradation of bodily effects reflects the nature of genuine religious affections versus other kinds of affections: their glory, he argues, is such that it is only appropriate that it would "overbear the body." Genuine religious affections would not be genuinely of God's glory if they did not overwhelm the body by its "sense of the majesty of God."[132] Such glory and majesty by definition ought to overwhelm accordingly; we should expect the body to be vulnerable in that way, to be "exceeding[ly] weak" compared to such glory and majesty.[133]

It is within this context—of varying degrees of affections leading to varying degrees of bodily effects—that Edwards's one passing paragraph on the passions makes sense. There he explains that "*affections* and *passions* are frequently spoken of as the same; and yet, in the more common use of speech, there is in some respect a difference."[134] Affections, he claims, refers to "all vigorous lively actings of the will or inclination." Passions refers to "those that are more sudden," but to what does "those" refer? Passions are those "lively actings of the will or inclination" that "are more sudden, and whose effects on the animal spirits are more violent, and the mind more overpowered, and less in its own command."[135] Inasmuch as Edwards suggests that passions are also a kind of vigorous exercise of the will and inclination, albeit exercises that are less in control by the mind, the passions are a kind of deformed, deficient affections that subject the body to great, heightened effects.[136] Thus, passions in an Edwardsean key are not to be taken as Thomistic passions (or what we have been taking as emotions). What Edwards appears to be pointing to with respect to the passions is a situation in which one's will and inclination is of the sort that one is led to emotional hysteria and, correspondingly, wild bodily movement.[137]

The Unreliability of the Emotions

That the passions have this kind of frenzied bodily emotional effect is in keeping with Edwards's claim that due to the soul-body unity, varying degrees of affections will necessarily move or alter the body in kind. But it would be a mistake to think that such wild bodily effects are consequences of only malformed and irreligious affections (the passions, for instance). Consider the observation that Edwards puts forward on the religious versus nonreligious affections. For Edwards, one's emotional state—the constitution of one's bodily existence—can be a consequence of genuine religious affections (the result of the indwelling of the Holy Spirit in the soul) as well as false religious affections and secular affections. As he observes,

> Great effects on the body . . . oftentimes arise from great affections about temporal things, and when religion is no way concerned in them. And if great affections about secular things that are purely natural, may have these effects, I know not by what rule we should determine, that high affections about religious things, which arise in like manner from nature, can't have the like effect. . . . No such rule can be drawn from reason: I know of no reason, why a being affected with a view of God's glory should not cause the body to faint, as well as a being affected with a view of Solomon's glory.[138]

If "great effects on the body" can arise from either religious or nonreligious affections, then the emotions (or the emotional state of the body) "are no sure evidences that affections are spiritual."[139] This is why Edwards, in part, held deep reservations over the kind of religious enthusiasm that accompanied the many evangelical revivals that swept through early eighteenth-century New England, especially those encouraged by the itinerant preaching of George Whitefield, among others.[140] It is not that Edwards disapproved of revivalism per se and the kind of enthusiasm that it generated. In fact, he departed from fierce critics of New England revivalism such as Charles Chauncy, copastor of Boston's First Church,[141] a departure that was made clear from Edwards's September 10, 1741, commencement address at Yale.[142] Edwards's concern was not that revivalism resulted in religious (bodily) enthusiasm; his primary concern was that the veracity of revivalism could not be judged "on the basis of its epiphenomenon."[143] For Edwards, emotions were "merely extrinsic manifestations" of a person's particular affective state and thus could not be determinative of whether a person's affective state was "the work of the Spirit of God or no."[144] Whether such enthusiasm is a genuine mark of holy conversion and, correlatively, the exercise of true religious affections in the soul or mind is questionable if such enthusiasm can arise from all kinds of affections or perceptual understandings of self and world, not just genuinely religious ones.[145] Furthermore, even those under the influence of genuine religious affections could not be expected to display or express the same kind and intensity of emotions among them, making the emotions even more problematic as a mark of holy conversion. This is why Edwards referred to the emotional experiences of those attending revivals as "not signs."[146] And accordingly, he later warned in a 1743 letter to Thomas Prince, pastor of Old South Church in Boston, regarding the revivals in Northampton, Massachusetts:

> The degree of grace is by no means to be judged of by the degree of joy, or the degree of zeal; and that indeed we can't at all determine by these things, who are gracious and who are not. . . . Some that have had very great raptures of joy, and have been extraordinarily filled (as the vulgar phrase is) and have had their bodies overcome, and that very often, have manifested far less of the temper of Christians, in their conduct since, than some others that have been still, and have made no great outward show. But then again there are many others, that have had extraordinary joys and emotions of mind, with frequent great effects on their bodies, that behave themselves steadfastly as humble, amiable, eminent Christians.[147]

A diversity of emotions is to be expected even among the regenerate, especially since the emotions of some, even if under the influence of the indwelling Spirit of God, could very well be functioning, Edwards puts it, as "*causa sine qua non*, or an occasional cause."[148] This is his way of saying that the emotions of even regenerate persons might be a function of "such things as corruption, errors of judgment, misguided love for God, false zeal, etc."[149] So, it is not that grace—and thus genuine religious affections—is absent in such persons, but we would not know that by simply looking at the emotions they are displaying because their emotional, bodily expressions may be a function of our propensity for error and misinterpretation:

> The truly gracious influences of the spirit of God, yea, and an high degree of love to God, is consistent with these two things, viz. a considerable degree of remaining corruption, and also many errors in judgment in matters of religion, and in matters of practice. And this is all that need to be allowed, in order to its being most demonstratively evident, that a high degree of love to God may accidentally move a person to that which is very wrong, and contrary to the mind and will of God. For a high degree of love to God will strongly move a person to do that which he believes to be agreeable to God's will; and therefore, if he be mistaken, and be persuaded that that is agreeable to the will of God, which indeed is very contrary to it, then his love will accidently, but strongly, incline him to that which is indeed very contrary to the will of God.[150]

In sum, while Edwards is willing to cede that the emotions of a regenerate person may essentially be due to God's gracious action and thus genuine religious affections influencing them, there is no surety to this fact just by looking at the regenerate person's emotions since the fervor or enthusiasm may also be due to the person's particular circumstances. In one sense, this can be seen as a result of the "weakness of human nature," or "a disposition to run into extremes and get into confusion," which he says "has always appeared in times of great revival of religion," including the Reformation and not just the revivals of his day. (In this regard, it is interesting to note how he also thinks the devil can cause such errors by causing emotional states that raise the affections that look religious: "Hence, through ignorance, the person being surprised, begins to think, surely this is the Holy Ghost coming into him. And then the mind begins to be affected and raised: there is first great joy; and then many other affections, in a very tumultuous manner, putting all nature, both body and mind, into a mighty ruffle." The emotions can raise some kind of affections, but only if they themselves are moved by some other cause, the devil certainly being one of them.)[151] But falling into error in another sense can also be taken as reflecting the morphology of conversion, Edwards suggests. Especially for those who are "in the beginning of something very extraordinary" by virtue of the work of divine grace, "a great deal of noise and tumult, confusion and uproar, and darkness mixed with light, and evil with good, is always to be expected," Edwards notes.[152] Whatever the case, the emotional fervor of a regenerate person may be different from another regenerate person for reasons other than whether one is under the influence of the Spirit more so than the other. This, then, is another indication that "the nature of the cause [i.e., religious affections via grace] is not to be judged of by the nature of the effect [emotions]."[153] If one's emotional state is not a sure indication of one's conversion, then the real signs of whether one is under the influence of the Spirit must be found elsewhere.

The Noncognitive and Relative Nature of the Emotions

While the affections may, to use a Thomistic description, "resemble" the emotions, they do so for Edwards because the emotions (qua movements of the body) are always "affected" by one's particular dispositions, inclinations, or commitments. The picture of the emotions I am trying to convey here is one in which the emotions are "activated" by some kind of affections. More specifically, the emotions are reflexive features of human experience and not functionally appetitive in the way Aquinas conceives of the emotions. Although the emotions are not the same as the affections, emotions "always accompany them"; they are "only effects or concommitants of the affections," as Edwards repeatedly insists.[154] Perhaps another way of putting the point is that for Edwards, the emotions are when the affections are, that is, when we are willing and inclined in a particular direction based on what we perceive or apprehend. Recall the following passage from Edwards: "So subject is the body to the mind, and so much do its fluids, especially the animal spirits, attend the motions and exercises of the mind, that there can't be so much as an intense thought, without an effect upon them."[155] Does this not convey a sense of the body's basic submissiveness (and, correlatively, its emotive movements) to the seat of the affections, to the activity and direction of the will and inclination or, ultimately, the mind? That would certainly be in line with his biblical appeals to the body's (necessary and expected) vulnerabilities to God's glory and majesty, as we saw earlier.[156] It also is in line with our nature as human beings, wherein "everything we do . . . is an exercise of the will and inclination," or the mind.[157] For Edwards, the primacy of the mind means that our bodies are, again as noted above, "subject to" or "attend" to its exercises.[158]

The emotions are necessary effects of the affections and thus of what we apprehend. That is the corollary to Edwards's insistence that our apprehensions or perceptions of self and world—if they are of the kind that incline us toward particular likes or dislikes, preferences, or values—necessarily move the body and therefore are necessarily accompanied by emotions, sometimes intensely, sometimes less so. We can understand, then, why Gustafson is able to readily identify affections as emotions. While we are disposed to react or respond to situations based on particular commitments, judgments of value, and so on, those responses are hardly emotionless. As Gustafson notes, "we assume something like this when we say about an event, 'That's going to make him very angry.'"[159] Such a statement assumes continuity between our judgments and emotions, which is captured in the term "affection." But Gustafson ends up conflating affections and emotions in a way that obscures the fine points of Edwards's understanding of affections and emotions. As simply concomitant effects or consequences of or arising from (necessarily, due to our soul-body nature) some kind of affections, emotions in themselves lack moral content.

It would not be wholly inappropriate, then, to think of the emotions in themselves as nonrational in a sense. At the same time, it would not be wholly inappropriate to claim them as having a cognitive dimension. But cognitive in what sense? That is a tricky question, requiring a good deal of nuance and precision. While emotions are concomitant with our affective knowing, it would not be entirely accurate to say that they are forms of thoughts about the fragility of one's attachments and relationships, as Martha Nussbaum would think of them.[160] While an extended discussion of the convergences and divergences between Edwards and Nussbaum is not possible here, suffice it to say for our purposes that unlike Nussbaum, Edwards suggests that emotions are cognitive only in the secondary or subordinate sense. They can appear to be object-oriented; one's emotions can appear to be in response to some experience of a thing, person, or event and thus seem as if expressing or manifesting judgments about them in one sense or another. But the emotive reaction arises from (is an effect of) the object-oriented nature of the soul's affective knowing or perception of reality. As such, emotions lack a cognitive structure; they simply are felt, embodied experiences that are caused by and accompany one's affectivity.

We might say then that emotions are relative rather than, as James E. Gilman contends, "bearing truths that are universally accessible, comprehensible, and normative."[161] That emotions are relative is perhaps an unsettling claim, especially from a Thomistic perspective, but it conforms to the kind of affective and emotive distinctions that emerge when reading Edwards with Thomas in mind. For Edwards, inasmuch as movements of the body are not reliable indicators of one's affective dispositions, there is nothing particularly informative in a normative way about a person's emotional state. Again, for

Edwards, one can be equally emotional from affections that are either religiously or nonreligiously constituted (and there can be different emotional states arising from affections of the same kind). One's emotional state is therefore not indicative of whether one is in fact under the influence of the spiritual sense imparted by the indwelling Spirit or under the influence of some other sort of affective understanding of self and world. The Edwardsean point is simply that while emotions are an intrinsic part of human agency and experience, the composition of one's emotional state is not normatively particular to certain kinds of cognitions and valuational dispositions. That point draws Edwards somewhat closer to a contextual account of the emotions advanced by the psychologist Lisa Feldman Barrett.[162] It also draws Edwards further away from Nussbaum's cognitive construal of the emotions, though Edwards would likely agree with Nussbaum that his approach does not necessarily mean that emotions are ultimately evil and require suppression, as the Stoics argued in their normative philosophy.[163]

That emotions are relative or contextual, that is, not indicative of specific dispositional attitudes, helps to explain why persons may be similarly angry while expressing such emotion in different directions, toward different objects of concern. For instance, take two young adults, both emotionally, visibly angry, but one is angered over anti-Black violence,[164] while the other is unmoved by such violations or, alternatively, is deeply angered by those protesting against such racism and their demands.[165] Through a Thomistic lens, we could venture to say that their anger is more common than it might initially appear: both are angry because of some common perceived injustice, and both "[desire] evil" toward the unjust.[166] But what they think is unjust is not the same, and their anger per se would not necessarily reveal why each young adult is angered by particular divergent conceptions of injustice (the injustice of racism versus the injustice of the perceived marginalization of white persons). From an Edwardsean perspective, we should not be surprised that both are equally angry even if the reasons for their anger are wildly divergent. Our perceptions of things (of self and world) are always felt (this is human nature), but there is no normative way of feeling about a particular judgment or perception. The emotive markers of our embodied existence (such as anger, sadness, fear, or delight) are common to all persons so long as we have bodies. But those emotive markers will take on different meanings as a consequence of one's affectivity, which is expressive of one's fundamental moral orientations. Our emotions may indeed signal (to others) our perceptions of things, but there is no emotion that corresponds to a particular perception. On this view, "righteous anger is not opposite of love" is true if anger in itself is to be seen as undermining righteousness.[167] Such a way of thinking about anger, however, would presume misleadingly that anger reflects a particular and definite moral orientation. But it does not. So, for instance, James Baldwin's claim that "to be a Negro in this country and to be relatively conscious is to be in rage almost all the time" should hardly surprise.[168] If anything, we should be surprised if those afflicted by racial injustice are not angry. To be angry is to be human, and from an Edwardsean perspective, we should fully expect the righteous to respond in anger as much as the unrighteous might do so. In short, there is no anger and, more generally, no emotion that is normatively righteous or unrighteous.[169]

Beyond Aesthetic Emotions and the Ambivalent "Power" of Art

Reading Edwards with Aquinas's account of the affections and emotions in mind allows for a differentiation between the affections and emotions in Edwards's thought that would otherwise remain opaque. The key to that differentiation is discerning the body as the locus for the emotions and the will for the affections. But while Aquinas will allow for some degree of independence between the emotions and will (thus allowing the emotions to serve as an additional source for moral deliberation), Edwards restricts their independence. This restriction does not mean that affections and emotions are, in the end, functionally the same; the delineation between the two is maintained. But what matters to Edwards is that we notice which of the two, affections or emotions or, more precisely, will or the body, is functionally dominant. For Edwards, emotions are bodily feelings that well up in response to affections of some kind. And because emotions function in this way, whether one's emotional state gives access to the content of one's affectivity is questionable, since persons with diverse moral dispositions (affections) can be similarly emotional (or persons of similar moral dispositions can be emotionally different). Such a view of the emotions problematizes the prospects of construing the emotions as cognitive experiences at least in some normatively revealing way and calls specific attention to the unreliability of human emotional life. It is this unreliability that complicates the reliance on and elevation of the emotions especially in modernist art discourse.

Before elaborating on this implication, it is worth emphasizing that their unreliability does not mean that the emotions are irrelevant. Edwards is profoundly attuned to the emotional dimensions of human life, that is, to the reality of our embodiment; so long as we have bodies, our thoughts, inclinations, and preferences will have an incarnate form. But he is equally attuned to the pitfalls of overemphasizing our embodiment, that is, to the tendency of claiming a significance to the emotions (to what they reveal or signal to ourselves and to others about our inner lives or thoughts or a particular state of affairs) that they do not in fact have. His skepticism is distilled in his repeated claims that the emotions are untrustworthy indicators of our moral orientations and as such the kind of worry he has over whether or not our emotions are, for instance, consequences of manipulation or exploitation. How would we know if one were subject to nefarious (or ungodly) influences? Could our emotional life lend that kind of insight? Edwards would be suspicious that our emotions could disclose to us such information given the inherently "democratic" nature of emotions: if persons of diverse dispositions can feel the same kind of emotions, then the usefulness of the emotions for moral and spiritual discernment comes into doubt. That was in part the kind of lesson Edwards drew from his experiences with revivalism in eighteenth-century New England. A person under the influence of a theatrical evangelist could be just as emotionally enthused about religion as one under the influence of a more conventional pastor, and not just pastors but also, as alluded to earlier, the devil itself:

> And there are some instances of persons, in whom it seems manifest that the first ground of their affection is some bodily sensation. The animal spirits, by some cause (and probably sometimes by the devil), are suddenly and unaccountably put into a very agreeable motion, causing persons to feel pleasantly in their bodies; the animal spirits are put into such a motion as is wont to be connected with the exhilaration of the mind; and the soul, by the laws of the union of soul and body, hence feels pleasure.[170]

On the question of the emotion's reliability, we can ask an analogous question with respect to art as modernism conceives of it. How would we know if one's emotive responses to an artwork are the consequence of the artwork itself, particularly its aesthetic forms, and thus revelatory of genuine art? In other words, how would we know if one is experiencing aesthetic emotions? A person under the influence of a particular artwork—a painting by, say, Matisse at the Centre Pompidou in Paris, such as his *Woman Reading* (1894)[171]—could be just as emotionally inspired as one under the influence of nonart, for instance, eating a croissant at a Parisian boulangerie. What makes the former an experience of aesthetic emotion and the latter something else if the emotive responses are similar despite the different objects to which each refers, unless we want to claim that both Matisse paintings and French pastries are artworks? But that would mean being open to the possibility that everything and anything can take on the status of art, since what would matter is the kind of feeling that something generated (since that is what defines art as art as pertaining to the realm of the emotions) rather than what the object actually is. But would that not vitiate the idea of art altogether?

The difficulty of this question to some extent is ignored in the general turn to literature and beauty in theological ethics. As noted in chapters 1 and 2, the special interest in the arts in recent theological-ethical discourse relies in part on the way the arts appeal to our emotions and thus broaden moral reasoning and understanding beyond Kantian rationality. What we know and how we know are more than a function of reason strictly understood and is more holistic and embodied and thus inclusive of the emotions; knowing (and ultimately doing), in other words, is also about feeling. In this sense, it is ironic that contemporary theological-ethical turns to literature and especially concepts of beauty are not unrelated to modernism in its focus on the emotions with respect to art's nature and functionality; this is ironic, because modernism's focus on aesthetic emotions is intended to protect the arts from nonaesthetic spheres, such as moral and social spheres, while theological-ethical appeals to the emotions by way of literature and beauty are meant to elevate the role the arts can play in informing, enlivening, and sustaining communities and the kind of moral thinking that is requisite for such support. But this linkage between the arts and the emotions does not necessarily demonstrate why it is the arts per se that can engender the kind of emotions that they are purported to be capable of engendering. Is there something unique to art—reading, looking, listening, even creating—that allows it to generate the kinds of feelings that are hoped for, even expected? What makes art's capacity to engender such emotions distinctive from the capacity of other objects, events, or experiences to engender such emotions (such as playing, eating, conversing, maybe even working)? This is one basic question that the theological-ethical turns to literature and beauty do not consider in any sustained manner.

The difficulty of this question, however, as we saw earlier, does not escape the attention of a modernist thinker such as Bell when he stipulates that knowing something about the artist's intentions for the artwork—which requires some level of training to be able to discern accordingly—is essential if we hope to have the artwork engender the right kinds of feelings (i.e., aesthetic emotions) and, correlatively, if we hope to know if whatever one is feeling is because of or in relation to one's attempt to discern the art object as art, especially the intentions of the artist. But if one's orientation or disposition to artwork (or how one approaches artwork) is the basis by which one is able to determine if one's feelings are associated with an art object, that would cast doubt on whether there is indeed a discernable phenomenon of feeling for something in a manner that is intrinsically aesthetic; alternatively, that would cast doubt on whether artwork itself is capable of eliciting emotions that are appropriate to itself. Emotions are what they are, or we feel the emotions that we do, in large part by the intentionality and perceptions we bring to them. But even then, as Edwards emphasizes with respect to the emotionalism of revivalism, there is no specific emotion that corresponds to or expresses a particular disposition, intentionality, or perception we might have. Just as there is no emotion (such as anger) that is necessarily linked to moral righteousness or unrighteousness, as discussed above, in what way, then, can we speak of an emotion that is necessarily aesthetic and another that is nonaesthetic?

This is not to say that artworks are powerless and incapable of moving persons in a particular way. Consider Edwards's insistence on the need for good preaching. While he never mentions preaching as an art form, it is clear that he believed in the importance of preaching that reflected strong aesthetic qualities if preaching is to do the kind of work it is intended to do. In responding to critics of revivalism, Edwards defended the position that "an exceeding affectionate way of preaching about the great things of religion, has in itself no tendency to beget false apprehensions of them, than a moderate, dull, indifferent way of speaking of 'em."[172] This, he says, is in keeping with the nature of how persons apprehend the truth. As he proposes in "Some Thoughts Concerning the Revival,"

> I know it has long been fashionable to despise a very earnest and pathetical way of preaching; and they, and they only have been valued as preachers, that have shown the greatest extent of learning, and strength of reason, and correctness of method and language: but I humbly conceive it has been for want of understanding, or duly considering human nature, that such preaching has been thought to have the greatest tendency to answer the ends of preaching. . . . [A]n increase in speculative knowledge in divinity is not what is so much needed by our people, as something else. Men may abound in this sort of light and have no heat: how much has there been of this sort of knowledge, in the Christian world, in this age? . . . Our people don't so much need to have their heads stored, as to have their hearts touched; and they stand in the greatest need of that sort of preaching that has the greatest tendency to do this.[173]

Here Edwards once again underscores the idea that true knowledge is constitutive of something beyond reason. In other words, only when our affections (our will) are engaged does our understanding move beyond notional knowledge of things. (So, to long for something lovingly is to know or perceive it in a manner that is quite different from simply knowing it in a way that does not incline you to it affectionately.)

But as is typically the case for Edwards, appeals to human nature are always confirmed if not founded in appeals to scripture, and his primary support for his claim to the importance of affectionate preaching is biblically based. For instance, invoking Isaiah 27, 40, 42, 52, and 58, Edwards proposes that "it seems to be foretold [in the Old Testament] that the Gospel should be especially preached in a loud and earnest manner." Then, he claims, "And 'tis worthy to be noted that the word commonly used in the New Testament, that we translate 'preach,' properly signifies to proclaim aloud like a crier."[174] On these and many other scriptural references, Edwards asserts that preaching in a highly affectionate manner "does in fact more truly represent" the truth of religion "than a more cold and indifferent way of speaking of them." Accordingly, preaching "with very great affection . . . has most of a tendency to beget true ideas of it in the minds of those to whom the representation is made."[175]

To "beget" true ideas of God suggests that affectionate preaching is far from ineffectual. It can, Edwards states, raise the affections of their hearers.[176] But it is interesting to note that the nature of this begetting is more nuanced than it first sounds. That affectionate preaching is indeed capable of arousing religious affections is one implication of Edwards's claim. But the more plausible implication is that affectionate preaching furthers rather than causes the divine work already under way. Consider more specifically when Edwards rejects those who claim that preaching ought to comfort rather than terrify. That claim falsely assumes that the work of God is more about comfort. Whatever we might think of the veracity of his theological belief that ascent to the Gospel requires a sense of terror of one's reprobate state, the larger point to notice is the role that lively, dramatic preaching ought to play in that ascent or, as Edwards puts it, in the awakening of conscience.[177] Inasmuch as a central tenet of God's truth is that we are sinners, it is wholly appropriate, according to Edwards, for the minister to preach in a manner that terrifies. But note here that such dramatic, affectionate preaching is characterized as letting "more light" into the conscience rather than letting light in. This is not an inconsequential distinction. More light is appropriate, since it is not the minister's preaching that is "enabling them to see their case to be, in some measure, as it is" but instead due to the "sinners' consciences [being] greatly awakened by the Spirit of God," which would be in keeping with God's absolute sovereignty.[178] As persons are being spiritually awakened, it is critical to increase their terror over their sinfulness, "for those that are most awakened have great remaining stupidity; they have a sense of but little of that which is; and 'tis from remaining blindness and darkness that they see no more; and that remaining blindness is a disease that we ought to endeavor to remove."[179] And it is only when we are increasing their sense of sinfulness—rather than thinking that our preaching is beginning to shine light in the consciences of persons as opposed to "Christ . . . beginning to open the eyes of conscience"—that ministers can be regarded as acting "as co-workers" with Christ's saving work. So, in this respect we might say that Edwards anticipates that affectionate preaching will do the kind of work that he says it will by virtue of an anticipation that God will work in them if not already so. And it is because persons will be disposed to hearing preaching that seeks the truth of God that affectionate preaching will raise their affections high, or higher; it will deepen their sense of the truth of the Gospel.[180] Without that prior orientation, preaching will have little effect.

Because of that prior orientation, persons can begin to notice what they ought to notice, that they are, as Edwards puts it, miserable and even more so than they may think on account of their original sin. For those disposed to the "real conviction" of the truth of the word of God, preaching that amplifies the terror of their sinfulness will be effective. Only in the case of melancholy should ministers soften their preaching, for as Edwards diagnosed, seeking the truth to melancholic persons will more likely lead to being "deceived, and led into error by it, through that strange *disposition there is in them* to take things wrong."[181] It is because of this disposition to falsehood that the preaching of truth will be less effectual, "unless the truth be spoken with abundance of caution and prudence, and consideration of their disposition and circumstances."[182]

Edwards's turn to affectionate preaching is not necessarily some formal and complete statement of art theory, and yet, it is clear that Edwards was concerned for the aesthetic quality of sermons. This concern alerts us to the limits and possibilities of art or, more broadly, the aesthetical. While scripture referred to loud and earnest proclamation of the word of God, this did not mean that ministers should simply shout or preach loudly, but for Edwards, scripture calls ministers to preach with the quality of aesthetic form in mind: a dull sermon is less likely to appeal to the hearts of persons than one that is more dramatic. However, it is not theatrics per se that appeal to congregants' hearts, for their effectiveness depends on congregants' "disposition and circumstances," as he underscores with respect to preaching to the melancholic. It is noteworthy that Edwards is particularly sensitive to the disposition that certain persons have and what that means for their receptivity to preaching.

He signals that what we notice in scripture and what is particularly felt (or not felt) is delimited by the particular temperament and outlook we bring to scripture.[183] So, the artistry or aesthetics of preaching is important, but not in itself. By the same token, perhaps we can say that the form of an artwork matters, but we will also need to ask what we can expect from persons who encounter artworks—however bold, beautiful, or thrilling they might be—except for what its viewers (or listeners or readers) are formed (i.e., willing or disposed) to see and feel. There is only so much a shape or color or sound can impart at first look or listen, and if you want them to do more than that, to communicate and effectuate something more particular, you may need to know something beyond what they alone—that is, beyond what just looking at or listening to them—can provide. As Edwards observes, "As for instance; when a person is affected with a lively idea, suddenly excited in his mind, of some shape, or very beautiful pleasant form of countenance, or some shining light, or other glorious outward appearance: here is something apprehended or conceived by the mind; but there is nothing of the nature of [divine] instruction in it: persons become never the wiser by such things."[184]

This is not to cast doubt on the possibility of persons coming to an artwork with one set of "eyes" or "ears" (or a particular disposition) and then having them replaced with different "eyes" or "ears" and to be moved by it in a way they were not moved originally. But it is to cast doubt on whether art itself—especially whether its way of expressing form such as line and color or its play on aesthetic technique, as modernists insist—can be the catalyst for such change, or transformation of vision. (We can ask similarly to non-modernists who might feel that what is depicted and how well it is depicted in art matters more.) If art is not powerless, then that is so because art, like affectionate preaching, deepens (or reinforces) rather than engenders one's vision. It may in some instances unsettle, especially upon first exposure. We might as a consequence gain a different perspective or new understanding "from strong ideas of shapes and colors, and outward brightness and glory, or sounds and voices,"[185] but there is only so much a shape or color or sound can impart at first look or listen, and if you want them to do more than that, then you will need to know something beyond what they alone can provide. Thus, whether the experience of being unsettled alone is powerful enough for such change may be expecting too much, not in the sense that change is impossible but instead that some may indeed be changed and others not at all. In other words, what we can expect is that such unsettling will be more consequential to some and inconsequential to others, which raises the question of how to account for such a pluralism of effects. To approach this question with Edwardsean eyes is to consider the inevitability of such pluralism to the extent that the perceptions we bring to art, like, again, affectionate preaching, will matter as much if not more than the quality of the art itself. In this case, knowledge is not necessarily power. Knowing more of what the artwork is about or knowing more than we might have known initially—the artist's intentions and influences, the artwork's history, what kind of aesthetic tradition it belongs to, why it focuses on the themes or subjects it does—does not necessarily inspire one to act in a particular way or value certain ideas and beliefs. More likely, such knowledge will engender disagreement of interpretation, disagreement over which features of the artwork are relevant or worth noticing or not as well as disagreement about how one should respond to the artwork or what kind of responses are appropriate and inappropriate. Additionally, some may not care to know such things about the artwork or think that they are irrelevant (as modernists broadly do). As such, the enterprise of knowing more about an artwork may in fact motivate multiple responses or courses of action rather than consensus and unanimity. To repurpose a line from Edwards, "the experience of the present and past ages abundantly confirms the same."[186] If knowledge alone does not engender the kind of conviction that is needed to motivate a particular course of action, then what are we missing? From an Edwardsean standpoint, receptivity and action are functions of one's disposition. Therefore, differences in disposition, to how and what we are inclined to, necessarily leads to differences in outcome, or reactions to circumstances, events, experiences. This complicates the kind of hope that is often placed on art to effectuate moral transformation and action.

THE PRIORITY OF ETHICS OVER AESTHETICS? WHO WE ARE IS WHAT WE SEE

Edwards's account of the affections is a statement of the nature of human knowing and ultimately agency: human agency is not simply a function of knowing what to do. For Edwards, human agency is constitutive of being inclined in a particular way. In other words, human agency requires affective knowledge, and it is this kind of knowledge (one's disposition) that constitutes "the springs that set men agoing, in all the affairs of life."[187] Allen Guelzo puts it this way: For Edwards, "The connection between perception and volition is in fact so close" that thinking and ultimately doing are functions of "a ceaseless interaction between preferences and perceptions." As Edwards writes, "the will always is as the greatest apparent good," but good in the sense of what is most agreeable to us, to what we desire.[188] Given the importance that Edwards places on inclination or disposition, or affections, in human agency, it makes sense that Edwards would think that the effectiveness of good preaching would depend on the affective state of its hearers rather than the affective state of its hearers depending on the effectiveness of good preaching. More broadly, it makes sense to expect how we respond to events, circumstances, and our wider environment will be shaped and colored by our tendencies or dispositions. This helps to explain why we should expect persons to have diverse responses to a single object or similar experience even if information about the object of their attention is the same: it is people's particular dispositions that are determinative of how they respond to and make their way through the world.

The language of expectation is important here inasmuch as the primacy of disposition calls attention to "a measure of predictability in human behavior."[189] In short, one's disposition matters with respect to one's receptivity to what one sees, hears, or experiences of the world and its influence on one's beliefs and choices moving forward. We should expect a correspondence between one's disposition and how one responds to what one encounters. "We do not live randomly, and the more intense our inclination toward a sort of behavior, the more likely we will act on it,"[190] hence, as Edwards asserts, the predictability or expectation of the "covetous man" in "his [greedy] pursuits" "of worldly profits" or the "voluptuous" size of a person "in his pursuit of pleasure and sensual delights."[191]

Perhaps another way of making the point is that one's lived experiences matter to how we see the world and what we think is valuable or not. Surely our experiences are also shaped by the world around us, but the impactfulness of the objects or events we encounter on our agency cannot be explained apart from the disposition that we bring to these encounters. As Edwards would say, it is one thing to know something of what is before us but quite another to have it move us in a transformative way. We may be saddened or distressed by learning something new or we may be angered, but whether that will engender particular moral behaviors or courses of action will depend on more than the kind of emotive responses we have. For some, such emotive responses may amount to inaction, for others moral resolve and activism, and for still others morally dubious choices. There is neither normative moral content to such emotive responses nor normative moral consequences for them. How one's emotive responses matter and impact our moral agency depends instead on the dispositional state, or affectivity in Edwardsean parlance, of the person. This is exactly what modernism aims to bracket: to sever our experiential circumstances from our acts of looking, reading, and listening as well as creating. To a large extent, that legacy is prominent in the way the wider public thinks about and treats art as that which is tangential to lived experience or to the broader concerns, issues, and questions that frame human life.

If it is our disposition that matters primarily to our agency, how we look or read, what we look at or read, what we notice or not when we look or read, and whether we want to read or look are tied inextricably to our basic orientations in life. For Edwards, the disposition that ultimately matters is one rooted in love of God or, to be more philosophical rather than theological about it, benevolence to being in general.[192] And whether one is in possession of such love or affection, or disposition, is discernable through the twelve signs of true Christian life he maps out in remarkable detail in his *Religious Affections*. These "signposts indicating the direction of the soul, whether it is toward God or away from God," include acts of selflessness, which does not exclude self-love if it is bounded by love of God (second sign) and conformity to the beatitudes (ninth sign).[193]

For Edwards, the insistence that one's affections always be "put to the test" followed from what he believed those of Arminian persuasion would find as an overexaggeration or misinterpretation: that redemption is God's work alone.[194] But for Edwards such a soteriological claim could only be the case, for if the world is created by God in order to glorify Godself, as Edwards maintained, then it is also God who is the principal in creation's actualization of that end.[195] But even if one were to recoil from Edwards's soteriological tenet (and what he sees as the fittingness of God's self-glorification via creation), Edwards's theological vision underscores a conception of the self that deserves attention especially with respect to thinking about art and ethics. In sum, we are our affections. The affections of some may be more lively than others, but the picture that Edwards paints is a world in which we make the kinds of choices and judgments that we do because of our inclinations and disinclinations. In other words, it is the habits of the heart that reveal the kind of person we are and why we make the kind of moral choices and judgments that we do. This vision of what we can call the "dispositional self" reflects how Edwards envisions God's own dispositional or affective nature.[196] When we are disposed to love of God and thus love of neighbor, Edwards claims, we are then in conformity to God's own disposition to communicate Godself (God's own goodness and glory) to creation.[197]

The vision of the dispositional self brings us back to Kennicott's realization that we encountered at the start of this chapter: if we ever thought certain kinds of images, mediums, or artworks could call us to action, to a just cause, then that was merely a conjecture if not a claim based on selective past experiences of such moral action. And if the latter, those instances of inspired moral action probably say more about the persons who bothered to look, read, or listen than about the moral potency of the act of looking, reading, or listening itself. Otherwise, we should be able to rely steadily on certain kinds or genres of artworks (again, Kennicott's interest is in genres that focus on capturing moments of human tragedy) to engender and sustain transformative social movements, but if history is any indication, we cannot; at least in the United States, we seem to be more divided and polarized as a society and more dubious about the merits of attending to others beyond our own borders at least since World War II, or so he observes.[198] Kennicott is hardly alone in making this claim. But to the extent that others notice the same but have a hard time accepting it, resorting to the mere hope that "novels and poems and songs and plays and paintings" and "iconic photographs" can be impactful, at least, "unconsciously," only reaffirms the difficult reality that art is hardly sufficient to inspire and actuate moral transformation and action.[199] We would certainly like to think—want to think—"there is a chance for change." But at what point does that hope amount to a kind of sentimentalism? We might respond that our moral vision and social realities can change so long as "what doesn't change is the authority of a human heart open to the pain of others." But for Kennicott, it is exactly our openness to others, to their plight, that changes. How else to explain the persistence of moral inaction? We might retort further, "Perhaps there are just too many photos [of human suffering] now[,] . . . too many . . . to focus for long on any one tragedy. Perhaps our distrust of technology, our suspicion that the images have been manipulated, or that we ourselves are being manipulated, makes it too easy to distrust our own response to them, too." But to be so cynical, skeptical, suspicious, or, at the very least, cautious and tentative and to invoke them as excuses for not being moved by what we see or read, even if their depictions are vivid, powerful, and unequivocal, would only seem to underscore lapses in moral character and draw attention to why such lapses are consequential more so than images or stories, however truthful they may be. It is this realization that prompts Kennicott to question whether we (by whom he means the American polity) are the kind of persons who are willing to be challenged by different perspectives, by the plight and suffering of those who are not like "us," and whether we have what it takes to be that kind of person.

That question is more of a lament for Kennicott, but it taps into an essential Edwardsean point. If our disposition matters above all else, that is, if who we are (i.e., our inclinations and desires, our likes and dislikes, what we love and do not love) is determinative of what we "see," then attending to who we are—who we really are—and the kind of person we ought to be should be paramount. This meant, for Edwards, engaging in at least three kinds of habits or practices aimed at putting our state of affections (or our moral character) to the test. The first habit or practice is critical self-examination as a means of unmasking the rationalizations behind our judgments.[200] "Without it the actual motivations of behavior [would] remain opaque. . . . [S]elf-knowledge, particularly of one's dominant dispositions, is a necessary part of wisdom that does not come without effort and attention."[201] The second habit or practice is "healing by contraries," a common practice in Christian spirituality that William C. Spohn traces to John Cassian of the fourth century.[202] For Edwards, healing by contraries took the form of practicing certain virtues to remedy vices. One virtue "can check or heal another because they are all inter-related, 'concatenated' or chained together. . . . [H]ope promotes love, faith evokes humility," and repentance tends to gratitude.[203] The third habit or practice involves justice, or the practice of "identifying with others,"[204] or, as Edwards implores, to "not seek your own things only, for you are not your own."[205]

With all these practices, it is not that Edwards thought that right moral perception is something we can achieve on our own; moral formation is ultimately God's own work. These practices are important nonetheless, since sin is still persistent even for those under the influence of the Spirit so long as we are human creatures, "hence the need for countervailing measures."[206] For those who feel, for instance, envy's movements will "'be alarmed at it, and will fight against it . . . and will cross the hateful disposition he feels in him and will go contrary to it in his outward practice.'"[207] Thus, moral formation, while its accomplishment is ultimately God's, is still work for us too, and it is challenging work, requiring constant practice.[208]

In sum, to know who we are and to become the person we ought to be is a formative task. We will need to be intentional and committed to examining ourselves and practicing those habits that counter our tendencies toward vice, especially selfishness. But this means tempering the kind of moral hopes we might want to place on art. Perhaps art, a picture, or an aesthetic (such as a particular form or style) can contribute to the hard work of moral formation, but it cannot do that hard work for us. A particular photo or a story can do moral work, that is, transform our judgments or choices, but only if we let it. But letting does not mean passivity on our part, or hoping and waiting for it to change us, but instead means to be alert to its potential moral meanings and call to action. This demands a moral sensitivity and posture that comes first; it must be there to begin with. Moral transformation requires moral formation, in other words, and it requires more than the work of aesthetic encounters; it requires moral encounters, encounters with actual others above all else.[209] Selfishness is only checked when we actually practice selflessness. The common good is only realized when members of a community actually "care for one another."[210]

NOTES

1. Gustafson, *Ethics from a Theocentric Perspective,* 1:2.
2. Gustafson, 1:117.
3. Gustafson thinks that when it comes to making or expressing a theological point, "images" and related forms are not only useful but also necessary, since "theology is an activity not only of the mind, but also of the heart, of the human spirit." In addition, "Poetry, metaphors, narratives, art, music, hymns, and biographies point to and express God's presence often more powerfully than theological arguments and creeds." Gustafson, "Participation: A Religious Worldview," 171, 172.
4. One's context matters when it comes to not only perceiving an artwork as religious or essentially aesthetic but also what kinds of artworks "enhance" one's construal of the world. For Gustafson, "the music that evokes, sustains, and expresses my Christian piety all is drawn from classic, even orthodox, Christian themes expressed in liturgical and other forms. Gospel music from earlier decades and 'praise music' of current usage are not in my repertory of Christian practices," due in part, he explains, to his ecclesial affiliation and upbringing (170n9).
5. Ellison, "A Very Stern Discipline," 742.
6. Ellison, "The Novel as a Function of American Democracy," 760.
7. Ellison, 761.
8. Ellison, 762.
9. Ellison, 767. This line was originally written as a question.
10. Ellison, 769.
11. Ellison's exhortation is not unlike Nicholas Wolterstorff's call for artists to create in a manner that, as John W. de Gruchy explains, is "more than simply self-expression" and is "akin to the role played by social prophets in ancient Israel." De Gruchy, "Art, Morality, and Justice," 427–28. Cf. Wolterstorff, *Art in Action,* 154. Art is liberatory when it provides "alternative images of reality" and not just images of an artist's idiosyncratic imagination. De Gruchy, "Art, Morality, and Justice," 427. So, not all art advances a liberatory cause, only a certain kind of art does so.
12. Ellison, "The Novel as a Function of American Democracy," 762.
13. Ellison, 761–64.
14. Conflict photography represents a genre of photographs capturing scenes of war and its consequences. See Havlin, "Photography and Modern Conflict." Such a form of photography is an iteration of disaster photography, a genre capturing or cataloging natural and human-made disasters and their effects on human populations and communities. See Garsd, "When Does Disaster Photography Cross the Line?" Arguably, one of the most wrenching and (in)famous examples of such photography is the Pulitzer Prize–winning photo taken by the South Vietnamese combat photographer Nick Ut officially titled "The Terror of War" but better known as "Napalm Girl," taken in 1972. While that photo is attributed to changing public perception about the Vietnam War, the photos of

Kennicott's concern have had no such influence. On "Napalm Girl" and its meanings and influences, see Nguyen, *The Gift of Freedom*, 83–132.

15. Kennicott, "We Used to Think Photos Like This Could Change the World."
16. Kennicott.
17. Others, especially within theological ethics, have attributed such apathy to the commodification of art, calling attention to the negative consequences of the prevalence of a consumerist mindset with respect to art. See, for instance, Cassidy, "Picturing Suffering." See also Flores, *The Aesthetics of Solidarity*, 136–41. This line of explanation, however, does not go as far as what I will suggest below is the overarching implication of Kennicott's explanation: if our responses (or lack of responses) to conflict art or disaster photography cannot be accounted for apart from our particular allegiances (including, as others argue, our consumerist desires), then art's moral potency does not reside in itself, and thus its moral efficaciousness is not intrinsic to the nature of art. Consequently, if we want art to do something (in this case advance justice), then allowing art to be art—that is, liberating it from economic, political, and cultural logics—will not necessarily get us there.
18. Kennicott, "We Used to Think Photos Like This Could Change the World."
19. Kennicott.
20. For a systematic study on Thomas's account of the emotions, see Cates, *Aquinas on the Emotions*. I will rely on Cates's account in part in my delineation of Thomas's definition of emotions and affections. For comprehensive accounts of Edwards's thinking on affections, see Smith, "Editor's Introduction"; and Martin, *Understanding Affections in the Theology of Jonathan Edwards*. I will note at least one difference of interpretation from Martin's account of Edwards's affections later in this chapter.
21. Dewey, "Art as Experience," 296.
22. See Kuklick, *Churchmen and Philosophers*; Crocco, "Edwards's Intellectual Legacy"; and Richardson, *A Natural History of Pragmatism*.
23. Dewey, "Art as Experience," 298.
24. Dewey, 296–97.
25. Dewey, 308. "By the same token, emotions are attached to events and objects in their movement. They are not, save in pathological instances, private" (308).
26. Lauter, "Re-Enfranchising Art," 23.
27. Lauter, 22.
28. "Take for example, those works once ascribed to 'masters' that lose their *aesthetic* value when they were reascribed to women. The *Portrait of Mlle. Charlotte du Val d'Ognes* is the classic example. When it was ascribed to David, critics praised its colors as subtle and singular and found its content (its 'merciless' view of 'an intelligent, homely woman') unforgettable. When it was reascribed to Constance Marie Charpentier (1767–1849), critics suddenly discovered weaknesses in its execution, attributable to the artist's use of literary rather than plastic values. Where before the painting had been unified by a single attitude, it became an 'ensemble made up from a thousand subtle attitudes' which all seemed to reveal the 'feminine spirit.'" Lauter writes further, "It is hard to look at quilts now in the wake of feminist research without asking how they came to be devalued by the dominant *formalist* aesthetic theory, since they (and their sisters, the woven coverlet or blanket) are often so obviously excellent in design, anticipating by half a century or more the principles of collage, of geometric abstraction, and even of art based on optical illusion. Nonetheless, quilts and their sisters in the larger category of needlework failed to qualify as art in the formalist theory because it was assumed that they were intended to be used

and so were not sufficiently separate from 'life.' They also failed to qualify because it was assumed that they did not express a unique point of view of a single creator." Lauter, "Re-Enfranchising Art," 23.

29. See Danto, "The Artworld." According to Estella Lauter, Danto observed that how the "artworld" may theorize about the nature of art underscores the extent to which those theories rather than the artworks themselves are critical to determining what art is or is counted as art. Lauter specifies Danto's general point in the following way: "Just as a bed by Rauschenberg is a work of art if seen through the artworld's filter, so work by women that seems identical in value to work by men may *not* be art (or good art) when the artworld's filters contain social biases about women along with precepts about art. In addition, to complicate the issue even further, items taken to signify feminine gender may not embody the condition or views of women at all, but instead may represent men's fantasies." Lauter, "Re-Enfranchising Art," 25.
30. Lauter, 25, is paraphrasing Danto.
31. Cronan, *Against Aesthetic Formalism,* 23. The cited line is Cronan's commentary on Alastair Wright's modernist interpretation of the significance of the artist Henri Matisse, who is regarded as the modernist flashpoint. Cronan refers to Wright, *Matisse and the Subject of Modernism,* 56.
32. Cronan, *Against Aesthetic Formalism,* 24. Cronan regards the distinction between modernist and postmodernist art as somewhat arbitrary (14, 24). For a comprehensive historical overview of the development from modernist to postmodernist art, see Foster et al., *Art since 1900.*
33. Cronan, *Against Aesthetic Formalism,* 27.
34. Cronan, 25.
35. Cronan, 32. Cronan refers to descriptions employed by modernist/postmodernist theorists Bois, "Painting as Trauma"; Deleuze, *Francis Bacon;* and Krauss, "The Im/pulse to See."
36. Cronan, *Against Aesthetic Formalism,* 33.
37. Cronan, 25, 15.
38. Tate Galleries, "Bloomsbury."
39. Bell, *Art,* 6. Compare this citation from Bell to Matisse's comment about color: "Colors . . . have in themselves, independently of the objects that they serve to express, an important action on the feelings of those who look at them. Thus simple colors can act on the intimate feelings with much more force, the simpler they are. A blue, for example, accompanied by the brilliance of its complementaries, acts on the feelings like a sharp blow on a gong. It is the same with yellow and red, and the artist must be able to play them according to necessity." Matisse, *Matisse on Art,* 195–96, as cited by Cronan, *Against Aesthetic Formalism,* 28, though whether this defines Matisse's views of art, as a formalist, is not necessarily straightforward, according to Cronan (28).
40. Bell, *Art,* 4, 7, 68.
41. Bell, 68.
42. Bell, 25.
43. Bell, 12.
44. Bell, *Art,* 11.
45. Bell, 52. "For it is only when things are *perceived* as ends that they *become* means to this emotion. It is only when we cease to regard the objects in a landscape [for instance] as means to anything that we can feel the landscape artistically. But when we do succeed in

regarding the parts of a landscape as ends in themselves—as pure forms, that is to say—the landscape becomes *ipso facto* a means to a peculiar, aesthetic state of mind" (79).

46. Bell, 52–53.
47. Bell, 59–60.
48. Bell, 60.
49. Bell, 61.
50. Bell, 62.
51. Bell, 63.
52. Bell, 66.
53. Bell, 65. Consider also Bell's remarks on descriptive art versus genuine art: "The hypothesis that significant form is the essential quality in a work of art has one merit denied to many more famous and more striking—it does help to explain things. We are familiar with pictures that interest us and excite our admiration, but do not move us as works of art. To this class belongs what I call 'Descriptive Painting'—that is, painting in which forms are used not as objects of emotion, but as means of suggesting emotion or conveying information. Portraits of psychological and historical value, topographical works, pictures that tell stories and suggest situations, illustrations of all sorts, belong to this class. That we all recognize the distinction is clear, for who has not said that such and such a drawing was excellent as illustration but as a work of art worthless? Of course many descriptive pictures possess, amongst other qualities, formal significance, and are therefore works of art: but many more do not. They interest us; they may move us too in a hundred different ways, but they do not move us aesthetically. According to my hypothesis they are not works of art. They leave untouched our aesthetic emotions because *it is not their forms* but the ideas or information suggested or conveyed by their forms that affect us." Bell, *Art*, 16–17 (emphasis added).
54. Invoking a fellow Bloomsbury thinker, Roger Fry, Bell outlines the "habits" that get in the way of seeing art for its own sake and the kind of habits that are necessary instead: "Mr. Roger Fry has pointed out that few can hope ever to see a charging bull as an end in itself and yield themselves to the emotional significance of its forms, because no sooner is the label 'Charging Bull' recognized than we begin to dispose ourselves for flight rather than contemplation. This is where the habit of recognizing labels serves us well. It serves us ill, however, when, although there is no call for action or hurry, it comes between things and our emotional reaction to them. The label is nothing but a symbol that epitomises for busy humanity the significance of things regarded as 'means.'" Bell, *Art*, 78. See also Fry, *Vision and Design*, chap. 1.
55. "Another way to put this is to say that reporting what a work makes one think of or feel is not advancing interpretations about what the work means. It is also to say that if the work is seen as requiring the beholder's response to give it meaning, then none of those responses can have any more purchase than another. Hence there can be no grounds to disagree about their significance." Cronan, *Against Affective Formalism*, 17; see also 109–64.
56. Cronan, *Against Affective Formalism*, 34.
57. Cronan, 7.
58. Cronan, 7.
59. Cronan, 12.
60. He thus sees this position as intersecting with Kant's concern in his *Critique of Judgment* (section 9) that "judging" must be given priority over "pleasure" in the beholder of

beauty, lest the beholder's feelings about it would be "unavailable" to others' scrutiny and lack "shared validity." Cronan, *Against Affective Formalism*, 5.

61. This of course assumes that there is such a thing as an art's intention and that we can in fact know it. For debates on this matter in art theory see Cronan, *Against Affective Formalism*, 11–12.
62. Cronan, 35.
63. Bell, *Art*, 49.
64. Bell, 49–54.
65. Eaton, *Merit, Aesthetic and Ethical*, 63–64.
66. Eaton, 21. See also her discussion of the duck-rabbit problem in art (63).
67. De Bolla, *Art Matters*, 17. Though de Bolla shares the centrality of emotive response with Bell, there is a distinction to be made between them. For de Bolla, art is only known through our affective experience of it; form may lead to it, but unlike Bell, form does not define art. There is no specific "'art' component" to an artwork per se (13). What makes an object rise to the status of art is the kind of emotional response we have of it, whereas for Bell, that emotional response is primarily a function of our attention to an artwork's form. That is not necessarily so for de Bolla, as he writes that "I find attempts to define particular qualities of those objects designated artworks as 'aesthetic' qualities—harmony, unity, intensity, and so on—unhelpful because they suggest that one's attention should be directed at the artwork rather than at an experience of it. This slippage or sliding away from what I take to be the proper object of attention confuses the location of the 'art' component because that 'art' is uniquely a feature of an *aesthetic* experience and not something within the object; although the tools we need to locate and understand that experience may *appear to the viewer* to reside in the object, this appearance is an illusion produced by our *affective* response" (18; see also 26–28.)
68. De Bolla, *Art Matters*, 17.
69. De Bolla, 31.
70. De Bolla, 17.
71. De Bolla, 21–22.
72. De Bolla, 20–22.
73. De Bolla, 22.
74. De Bolla, 51.
75. Consider, for instance, extreme cases of swooning before artwork, which the medical profession has categorized and diagnosed as aesthetic syndrome or, more popularly, Stendahl syndrome. See Palacios-Sánchez et al., "Stendhal Syndrome."
76. De Bolla, *Art Matters*, 26.
77. De Bolla, 47 (emphases added). For more on Barnett Newman's *Vir Heroicus Sublimis*, see MoMa, "Art and Artists," accessed August 19, 2022, https://www.moma.org/collection/works/79250.
78. De Bolla, *Art Matters*, 25.
79. De Bolla, 21.
80. De Bolla, 55.
81. Cronan, *Against Affective Formalism*, 14, 27. This explains his labeling of modernism as "affective formalism." See especially 27. Cronan refers to postmodern approaches to art as the second affective turn in formalism (14).
82. De Bolla, *Art Matters*, 25.
83. Gustafson, *Ethics from a Theocentric Perspective*, 1:198 (emphasis added).

84. Gustafson, 1:199; cf. 1:119, 229.
85. Gustafson, 1:171–78.
86. See Cates, *Aquinas on the Emotions*; Cates, "The Religious Dimension of Ordinary Human Emotions"; Gilman, *Fidelity of Heart*; and Lauritzen, *Religious Belief and Emotional Transformation.*
87. Gustafson, *Can Ethics Be Christian?*, 43. Cf. Cates, *Aquinas on the Emotions*, 44.
88. In this essay, I follow Diana Fritz Cates's lead in taking Thomistic passions (*passiones*; *passio*) as emotions. She notes that while some argue that Thomistic passions are noncognitive and therefore nonemotions, she argues that insofar as passions are object-oriented in Thomas's thought (passions are caused by an apprehension of an object), passions translated as emotions makes sense. Cates, *Aquinas on the Emotions*, 74–75n1.
89. Aquinas, *Summa Theologica*, Q. 22, Art. 2, 2:692.
90. The murkiness of Aquinas's use of the term passion and affection appears elsewhere too, primarily as a matter of proper translation. For instance, regarding Aquinas, *Summa Theologica* II, Q. 60, Art. 2, John A. Oesterle refers to "interior affections, which are called passions of the soul." Aquinas, *Treatise on the Virtues*, 100. However, the Dominican Fathers' translation of the same text refers to "interior emotions which are called the passions of the soul." Aquinas, *Summa Theologica*, 2:842.
91. Aquinas, *Summa Theologica*, Q. 22, Art. 3, 2:693 (emphasis added).
92. Aquinas, Q. 82, Art. 5, 1:417.
93. Aquinas, Q. 59, Art. 4, 1:296.
94. Cates, *Aquinas on the Emotions*, 67.
95. Aquinas, *Summa Theologica*, Q. 26, Art. 1, 2:704.
96. Aquinas, Q. 26, Art. 2, 2:705.
97. Aquinas, Q. 26, Art. 1, 2:704; and Aquinas, Q. 26, Art. 2, 2:705.
98. Aquinas, Q. 82, Art. 5, Reply Obj. 1 (emphasis added), 1:417.
99. Aquinas, Q. 22, Art. 3, 2:693.
100. Aquinas, Q. 22, Art. 2, Reply Obj. 3, 2:692.
101. Aquinas, Q. 22, Art. 3, 2:693.
102. Aquinas, Q. 22, Art. 3, Reply Obj. 3, 2:693 (emphasis added).
103. Aquinas, Q. 59, Art. 5, Reply Obj. 3, 2:841.
104. "Love and joy, in so far as they are passions, are in the concupiscible appetite, but in so far as they express a simple act of the will, they are in the intellectual part." Aquinas, Q. 59, Art. 4, Reply Obj. 2, 1:297.
105. Aquinas, Q. 24, Art. 3, Reply Obj. 1, 2:699; cf. Aquinas, Q. 31, Art. 3 and 4 on joy and delight, 2:722–24.
106. Aquinas, Q. 59, Art. 5, 2:841.
107. Cates, *Aquinas on the Emotions*, 202.
108. Cates, 194.
109. Aquinas, Summa Theologica, Q. 24, Art. 3, 2:699.
110. Edwards, "A Treatise Concerning Religious Affections, in Three Parts," 96.
111. Edwards, 97.
112. On the will and intellect as both constituting "perceptual" understanding in Edwards, see Choi, "The Role of Perception in Jonathan Edwards's Moral Thought." It is important to note that while our will may move based on our perception of something, this is not the same as how some interpreters of Thomas understand the relationship between the intellect and will as separate and thus the former deliberating and the latter then executing the

intellect's judgments. As Allen Guelzo notes, "Minds, after all, cannot deliberate between perceived alternatives without willing or choosing actually getting mixed up in the process of what [Thomist] intellectualists mistake for a purely intellectual sequence. Thinking itself is a ceaseless interaction between preferences and perceptions." Guelzo, "After Edwards," 55.

113. Smith, "Editor's Introduction," 14.
114. Edwards, "A Treatise Concerning Religious Affections, in Three Parts," 101.
115. This also reflects Edwards's engagement with Lockean epistemology.
116. Goen, "Editor's Introduction," 83.
117. Edwards, "A Divine and Supernatural Light," 111. Cf. Edwards, "A Treatise Concerning Religious Affections, in Three Parts," 272–73.
118. Edwards, "A Divine and Supernatural Light," 111.
119. Edwards, 112. This is why he refers to sensible knowledge as "heart" knowledge; it pertains to affectivity, our will, or how we are inclined toward some thing.
120. Smith, "Religious Affections and the 'Sense of the Heart,'" 110 (emphasis added).
121. Smith, "Editor's Introduction," 14–15.
122. Edwards, "A Treatise Concerning Religious Affections, in Three Parts," 113.
123. Edwards, 118.
124. Edwards, 113.
125. Edwards, 98.
126. Edwards, 113.
127. Edwards, 98. Also note the very interesting insistence that if we purposely restrain the body, especially in relation to the exercise of spiritual things, we will end up restraining those holy affections. See Edwards, "Miscellanies" 101, 269.
128. Edwards, "A Treatise Concerning Religious Affections, in Three Parts," 98.
129. Edwards, 131–32.
130. Cf. Edwards, 98.
131. Edwards, 133–34.
132. Edwards, 134.
133. "Because the Scripture teaches us often, that if these ideas or views should be given to such a degree, as they are given in heaven, the weak frame of the body could not subsist under it, and that no man can, in that manner, see God and live. The knowledge which the saints have of God's beauty and glory in this world, and those holy affections that arise from it, are of the same nature and kind with what the saints are the subjects of in heaven, differing only in degree and circumstances: what God gives them here, is a foretaste of heavenly happiness, and an earnest of their future inheritance." Edwards, "A Treatise Concerning Religious Affections, in Three Parts," 133.
134. Edwards, "A Treatise Concerning Religious Affections, in Three Parts," 98.
135. Edwards, 98.
136. In contrast, Ryan Martin sees passions, or at least this reference to the passions in Edwards's *Religious Affections*, as pertaining to not the will or inclination, and thus not a form of affectivity (even a deformed affectivity), but rather the body alone. But this interpretation of the reference to the passions in Edwards's *Religious Affections* is not supported by the text and instead is based primarily on association, that is, reading Edwards through what Martin refers to as "occurring themes" of Edwards's Calvinist forebears and especially, he speculates, through the influence of the French thinker Nicholas Malebranche. This speculation colors Martin's approach to the passions unnecessarily. Martin, *Understanding Affections in the Theology of Jonathan Edwards*, 178–84.

137. In this respect, Edwards's use of "passions" is not unlike the way we typically use the term in common contemporary speech, that is, as sometimes associated with or a description for a highly charged situation where persons' emotions are running high because of how they perceive a particular state of affairs.. Note this use of the word "passion" in reference to protests of residents of the East Village neighborhood in New York City, in opposition to street closures and sidewalk dining policies implemented by the city's mayor in response to COVID-19: "It's like the old days," remarked Linda Johnson, an eighty-two-year-old member of the land use committee, referring to the riotous confrontations that once broke out regularly at Community Board 3 meetings. "People are passionate." See Offenhartz, "'This Isn't Paris!'" Those "riotous confrontations" refer to East Village community board meetings during the 1990s. See Jacobs, "The Wild, Wild Lower East Side."
138. Edwards, "A Treatise Concerning Religious Affections, in Three Parts," 132.
139. Edwards, 132.
140. Marsden, *Jonathan Edwards*, 211–12.
141. Goen, "Editor's Introduction," 62–65.
142. Edwards, "The Distinguishing Marks of a Work of the Spirit of God," 226–88.
143. Goen, "Editor's Introduction," 53.
144. Edwards, "Distinguishing Marks," 228.
145. Consider also Edwards's reflections on impassioned speech, which he thinks is no sure embodied sign of genuine religious affection, for one can speak with emotion and feeling from other sorts of affections: "That persons are disposed to be abundant in talking of things of religion, *may be from a good cause, and it may be from a bad one*. . . . It is very much the nature of the affections, *of whatever kind they be*, and whatever objects they are exercised about, if they are strong, to dispose persons to be very much in speaking of that which they are affected with . . . to speak very *earnestly and fervently*. And therefore persons talking abundantly and very fervently about the things of religion, can be an evidence of no more than this, that they are very much affected with the things of religion; but this may be (as has been already shown), and there be no grace." Edwards, "A Treatise Concerning Religious Affections, in Three Parts," 136 (emphases added).
146. Edwards, "Distinguishing Marks," 228.
147. Edwards, "To The Rev. Thomas Prince of Boston," 556.
148. Edwards, "Some Thoughts Concerning the Revival," 316. Goen refers to this as Edwards's "occasionalism" but in this context may be using it somewhat differently from other scholars who refer to Edwards as an occasionalist (Goen, "Editor's Introduction," 67). See, for instance, Cochran, *Receptive Human Virtues*, 16.
149. Goen, "Editor's Introduction, 67.
150. Edwards, "Some Thoughts Concerning the Revival," 316. Edwards cites the examples of Luke 9:51–56, Numbers 12:3 and 20:7–12, Romans 14:6, and 2 Corinthians 2:6–11 and 7:11, among other passages in scripture (316–19).
151. Edwards, "A Treatise Concerning Religious Affections, in Three Parts," 269.
152. Edwards, "Some Thoughts Concerning the Revival," 318
153. Edwards, 316.
154. Edwards, "A Treatise Concerning Religious Affections, in Three Parts," 98.
155. Edwards, 132.
156. See, again, Edwards, 133–34.
157. Edwards, 97.
158. Edwards, 132.

159. Gustafson, *Can Ethics Be Christian?*, 44.
160. Nussbaum, *Upheavals of Thought*, chap. 1.
161. Gilman, *Fidelity of Heart*, 24. Enlisting Edwards's account of the affections, James E. Gilman strives to affirm "that emotions are powerful moral forces and very often, when properly cultivated, function as reliable moral guides." Gilman, *Fidelity of Heart*, 7. My reading of Edwards, however, raises the question of the type of moral guides the emotions represent.
162. Barrett proposes that just as there is no distinct neural entity with respect to particular emotions, there are no normative emotive acts or patterns of the body; emotions are dependent on the situation. As such, emotional expressions do not necessarily correspond to one's particular inner feelings, perceptions, or commitments in some "natural" or biological way. The spirit of that thesis is not unlike what I am proposing as the relative nature of the emotions in Edwards's thought. See Barrett, "Are Emotions Natural Kinds?" Barrett's thesis is laid out in more detail in *How Emotions Are Made*, chap. 4–7. See also Mesquita, *Between Us*.
163. Cf. Nussbaum, *Upheavals of Thought*, chap. 3. While Edwards would disagree with the Stoic suspicion of the emotions, Edwards and the Stoics converge in other ways, especially with respect to virtue. See Cochran, *Receptive Human Virtues*.
164. Sullivan and Groves, "'We're Sick of It.'"
165. *New York Times*, "Inside the Capital Riot: An Exclusive Video Investigation." This video report opens with a visibly angry white man and is titled *Day of Rage: An In-Depth Look at How a Mob Stormed the Capitol*. Cf. Kranish, "How Tucker Carlson Became the Voice of White Grievance." More pointedly, the cable news network host is described as "the preeminent voice of angry White America."
166. Aquinas, *Summa Theologica*, Q. 46, Art. 7, 2:783.
167. Pierce, "Righteous Anger, Black Lives Matter, and the Legacy of King."
168. James Baldwin as transcribed from a radio interview. See Baldwin et al., "The Negro in American Culture."
169. Thus, we will need to question additional accounts of anger such as that of Martha Nussbaum, who sees the desire of retribution as structurally part of the emotion of anger, rendering it morally problematic. See Nussbaum, "Transitional Anger," esp. 51–52, 54. Unlike Nussbaum, Willie James Jennings sees anger as morally crucial so long as it does not devolve into hatred. But if emotions have no particular moral orientation from an Edwardsean perspective, then even this more positive construal of anger will need greater scrutiny. See Jennings, "Anger Is the Engine of Hope Now."
170. Edwards, "A Treatise Concerning Religious Affections, in Three Parts," 269.
171. See Henri Matisse, "Henri Matisse Complete Works 5"; and Henri Matisse, "Selected Henri Matisse Paintings."
172. Edwards, "Some Thoughts Concerning the Revival," 386–87.
173. Edwards, 387–88.
174. Edwards, 389.
175. Edwards, 387.
176. Edwards, 387.
177. Edwards, 391.
178. Edwards, 390.
179. Edwards, 392
180. See Spohn, "Spirituality and Its Discontents," 262.
181. Edwards, "Some Thoughts Concerning the Revival," 392 (emphasis added).
182. Edwards, 392–93.

183. A more generalized version of this point is brought to the fore in Cep, "Reading the Old Testament While Pregnant," where she claims that in her current stage of life—she is an expectant mother—passages of motherhood in the Bible are particularly resonant to her. That reading scripture is a social, ethical enterprise, not insulated from moral context but always linked to social location, is emphasized in Fiorenza, "The Ethics of Biblical Interpretation."
184. Edwards, "A Treatise Concerning Religious Affections, in Three Parts," 267.
185. Edwards, 268.
186. Edwards, "Some Thoughts Concerning the Revival," 387.
187. Edwards, "A Treatise Concerning Religious Affections, in Three Parts," 101.
188. Edwards, "A Careful and Strict Enquiry into the Modern Prevailing Notions of that Freedom of the Will," 144. See also Guelzo, "After Edwards," 55.
189. Guelzo, 57.
190. Guelzo, 57. See also Edwards, "A Careful and Strict Enquiry into the Modern Prevailing Notions of That Freedom of the Will," 150.
191. Edwards, "A Treatise Concerning Religious Affections, in Three Parts," 101; see also 283. Or, one acts according to what is most agreeable to the person: "Thus, when a drunkard has his liquor before him, and he has to choose whether to drink it, or no; the proper and immediate objects, about which his present volition is conversant, and between which his choice now decides, are his own acts, in drinking the liquor, or letting it alone; and this will certainly be done according to what, in the present view of his mind, taken as a whole of it, is most agreeable to him" (Edwards, "A Careful and Strict Enquiry into the Modern Prevailing Notions of That Freedom of the Will," 143).
192. See Edwards, "Dissertation II," 540–42.
193. Smith, "Editor's Introduction," 12. For the second sign, see Edwards, "A Treatise Concerning Religious Affections, in Three Parts," 240–52; for the ninth sign, see 357–64.
194. Smith, "Editor's Introduction," 48.
195. See Edwards, "Dissertation I," 446: "God may have a real and proper pleasure or happiness in seeing the happy state of the creature: yet this may not be different from his delight in himself; being a delight in his own infinite goodness; or the exercise of that glorious propensity of his nature to diffuse and communicate himself, and so gratifying this inclination of his own heart."
196. Referring to Edwards's account of the self as dispositional—or what I am calling his "dispositional self"—is my generalization of his anthropology from his larger "dispositional ontology," a description coined by Sang Hyun Lee. See Lee, *The Philosophical Theology of Jonathan Edwards*.
197. "This knowledge [of God's goodness and glory] in the creature is but a conformity to God. 'Tis the image of God's own knowledge of himself. 'Tis a participation of the same: 'tis as much the same as 'tis possible for that to be which is infinitely less in degree: as particular beams of the sun communicated, are the light and glory of the sun in part." Edwards, "Dissertation I," 441.
198. Consider further the findings of an August 2022 poll: a majority of Americans believe that the United States is being invaded by immigrants crossing the southern US border. Rose, "A Majority of Americans See an 'Invasion' at the Southern Border, NPR Poll Finds."
199. If Kennicott's op-ed on conflict and disaster photography underscores the moral powerlessness of art, then Margaret Renkl's op-ed on the same kind of art represents a rebuttal. See Renkl, "When a Picture Is Worth a Thousand Tears."

200. See Spohn, "Spirituality and Its Discontents," 264–65. This is one of three sets of practices that Spohn categorizes from the thirteen sermons published in Edwards, "Charity and Its Fruits."
201. See Spohn, "Spirituality and Its Discontents," 265.
202. Spohn, 266.
203. Spohn, 267. Spohn also refers to Sermon Twelve, "Christian Graces Concatenated Together," in Edwards, "Charity and Its Fruits," 326–38.
204. Spohn, "Spirituality and Its Discontents," 269. See also Sermon Seven, "Charity Contrary to a Selfish Sprit," in Edwards, "Charity and Its Fruits," 262.
205. Spohn, "Spirituality and Its Discontents," 268.
206. Spohn, 267.
207. Spohn, 267, citing Sermon Five, "Charity Contrary to an Envious Spirit," in Edwards, "Charity and Its Fruits," 222.
208. The integrity of human agency in conversion is underscored in Elizabeth Agnew Cochran's study of Edwards's virtue theory. See Cochran, *Receptive Human Virtues*.
209. On the work of encounter, see Francis, *Fratelli Tutti*; and Mescher, *The Ethics of Encounter*. The morally formative work of encounter will also entail the work of being vulnerable. See, for instance, Butler, *Precarious Life*; Gilson, *The Ethics of Vulnerability*; Hogan, "Vulnerability"; Keenan, "The World at Risk"; Keenan, "Linking Human Dignity, Vulnerability and Virtue Ethics"; Keenan, "Building Blocks for Moral Education"; and Keenan, "Social Trust and the Ethics of Our Institutions."
210. Edwards, "Charity and Its Fruits," 270.

5

THE MISEDUCATION OF ART

I have endeavored to defend the idea that one's disposition is critical to how one is receptive to a number of aesthetic practices, that is, how one looks, hears, and reads as well as creates and how such aesthetic practices in turn impact one's state of being. I have attempted to advance this idea by turning to a normative account of what we could call the dispositional self: that we are not rationalist beings whose choices or judgments are solely functions of calculated, measured discernment; instead, our choices or judgments are expressions of our dynamic inclinations (or disinclinations) toward what we like or love (or do not). This vision of the self follows the larger structure and logic of Jonathan Edwards's theology, which is a vision of the world defined by a sovereign God who intends for all of creation to be actualized toward God's glorification.[1] Edwards's emphasis on inclination or disposition reflects this divine intentionality for humanity, and the state of our disposition indicates our participation in creation's actualization of God's glorification.

Though this vision of the self is theologically particular, it is descriptively sensitive, turning to our experiences for its veracity. In other words, this vision of the self accounts for the multiplicity of ways we respond to events and circumstances. More specifically, there is no one set of emotional responses to any kind of event or circumstance, as Edwards so keenly observed with respect to the revivals of the Connecticut River Valley in early eighteenth-century New England; thus, it cannot be our emotional life but rather our affective life (disposition) that reveals and determines what we understand or perceive and ultimately do.

We can extend Edwards's suspicions of the emotions to contemporary claims that art generates its own kind of emotive responses. Contrary to such claims, if the kind of emotive effect that art elicits is always varied, perhaps even unpredictable and not particular to art itself, then the notion that how we are disposed to art matters to how we respond to art has a good deal of explanatory appeal. Such appeal spills over to the realm of art and ethics. Art is not morally consequential because it appeals to our emotions in ways that form our moral agency; such a way of thinking about the connection of art to ethics assumes mistakenly that there is a special relationship between art and ethics or that there is a predictable relational flow of art, emotions, and then moral knowing and doing. But just as there is no emotive predictability, there is no moral predictability with respect to looking, reading, and listening. Thus, the emotive unpredictability of art parallels the moral unpredictability of art, or what I have been calling art's moral pluralism, with art's moral failure (the fact that the kind of moral hopes that are sometimes placed on art do not in fact materialize) occupying one end of that moral pluralism spectrum. Accordingly, if art does not always achieve the kind of moral salience or effectiveness that a number of ethicists claim it can, no matter how "great," "classic," "beautiful," or "provocative" the artwork, then the art-audience relationship merits our critical attention as an important determinant of art's moral salience.

This is not to say that analogies that are employed in artworks, such as poems, songs, and novels (and even metaphors and, more generally, appeals to our imagination), are inconsequential;[2] on the contrary, they can aid us in understanding an idea, a thesis, and a dimension of the human condition more clearly, maybe even differently. However, the question that uncomfortably looms over such a proposition, one that is too often ignored, is what makes their use successful—if indeed they are successful at all or, alternatively, unsuccessful—with respect to moral knowledge and the changing of minds? Is it the analogies themselves (their artistic renderings) or something that works in concert with them or even something that foregrounds their impact? Critical attention to the audience's relationship to art calls attention to the latter, and this proposal draws attention to an Edwardsean thesis on the determinative function of the affections, or our disposition, with respect to what we perceive: "But there is a great difference between these two things, viz. lively imaginations arising from strong affections, and strong affections arising from lively imaginations."[3]

With that in view, it is worth noting that my efforts thus far have shied away from making the case for a certain kind of art or proposing that a community's flourishing depends on valuing one form of art over another or, for example, whether certain kinds of novels are morally beneficial more so than others; whether artists should stick to painting in a realistic, representational manner over focusing primarily on color and technique; whether we ought to promote the mural arts or other forms of participatory art forms over promoting, say, portraiture; or whether character-driven plays and off-Broadway community theater rather than feel-good, big-budget musicals ought to be supported. These are issues worth debating, but they can also bog us down until we see them as "a crucial part of a civic dialogue about what matters to *us*, what *we* value."[4] The emphasis on us/we underlines the critical importance of the moral posture of persons and communities as the valuational framework for their aesthetic judgments.

Consider once more the case of the Lady of Guadalupe. As we saw in chapter 2, Roberto Goizueta sees the Guadalupe story as an aesthetic prerequisite to the practice of justice. Nichole Flores proposes similarly when claiming that the Guadalupe story is an aesthetical political theology; it is through the Guadalupe story that a particular kind of community is made possible. This way of thinking about the aesthetical dimension of the Guadalupe story is made more explicit when Flores calls attention to the method of aesthetic interlacing.[5] This method allows those who are watching or witnessing or hearing the Guadalupe story to identify with what Juan Diego of the Guadalupe story endures. When interlaced in this way, the Guadalupe story is not just a political theology but instead becomes a template for imagining, interpreting, and giving shape to one's own experiences in the form of Guadalupe's political theology. (In other words, the aesthetics of the Guadalupe story is the very means by which the story calls us to be its underlying political theology.)

But it is interesting to note that Flores hints at a more complicated view of how the Guadalupe story functions as a moral template. This more complicated view is embedded in her heavy reliance on a particular version of the Guadalupe story, the Guadalupe story reimagined through the play titled the *Miracle of Tepayac*. This version, as Flores describes it, intermingles the Lady of Guadalupe's appearance to Juan Diego "with the story of a Hispanic Catholic parish in a fictional Colorado tourist town"; this parish was "once-thriving and beautiful" but is "fighting to survive" while "also struggling to meet the immense spiritual, economic, social, and political needs of its members and the broader community with few resources or support from their bishop."[6] It is because the Guadalupe story is recast (or interlaced) in this way that it has the capacity to resonate with and speak to Latinx communities, including Denver's Chicanx community as it struggles with issues related to farmworker rights, immigrant justice, political disenfranchisement, social and cultural marginalization, and gentrification.

For Flores, the Guadalupe story is morally formative (i.e., it invites the cultivation of solidarity and social transformation)[7] in the *Miracle of Tepayac*'s version of the story. If this version of the Guadalupe story is morally effective because it is interlaced with a political critique of the laws and structures that have devastated certain Latinx neighborhoods, then it would seem that what ethically matters is not the Guadalupe story per se but rather what kind of Guadalupe story is told and who that particular version of the story is intended to affect. More directly, not any rendering of the Guadalupe story will do,[8] certainly not the way in which the Guadalupe story is depicted and displayed in the Mexico City Headquarters of Banamex, the second-largest bank in Mexico, or the way it is appropriated and displayed by particular Catholic pro-life groups.[9] For Flores, the problem with these depictions of the Guadalupe story is not that they are aesthetically displeasing; what is displeasing about them is the social ends to which they are employed by particular communities, organizations, and institutions. In short, all depictions of Guadalupe are not equally valid; some are more valid than others, and the measure by which their validity is determined is the kind of moral life and community they aim to generate or support.

Whether this or that kind of art object and art form ought to be valued over others is inseparable from what is morally important to a particular person and that person's community. (In other words, unless we get our ethics straight first, we will lack the framework to discern the kind of aesthetics we think is important or the kind of aesthetics we think we need.) One might propose a theological aesthetic or a philosophical account of what constitutes attention-worthy art, but the adjudication of such arguments will require some sense of what kind of community one wants or believes is valuable and the kind of art and aesthetic that is befitting of such an account of community. While questions of aesthetic judgment are important, they are not necessarily the right starting point for their own adjudication. And it bears noting that given the challenges of coming to any kind of moral agreement on what constitutes the good life—even what counts as community is deeply contestable—it is not difficult to see why societal-level consensus on what counts as good or bad art can often be illusive.

I am therefore less interested in navigating the question of which aesthetic objects or experiences ought to be valued and more interested in the underappreciated question of art's moral pluralism. Stated differently, I am doubtful of the value of thinking through the question of what kind of art and aesthetic activities are morally important without first grappling with the following kinds of questions regarding art's unpredictability: Why does our advocacy for certain kinds of art or our belief in the moral importance of certain kinds of art forms and their correlative practices (reading, looking, and listening) often fail in having moral effect? More specifically, why do photos of tragedy fail to engender moral action? Why are some critically acclaimed works of literature subject to division, polarizing to some and not to others? And why do some "good" people love morally questionable art (or what some might say is morally questionable, such as romance novels, heavy metal music, gangster rap, some kinds of avant-garde and pop art, and horror cinema or, its more extreme sibling, gore movies), while other "good" people do not care for art at all (but should love art because, well, they are good people)? Then there are those who are "vile" and love beautiful art, or what some might characterize as beautiful: Mozart, Beethoven, Michelangelo, and the like. How are we to make sense of these persons and their aesthetic loves? Critical attention to these sorts of questions led to the following proposal in chapter 4: the moral power of art cannot be accounted for apart from the role or influence that the beholder's disposition has in what art effects. This proposal included the additional claim that we ought to prioritize the hard work of moral formation—of forming our disposition toward the good—if we want art to do the kind of moral work we hope it will do (or think it can do). This might entail discernment of whether particular artworks or aesthetic themes can enhance such work, but its role of enhancing (rather than engendering) complicates the essential moral character of art.

What, then, does this mean for art with respect to ethics? From the very start of this book, borrowing from Marcia Muelder Eaton, I have characterized a number of theological-ethical approaches to art and ethics as consequentialist. And inasmuch as art and its correlative practices of reading, looking, and listening are morally consequential—that is, they can form our agency and thus change what we know and move us accordingly—art and its practices extend the scope of experience as a source in theological-ethical method.[10] But if the disposition of the one who looks, reads, and listens is critical to what art can do, is a morally consequential account of art essentially problematic? Correlatively, can it be counted as an essential theological-ethical source or a distinctive source of revelation, or is it simply an expression of a particular theological-ethical point of view?[11]

It would seem that my proposal casts a good deal of doubt on the importance of art for ethics to the extent that it is ethics that makes art morally worth talking about. As I note later in this chapter (and as I noted in chapter 3 via a discussion of Scarry in particular), I do not think that all responses to art are attributable to one's moral posture; that would be too totalizing and distort the complexity of our experiences with art. But on the narrower question of whether art elicits moral responses in us, adds to our evaluative and normative judgments on justice, or morally changes us, this is indeed a matter of one's moral posture.

Consider one more case: a literary illustration.[12] Kathleen Wall describes the protagonists of Zadie Smith's acclaimed novel *On Beauty* as "ethically [blind] to the particularities of the individuals in their world; they violate their intersubjective relations with others, treating wives, students, and children as adjuncts to their reputations and desires."[13] The ethical blindness of the main protagonist, Howard Belsey, a professor of art history, leads to marital infidelity and the eventual breakup with his wife, Kiki. Smith suggests that Howard's ethical lapses are remarkable given his expertise in and love of Rembrandt's art. (The moral shortcomings of the novel's other characters are shameful too, especially against the backdrop of their various aesthetic pursuits.) But the end of the novel offers a glimmer of hope, a possible reconciliation between Howard and Kiki. Howard, while harried in his trek to deliver an art history lecture (his tenure is at stake, we are told), loses his notes in a cab and resorts to explaining from memory the slides of paintings that anchor his lecture. When the slide of the Rembrandt painting "'*Hendrickje Bathing,* 1654'" appears, Howard notices Kiki in the audience: "Howard looked at Kiki. In her face, his life. Kiki looked up suddenly at Howard—not, he thought, unkindly."[14] He then looks at the slide once more, admiring its subject. Shortly afterward, he turns to the audience again "and saw Kiki only. He smiled at her. She smiled. She looked away, but she smiled. Howard looked back at the woman on the wall, Rembrandt's love, Hedrickje."[15] And with that, Smith intimates a new future for both Howard and Kiki.

This ending raises a question: Is it the Rembrandt painting that facilitates Howard's renewed regard for Kiki or something else? For each character in the novel, art is an integral part of their daily lives, however troubled their lives may be. The closing scene of the novel does not deviate from that basic narrative pattern: Howard and Kiki see each other again, possibly as husband and wife, while they happen to be in the presence of art. In that moment Howard sees himself as Rembrandt, that is, as the one staring and painting the subject of Rembrandt's love, Hedrickje. For Howard, his Hedrickje is Kiki, his estranged wife. But would Howard have seen Kiki as Rembrandt saw Hedrickje had it not been for the tumultuous events that preceded this final scene, that is, how Howard and his family had to navigate through his indiscretions and its consequences, the airing of grievances and resentments, and the resulting new understandings of one another? Smith is somewhat ambiguous on the question, or at least she leaves it up to the reader to decide, though others have made a more definitive interpretation.[16] It would be difficult, however, to separate the importance of those prior events in Howard's moment of renewed attention to Kiki; those prior events had changed Howard, and as a consequence, he was positioned to see Kiki anew by the novel's end. So, if Rembrandt's painting had any part in the possibility of reconciliation between Howard and Kiki, such power coincided with, if not was exerted by, the fact that Howard was a different person at that moment when he saw Kiki sitting in the audience as the Rembrandt slide appeared. In other words, the painting had moral power because of Howard's disposition; he was disposed (or maybe redisposed) to a faithful love rather than an egotistical love because of all that had transpired between the time of his infidelity and his reencounter with Kiki at the lecture. This encapsulates the notion that I am trying to defend: that the moral power of art cannot be understood apart from our moral posture, the disposition that frames our approach and receptivity to art.

If our moral posture has as much if not more to do with art's morally transformative possibilities, then the claims that we make about art's moral salience is a derivative claim and not a necessary one; it is always driven by a particular moral theory and must be so.[17] There is perhaps a circularity here, but there is also something relatively obvious about the notion that art's moral relevance is dependent on particular moral theories,[18] obvious in the sense that it would not make much sense to suggest that art is important to the moral life unless one assumed, explicitly or not, what the moral life is or held a particular definition of it. Even a seemingly straightforward claim such as "a good novel teaches us to appreciate life" must assume some sense of what a life worth appreciating entails for it to be a meaningful statement. And it is this assumption that provides the warrant to contest another's account of art's moral salience and to advocate for another (e.g., "therefore a good novel does more than just make us critical thinkers"); it also provides the warrant to claim one kind of art form as more morally salient than another (e.g., "consequently, science fiction can't count as a good novel because it's all about ingratiating one's fantasies"). It is because of a preceding moral notion that our moral claims about art are intelligible and, for that matter, can be made at all, lest our intent is to simply utter an empty sentence, or a sentence that only makes sense to oneself.

But to make more explicit the obvious—that is, the need for an ethical theory in any account of art's moral salience—is to call specific attention to the flip side of this claim that is not necessarily noticed and appreciated: the turn to art, to its moral salience, is not so much about art per se. If art can indeed do something to or for us at least with respect to ethics, it can do so not by virtue of something unique to art but instead by virtue of the moral theories one is trying to elevate through the turn to art. In this respect, art becomes an aesthetic counterpart, mirror, or even companion to a particular moral theory (and thus view of the self, view of the good, and corresponding values and norms), which helps to explain why some are particularly interested in literature while others think that the nonliterary arts such as music and dance track more closely to the shape and texture of the moral life.[19] Contemporary aesthetics-ethics discourse therefore requires greater precision, which is to say that we need to acknowledge more explicitly the moral assumptions (i.e., the moral ends or goals) driving our moral appeals to art.

In defending the idea that the moral power of art is constitutive of one's disposition, I am raising the question of the extent to which the moral power of art is a statement about the power of art per se or, more so, a statement about what the moral life is and the kind of work that is required to advance a particular account of the moral life. The trajectory of this book leans toward the latter, which demands that we pay closer attention to how art's moral power (its capacity to effectuate, motivate, or inspire particular choices or actions) must rely on something other than itself.

So, can art be considered morally consequential and, relatedly, an integral source for ethics, and if so how? In this chapter, I want to make the case that art can and ought to be regarded as an integral source but in a way that is more complicated than we might expect (or even want) it to be given the claims that I have made above. Part of this case will require some clarification of what I mean by disposition or, more specifically, that it is one's disposition that matters with respect to one's receptivity to what one sees, hears, or experiences. To be sure, one typical way of conceptualizing one's disposition is in terms of the virtues or character. In chapter 4, I frequently alluded to such a way of thinking about disposition in moving back and forth between disposition talk and the language of who we are (e.g., who we are affects how we look or read). Such language, however, is more opaque than it might seem. In other words, it is sufficiently vague that it can mask a more specific account of disposition that I think is central to understanding the nature of our receptivity to art and its correlative impact on our agency. The key elements of this account are sprinkled throughout chapter 4, where I have also referred to disposition, again following Edwards, as one's orientation as a function of one's likes and dislikes, or inclinations. But for Edwards, disposition is also more complex than these descriptions, which is signaled in his language of disposition as affections (or affective perception) and further indicated in the moral dimensions of the signposts of genuine religious affections, to which I made passing reference at the end of chapter 4. Furthermore, in chapter 3 (and again at the start of chapter 4 and, finally, briefly above), I anticipated the critical role of this more complex account of disposition when discussing the importance of community for our conceptions of art's moral value. Bringing these additional descriptions together into a coherent account will clarify how art should be regarded in the task of ethics. My commitment to the general claim will be constant: disposition matters in our receptivity to art and its moral influence on us. But my interest will be in addressing the social conditions from which our dispositions manifest or expresses themselves. To parse out what I mean by this, I will proceed by mapping out at least two ways that I believe art should not be considered as an integral moral source: not as social capital and not as a source of moral lessons. Working in this *via negativa* manner, my aim will be to underscore the inevitability of moral disagreement and conflict and how thinking about art can make sense of such outcomes. Because art leads to discord—or, more generically, moral pluralism—art is critical to identifying society's competing attitudes and habits of mind and, in turn, wrestling with the limits of moral knowledge and social cooperation. It is this paradoxical account of art's moral salience that respects the complicated moral outcomes of art while preventing such complexity from mitigating the value of art for ethics.

QUESTIONING ART AS SOCIAL CAPITAL

Based on the proposal that the moral power of art is constitutive of one's disposition, I suggested in chapter 4 (aided by an interpretation of Edwards's advocacy of good preaching) that art's moral power would have to be regarded more as reinforcing and deepening rather than engendering moral knowledge and action. This is complementary to Gregorie Currie's proposal that we think with art and not necessarily in and through art. That we think with art suggests that it gives us the kind of moral knowledge that can also be had apart from it. Focusing on literature, Currie claims that the practice of reading is not the "process by which we learn facts about what is right and wrong" but rather that which aids in the refinement, reinforcement, or, in some cases, rejection of what we have come to believe is right and wrong.[20] At times, Currie can sound as if certain kinds of moral knowledge are available only through the practice of reading inasmuch as literature is what allows us to understand the "rewards and costs" of particular moral choices through the lives of fiction's characters. But those intimations are tempered by his references to how literature adds to rather than provides moral knowledge coming from our daily experiences. Currie cites George Eliot in this regard. "'Art is the nearest thing to life, it is a mode of amplifying experience and extending our contact with our fellow-men beyond the bounds of our personal lot.'"[21] Currie then explains his intentions further. "What I want to do is offer a defense of Eliot's remark that shows how fiction supplements the moral lessons of experience in a way that *more experience* could not easily do."

For Hilary Putnam, this means that what he calls empirical knowledge is distinct from conceptual knowledge, and it is conceptual knowledge that literature provides:

> If I read Celine's *Journey to the End of the Night* I do not *learn* that love does not exist, that all human beings are hateful and hating (even if—and I am sure this is not the case—those propositions should be true). What I learn is to see the world as it looks to someone who is sure that hypothesis is correct. . . . But all this is not empirical knowledge at all; for being aware of a new interpretation of the facts, however repellent, of a construction that can—I now see—be put upon the facts, however perversely—is a kind of knowledge. It is knowledge of a possibility. It is *conceptual* knowledge.[22]

Currie would add that such knowledge is at its core practical knowledge insofar as novels, "with their descriptions of fictional characters and their activities, are capable of calling forth from us imaginative responses that are similar to those called forth by our encounters with real people."[23] But it is precisely because fictional descriptions of characters in novels resonate with the moral knowledge we gain from daily experiences that such descriptions can spark such imaginative responses or evaluative moral work. Thus, without the moral knowledge we gain from daily experience, whatever knowledge novels provide, they would be less salient; their salience, in other words, is dependent on experience that is independent of our aesthetic experiences.

Such dependence changes the calculus on the relationship between art and social capital. More specifically, it demands closer scrutiny of claims that art is integral to fostering the social capital necessary for human flourishing and, more specifically, democratic life. Robert Putnam describes social capital as the value of the social connections that are marked by reciprocity, honesty, and trust or, more specifically, the value of the norms of reciprocity and trustworthiness that arise from connections among individuals.[24] Social capital is not unlike the idea of social virtues but with the stipulation that virtues that facilitate society's flourishing are "most powerful when embedded in a dense network of reciprocal social relations."[25] Putnam does not mention the role of the arts in fostering social capital, but the notion that arts and social capital are integrally linked, and thus a public good and not simply a private good, is not uncommon.[26]

John W. De Gruchy can be seen as an advocate for such a view of art in his insistence on the public role of art and its capacity to foster public accountability. Art can do this, de Gruchy claims, because it "has the potential to change both our personal and corporate consciousness and perception, challenging perceived reality and enabling us to remember what was best in the past even as it evokes fresh images that serve transformation in the present. This it does through its ability to evoke imagination and wonder, causing us to pause and reflect and thereby opening up the possibility of changing our perception and ultimately our lives." Therefore, without art, identifying and building bonds with "society's victims; the ability to unmask hypocrisy; and the ability to evoke hope" are less possible. De Gruchy then claims, perhaps not surprisingly, that "artists are an essential element within civil society,"[27] but not any kind of artist. If we want art to serve its public function, then what is needed is a certain kind of art, specifically prophetic art, or art that combines the tradition of the Hebrew prophets and avant-garde activism. "As social critics, then, artists continue the iconoclastic tradition of the prophets, but like the prophets they also express the possibility of healing and redemption and thus envisage new futures."[28] De Gruchy draws this conclusion based on the role that artists have had in particular social movements. As a theologian from South Africa, he is especially interested in protest art that emerged in South Africa's era of apartheid and specifically as it "emerged during the years which followed the Soweto uprising in 1976."[29] With growing protests against apartheid came the growing movement to cultivate art as a means of political resistance. More sharply, without that growing political struggle, the call for a complementary form of art would have gained less traction.[30]

De Gruchy's account of the emergence of protest art in South Africa is a good example of how the advocacy of art as a social good or, more specifically, as fostering social capital runs inevitably along two tracks. The first is the claim that certain forms of art—such as mural arts and other forms of collaborative art projects,[31] or resistance or social protest art, in De Gruchy's case—can foster certain kinds of intergroup social bonds that are integral to justice and democratic life. The second is the assumption that such art forms and their aims are dependent on or, at the very least, run (or should run) parallel with ethical transformation. Such transformation is either already afoot, in the case of De Gruchy's example of protest art caught up in the push against apartheid, or is seen as a necessity for the success of the kind of art that is regarded as essential to the development and possession of social capital.

Consider further the kind of aesthetic analysis that is provided by M. Shawn Copeland. Copeland's analysis of pop culture aesthetics is a revealing instance of aesthetic analysis as a form of critical social commentary. Her rejection of contemporary rap and hip-hop aesthetic and then advocacy of Black preaching is premised on the idea that certain kinds of art and art forms—or a certain aesthetic—are more contributory to liberatory social bonds. More specifically, Copeland's critique of rap music and hip-hop culture is not just that she thinks it misrepresents women and the diversity of their experiences or that women are more than how such an aesthetic depicts Black women: this would simply assume that rap and hip-hop representations of women are just one of many possible representations without necessarily passing moral judgment on any particular representation. However, Copeland's aim is to level a definite critique of rap music and hip-hop culture and to name their aesthetic as misogynist, sexist, and patriarchical; as such, what she seeks is a critique of the "ordinary practices of everyday interaction" that rap and hip-hop culture perpetuates.[32] In her advocacy of the aesthetic of Black preaching, she is motivated by a different relational vision, by the kind of social bonds that are just and thus liberating. "The sermon is a rhetorical space in which preacher and people 'articulate the self, challenge the dominant culture's ordering of reality, and contest its authoritative discourse.'"[33] The practices of "nonviolent personal and social transformation, human and holistic relationships," ought to form our perception of self and one another.[34] But note her proviso that the Black sermon "achieves an aesthetic function," by which she means that it serves as an instrument in recovering and healing justice and liberation, "*only insofar as* preacher *and* congregation participate in the retrieval of those meanings and values" that liberate.[35] In other words, the aesthetic power of Black preaching is only as successful as the social bonds that accompany it or the social bonds that are lived along with it. Thus, while Black preaching can foster social capital, that is, advance the social bonds integral to freedom and just community, it may not function this way if those who listen or hear it are disposed to divergent forms of relationship.

Copeland's proviso is an important acknowledgment—however brief it is (it arrives in the last paragraph of the chapter)—of the possibilities of art in forming particular kinds of social bonds as well as the limitations of what art can do to form such bonds. There is no moral inevitability to Black preaching; it does not necessarily foster life-affirming social bonds unless we are actively participating in that sort of community. This is a proviso that finds its way in minor and conceptually unformed ways in a number of arts as social capital campaigns. For instance, in a study on the social impact of the arts in King County, Washington, the nonprofit organization ArtsFund identified almost a dozen cases of art connecting people and bridging cultures.[36] "The stories of [art's] impact ripple beyond direct participants to contribute to thriving neighborhoods and community spaces, health-promoting social fabric, and stronger shared understanding of complex issues like homelessness," according to the study.[37] At the same time, the vision of art's strong, direct social impact is restated in the study when it elaborates on why those surveyed in the study did not recognize the social impact of the arts: it is because, the study suggests, the "arts['] impact comes from how it integrates with other interventions, *complementing and reinforcing* them, rather than replacing them."[38] Art is impactful, it will then state, when "paired" with social programs.[39] In sum, the ArtsFund study provides concrete support for the claim that arts are necessary because of their social impact; it is valuable in fostering the kinds of relationships and social bonds that are integral to the maintenance and health of a democratic society. But the ArtsFund study also demonstrates how such a claim can be trimmed when resorting to the language of art as supplementing, reinforcing, or playing a supporting role in the generation of social capital. According to the study, its supportive role is tied to the success of nonaesthetic practices (i.e., social service programs) in creating the conditions for democratic social capital to be generated; thus, without such social service programs, the arts would be less impactful. Such a qualification raises the question of whether art can be a source for or contribute to ethical transformation in the absence of other means of ethical transformation. Probably not, at least not without their reliance.[40]

QUESTIONING ART AS A SOURCE OF MORAL LESSONS

If ethical transformation is too tall an order for art alone to facilitate, maybe we do well to think of art's moral salience in a more modest way as providing or teaching moral lessons. In chapter 1, we saw one version of this proposal. Eaton provides a helpful refresh:

> Art, especially narrative art, . . . *shows* readers what is morally salient in the lives of the characters whom the reader is asked to imagine. . . . And although it is not always explicit, a kind of Aristotelian view of virtue lies behind the explanation of why art can therefore be morally valuable. If morality is a matter of exhibiting virtue and if one acquires moral understanding and habits by following examples of virtuous behavior rather than by simply trying to apply moral principles, then anything that *shows* such behavior will be morally valuable. This is true of both virtuous people and of stories about virtuous people (or their oppositions, of course), for both invite (or discourage) imitation. . . . Fiction approached seriously demands that one imagine what happens when one does or does not tell the truth, share things, or persevere in the face of daunting obstacles or conflicts.[41]

That what a novel displays matters to its capacity to serve as a moral training ground explains why, according to Eaton, some emphasize the salience of Greek tragedy and others focus on the novels of Henry James or George Eliot.[42] Eaton is sympathetic to such a view of art, as art can teach us moral lessons; it can train us for or school us in a particular form of life. But, she adds, "if one is to explain how art, or at least the narrative arts, uniquely play a role in the development of moral understanding, it seems to me that we must attend not only to the content of such works but also to *how* they contribute to moral development—that is, to the particular properties works of art have that make it possible, even likely, that the kind of *showing* that is at its heart will be successful."[43]

For Eaton, if art is to be morally effective—"if it succeeds in stimulating serious moral thought, brings one to put oneself in others' shoes, increases moral understanding, broadens moral perspective, introduces or deepens reasonable moral guidelines, instantiates correct moral principles to the extent that these exist, or contributes to moral development"[44]—then what it says matters as much as *how* it says it. "Aesthetic properties are not frills or add-ons that make moral lessons more palatable." Instead, their appeal to us, or our desire to pay closer attention and consider them seriously, is tied to how artists "show" the content of their work. "Some works of art . . . have a moral content, and sometimes we accept, or at least do not dismiss outright, the moral perspective presented or represented. The task is to see how the aesthetic properties of those works contribute to the ethical success of the work," Eaton claims.[45] But note the absence of any possibility that the moral success of art depends on more than the aesthetic properties that frame its content. This absence is important to notice, because if the aesthetic properties of those works contribute to its ethical success, then what can we attribute to its ethical failure? Presumably if its aesthetic properties are such that those who pay attention to them will be morally impacted and changed, then why does it not always lead to this sort of success? Perhaps they do not know enough to notice or appreciate those properties, but if that is the case, then the aesthetic properties themselves are not sufficient to effect moral success.

Consider the example Eaton provides to show otherwise:

> One can almost at random pick a sentence from [Henry James's] fiction that *shows* how difficult it is to make sense of the lives of others and of oneself. Here is a case in point: "I verily believe it hung in the balance a minute or two that in my impulse to draw him out, so that I might give him my sympathy, I was prepared to risk overturning the edifice of my precautions." The reader is forced to reread many of his

> sentences to figure out what is going on, what is being said. Without this, the point about the world's complexity would be less forceful.[46]

Rereading may indeed be required to appreciate the force of what James is trying to convey, but Eaton's conclusion assumes that the complexity of the sentence will necessarily engender multiple attempts at reading. However, that is hardly a guarantee, and that much is plain to any college professor who has spent time in the classroom, especially with students who are there because they are required to be there. Students who will find a dense sentence from a James novel or some other novel irrelevant are just as likely as those who might find such an opaque sentence interesting and desire to attend to its meaning repeatedly. But it is oftentimes the case that students have to be induced, cajoled, or "threatened" under the penalty of a poor grade to continue to read and reread, and once forced (or, more euphemistically, incentivized), the sentence may indeed break through to students, at least to some of them. A student's positionality or disposition, in short, matters to the success of the novel.

Eaton will admit that the aesthetic choices made by an artist to express or convey the content of her work will be effective in sustaining the attention of her audience and drawing them closer to her work if and only if the audience is ready for it; the artist's audience "must, in the end, be able to match their experiences to" the art, she states.[47] This is particularly the case with literature. The showing of a novel's moral content "is successful when vivid, memorable images are created by foregrounding features, by using words and patterns that enable readers to form these images. Authors must attend to questions of accessibility—what images are likely to be formed, *given the age, gender, social status, and other characteristics* of the reader?"[48] This question pertains to the social contexts and experiences of the author's or artist's audience and serves as the bridge between the moral success of particular kinds of art and the kind of aesthetic strategies that contribute to their success. This position is latent throughout Eaton's reflections on art and ethics, and sometimes it is more explicit, though it can get lost in her effort to punctuate the point that ethicists need to pay attention to aesthetics.

At any rate, bringing this position to the fore draws attention to the extent to which we would be mistaken to think that art can do the kind of moral work we want it to do on its own, that is if we only paid closer attention to its aesthetic features and to what those features are trying to convey to us. The proposition that art is a source of moral lessons is therefore not as straightforward as one might expect. That it is a source of moral lessons is misleading unless we take seriously the extent to which it resonates with and perhaps depends on the values and interests that we draw prior to reading from our lived experiences.[49] In other words, the success of an artwork's moral content cannot be attributed to the power of the artwork's aesthetic features themselves (by aesthetic features I mean the artwork's use of repetition, rhythm, and many other aesthetic techniques or elements of form or style). This is one implication of my claim that art—what it is capable of effecting—is constitutive of its audience's disposition or orientation to it.

In saying that art's moral success will depend on its audience's disposition, I do not mean that art is incapable of any kind of moral work apart from its audience's disposition. Furthermore, I do not mean to imply that instances of art's moral failures are all attributable to one's particular disposition. Art and its forms can also be therapeutic and edifying, especially personally, as a way of working through one's struggles, making sense of dreams deferred (e.g., *A Raisin in the Sun*), and can be a medium for self-exploration and meaning making, and so forth. Furthermore, as I have noted throughout this book, art can be utilized to make a point clearer and more vivid, and art in that way can be performatively impactful, that is, can move its beholder emotively, to move the beholder to read or look more intently, perhaps with dumbstruck wonder. Elaine Scarry articulates iterations of such responses in her notion of art's forward momentum, art's seemingly powerful capacity to engender repeated acts of looking or attention, sometimes through replication or re-creation (leading to more art,[50] even philosophical musings). Eaton, as we saw in chapter 3 as well, observes how art objects, depending on what they are, incite one to invite another to take a look or read along; this creates a temporary focus group, as she calls it. To these instances, we can add the way in which a particular feature of art—a particular use of technique or form such as a pop of a peculiar color, the dimensionality of a brushstroke, or the musicality of a lyric or even the dissonance of an instrumental arrangement—can induce a moment of delight, can be energizing, or even be transporting (recalling Iris Murdoch's experience of noticing a hovering kestrel from her window.)[51] And if one is not affected by art in any of these ways, this could easily be attributed to simple inattention or being distracted by the many mundane demands of life (homework, housework, and the like).

But the question of concern is not whether art can do something to someone who is in its presence and is actively reading, looking, or listening (art can and often does something to a person engaged in such a practice). Rather, the concern is whether art can, more specifically, "have an effect on one's *moral life* that *lasts* after a book has been put down or after one has left the museum or auditorium."[52] Eaton thinks that art can have such an effect, but we cannot simply rely on its content to do that kind of work. If the content of an artwork is intended to have lasting moral impact, then how it is presented must be taken into consideration. Art that incorporates narrative (literature, specifically) as well as art that cannot easily avail itself of the use of words (some genres of music and visual arts are what she has in mind) can have the kind of moral effect she describes above, and for Eaton this will be primarily a function of the kind or quality of the aesthetic forms it employs. It is the aesthetic properties that an artwork employs that makes its content "challenging and convincing" and thus "sufficiently memorable," Eaton proposes. But whether that will have a discernable and enduring impact on one's moral life after one has finished reading, looking, or listening is one question that concerns me primarily, and to claim that the quality of the aesthetic forms an artwork takes on is what determines such an impact is to give too much power, perhaps authority, to the quality, form, or type of the artwork, or so I have been arguing. It is one thing to say that an artwork's form can make its content sufficiently memorable but another to say that it therefore is the means to change one's viewpoint or regard or to inspire or motivate a particular course of action. The particular use of color, for instance, may enliven one's senses and mood, but that is different from having an impact on persons in such a way as to actually transform their relationships with one another.[53]

ART, SOCIAL PRACTICES, AND THE HABITS OF DIALOGICAL AND DIALECTICAL MORAL REASONING

In questioning the authority that art—its content and especially its aesthetic properties or its aesthetic presentation—has with respect to what it is able to actually effect in the moral sphere, I mean to signal the importance of the kind of relationships that form who we are and thus inform what and how we perceive persons, events, and circumstances. Accordingly, what I want to draw attention to is the necessary intersection between our moral perceptions and aesthetic perceptions and experiences (acts of reading, looking, and listening) and the relational dynamic that is always at play in how and what we read or look at. In other words, the authority or weight we give to art is constitutive of the relationships that matter to us or that we simply assume as important. Jeffrey Stout underlines this importance when speaking of moral observation, especially of the noninferential kind. One can make observations that "play as premises in inferences that *lead to* ethical conclusions." Observations of this sort are not explicitly value-laden but can be employed to make value-laden moral explanations of a particular event, incident, or development.[54] This is the basic structure of a moral argument or defense of a particular moral position. In contrast, observations of the noninferential kind "essentially employ evaluative terms" in the observation itself; they are "prereflective, intuitive responses . . . [such as] 'That is unfair!' Another might be to whisper to your companion, 'Such splendid courage she shows.'" (Stout is referring to possible noninferential observations one might have made in witnessing the arrest of Rosa Parks.) In some of our moral observations or responses we don't necessarily "move through a series of inferential steps when making a judgment"; our judgments are not a function of reasoned determination in every instance. In short, some of our noninferential observations are in themselves ethical perceptions; they do not require a reasoned argument for its moral force.[55]

For Stout, noninferential moral observations are acquired through discursive training and therefore are not self-generated. "We are trained to respond noninferentially"; for example, "we are conditioned to respond noninferentially to instances of cruelty by using the term 'cruelty' and to instances of courage by using the term 'courage.'" "But the social conditioning of observation does not stop there," Stout explains further. The moral terms we are conditioned to use (or the moral, noninferential responses or observations we are trained to make) are prescribed within a set of particular social practices or norms. These norms tell us the kind of linguistic responses as well as the actions to perform that are appropriate in a given circumstance.[56]

Many of the social practices or norms to which we ascribe moral authority are defined by a select group of persons who have specialized ways of perceiving the world. This is certainly the case in many religious communities in the kind of authority that is given to the roles of "sages, imans, spiritual advisors, rabbis, and confessors."[57] In democracies, those we rely on and trust with respect to how we ought to "perceive people, actions, and events" are those we think deserve moral authority: "Moral authority belongs not to a class of ordained experts, but rather to anyone who proves his or her reliability as an observer and arguer in the eyes of the entire community." So, note that even though democracies are purportedly about respect for the freedom of individuals, Stout reminds us that even those who live in a democracy are not unattached monads. Democratic citizens like any other persons are formed by those who are found to be morally authoritative. "All discursive practices involve authority and deference to some extent. The notion that ethical discourse in democratic society is 'nondeferential' therefore requires qualification. It is more accurate to say that such discourse is *relatively* nondeferential. The difference is a matter of how, when, and why someone defers or appeals to authority, not a matter of whether one does so at all."[58]

Whether in a modern democracy or a theocratic political order, moral observation is always a relational affair. For Stout, it is democratic relationality that ought to be prioritized, and our moral observations ought to conform to the social practices or norms that are appropriate to democratic relationality. My interest is less in Stout's defense of democratic relationaltiy and more in the basic point about the inherent relationship between moral observation and relationality (or the relational conditions for moral observation).[59] The language of relationality is not employed by Stout, but his belief that our moral observation is reliant on some moral authority underscores a relational grounding for whatever moral observations we have. It is because someone is morally authoritative to us—in a democracy we get to determine who is morally authoritative and thus deserves our deference, while in other forms of political community such agency may not be there—that their stories or narratives or, more generally, instructions are received and train us "not only to reason in a certain way, but also to see some people or actions in a moral light."[60]

This point about the relational grounding of our moral observation is helpful, I think, in making sense of why Stout thinks that social criticism of the sort produced by "writers like William Cobbett, Harriet Martineau, George Orwell, James Agee, and Meridel Le Sueur . . . has done much to shape modern democratic sensibilities."[61] Their observational reports—"what life was like for the rural and urban poor, for the homesteaders of the American West, for the coal miners of England"[62]—were often paired with other media or, essentially, certain kinds of art forms:

> Once we begin to focus on the role of observation and observation reports in ethics, it becomes plain that the study of ethical discourse must take the full range of media into account, not merely those that are primarily verbal. It is obvious that the printing press, newspapers, pamphlets, books, and now the Internet have all played important roles in modern democracies as vehicles for the exchange of arguments. But the story of ethical discourse in modern democracies is also tied up with the history of photography, moving pictures, radio, and television—with all the ways in which we have come to record and disseminate our observations of the world.[63]

Such observations were able to shape modern democratic sensibilities because their producers—writers, photographers, and so on—were "trust[ed] in their reliability as witnesses."[64] And presumably they were taken as reliable because their observations and judgments were appropriate to the norms of their fellow democratic citizens, or at least the norms they aspired to. (I say presumably since Stout discusses the social criticism of Agee and others to simply underscore that they were taken as reliable and thus influential in forming democratic sensibilities and does not state explicitly why they were taken as reliable. It would make sense that they were taken seriously, however, inasmuch as they appealed to a sympathetic public.)

It may be unfair, one might say, to detect an aesthetic theory that corresponds to or is assumed in Stout's reflections on how the habits of moral observations are inculcated (since an aesthetic theory is not what Stout is after). Still, it is noteworthy that Stout gives some acknowledgment to the role of multiple artistic media in the formation of our moral observations and the extent to which that role is constitutive of how reliable we deem the one who is making moral observations through such media. It is this relationship that matters to understanding the morally formative role that the stories, narratives, and prose from authors such as Orwell and Agee had almost a century ago. Whether we find one's moral observations authoritative has a good deal to do with whether we trust them.

Perhaps another way of putting this is to say that if stories and narratives are formative, it is because they resonate with our social experience. James Gustafson reminds us that "experience is always prior to reflection," but its meaning—that is, making sense of experience—is always social.[65] And what we think is relevant or not is conditioned by that sociality, or the norms or social practices that are authoritative within a particular discursive community, to return to Stout's way of putting things. (This is why, as we saw at the start of chapter 4, Gustafson thinks that the kinds of distinctions we make, for instance, between what is aesthetic and religious—or when it is appropriate to pay attention to something as either aesthetic or religious—only makes sense within the context of our communal conditioning and the social norms that we believe are authoritative.) But sources of authority (and thus discursive communities) differ, and thus we are disposed to perceive and value things differently, a point that Stout makes in reference to Edmund Burke's and Thomas Paine's vehement disagreement on the legitimacy of monarchy and aristocracy versus democracy. As Stout notes, "Burke opposed the [American] Revolution and deferred to certain figures of authority, while Paine differed from him on both points. . . . [It] becomes clear that they were also disposed to have different *noninferential moral responses* to the events, persons, and actions of their time."[66]

Let me pause here to summarize at least two key points that I have made, or at least alluded to, so far. First, the linkage between moral observation, on the one hand, and social practices, on the other hand, sharpens our attention to the conditions from which we perceive (look, read, and listen) and, correlatively, the conditions that define their influence on us. Our disposition to perceive or experience "persons, actions, and states of affairs" correlates with particular social practices, which are reflective of a particular vision of relationality or expressive of particular relational loyalties or preferences, identifications, and values.[67] But it may be more accurate to say that our particular social practices or relationships are prior to our perceptual disposition (i.e., to how we respond to others, occurrences, and circumstances), since those relationships are morally authoritative or formative. Another way of putting the point is that what we perceive, or what we tend to and prefer to perceive, as well as what we want others to perceive—and the kind of arguments we make in our advocacy and defense of such perception (what Stout refers to as matters of making ethical or political inferences)[68]—are reflections of the kinds of social bonds or social order we embody or think we should embody. Looking, reading, and listening therefore are not insulated, separate activities from our moral perceptions but are themselves particularized moral experiences. In other words, how we look, read, or listen and what we are willing to look at, read, or listen to is, more specifically, informed by our relational formation. Thus, this is more than a matter of, as the saying goes, "seeing or believing what you want to see or believe." If what we perceive is a function of our social practices, then it is not necessarily a matter of desire or choice, as the saying might suggest, nor is it a matter of willful ignorance. Instead, it is about the relational situatedness of our moral perceptions and thus the relationally formed nature of our moral perceptions (and its influence on our acts of looking, reading, and listening). Accordingly, we are not always conscious of the formative nature of our relational loyalties; those who are making claims, inferentially, will be more cognizant of their social allegiances and sources of moral authority even if they are not aware in those terms. But most if not all, simply as a matter of course, make observations (noninferentially) in reflexive ways; our relational loyalties are thus simply assumed and express themselves habitually in terms of what we perceive and do. Thus, separating out our relational formation from our daily activities or practices overlooks the social context of lived experience.

Second, if our social practices and thus our relational loyalties or identities are intimately linked to what we value and how we go about thinking, saying, and doing what we do, then reading, looking, and listening, even if the object of such activity has explicit moral content, will not necessarily lead to a moral outcome that corresponds to such content. In other words, it is not the moral content of an art object that is morally determinative necessarily but rather the social-relational loyalty or identity of the art object's audience. And since there can be a diversity of social-relational loyalties or identities, so too with ways of reading, looking, and listening. Consequently, discordant or conflicting responses to art should not surprise us. Of course, some of this divergence may be out of simple inattention or momentary distraction, as I noted earlier, but in instances of active attention to art, how shall we account for possible divergences in moral response? Some art may intend, even overtly, to communicate moral lessons (or have moral meaning), and some may not. Regardless, the former may not affect some, while others may be moved morally by the latter kind of artwork. There is also another possibility: some may detect moral meaning in an artwork that is contrary to its intended moral meaning, and if we were to imagine someone pointing out the need to be trained or schooled to look, read, and listen in a particular way so as to detect the right or intended moral meaning of the artwork in question, then this specification magnifies the larger point that art's moral effects, its successes, are relationally dependent (because to be trained to understand the artwork "correctly," as it was intended to be understood by its creator, is a function of a particular relationality, of a particular social practice). Another possibility still is a dispute over the same recognized content of an artwork. In this scenario, all parties involved acknowledge that a particular artwork is morally salient, but the artwork engenders intense disagreement and conflict over the nature (or merits) of that salience. Certainly, not all disagreements are troublesome. There can be reasonable disagreements about art: whether a particular artwork or style of art is good or not (e.g., "I prefer midcentury modernism over the excess of rococo" versus "it is that very excess that makes rococo so interesting"), whether one likes the inclusion of particular instruments in a musical score (e.g., "the horns are hauntingly beautiful in *Tristan and Isolde*" versus "the horns makes its music too languishing") or the style or narrative structure of a novel (e.g., "I love Faulkner because he writes the way I think!" versus "I can't follow what *Absalom, Absalom!* is about. Where are all the periods?"), and so on. But these kinds of disagreements are not necessarily moral disagreements or conflicts over the moral meaning or salience of art or a particular kind of art: that is, whether it is something we ought to endorse or curtail, even censor; whether others ought to be encouraged to look, read, or listen to it; or whether it warrants the support or investment of public resources. Art that intentionally aims to provoke, such as obscenity art (as well as protest art), raises those questions typically (though even art that is not intentional in this way can have the same effect). Such art creates discord and polarizes its audience, and while many might say that what they are looking at is obscene, some if not many others will not, and that some will find it offensive and others will defend it in the name of "art" or will plainly find it not offensive and obscene (maybe beautiful even) underscores the extent to which different moral perceptions and social practices, interests, and values are at play in the reactions and assessments of such art. What counts as obscene or not is usually not just a divergence of feelings, nor is it self-evident (contrary to what US Supreme Court justice Potter Stewart claimed).[69] Instead, what counts as obscene or not is a matter of the social norms or the kind of social relationships we think or assume are integral. That moral observations are relationally constitutive in nature raises the prospect that such diversity of outcomes with respect to art reflects the influence of the beholders' social-relational context as much as we might think it pertains to the aesthetic quality of the artwork itself.

This prospect complicates what we can expect from art, morally speaking, or how we should think about art's relevance for ethics. At the very least, I would like to propose that rather than seeing art as a site for potential moral lessons, lessons that would be more felt and thus effective depending on the strength of its aesthetic presentation, art is always a site for potential moral disagreement; because we can only speak of relational loyalties or identities in the plural, moral observations are necessarily plural and often competing. This is one lesson we began to discern in chapter 3. But are art and its moral pluralism evidence of the intractability of disagreement? I think that is certainly one distinct possibility, and numerous instances have been provided throughout this book (again, especially in chapter 3) in which disagreement more so than consensus and mutual understanding is the consequence of art. Of course, one can also point to instances in which the converse is the case. But just because one can point to such instances does not necessarily demonstrate that art will be successful in engendering agreement and understanding; it only ends up, I contend, underscoring the reality that art engenders, necessarily, a pluralism of responses.

Yet, if there is indeed an inextricable link between differing visions of social relationality and the pluralism of moral responses to art, then it is possible to conceive of art as an important site for assessing competing visions of social goods (or what constitutes community) rather than evidence of the intractability of moral disagreement. Disagreement need not be interpreted as matters of difference "all the way down," wherein difference means epistemically distinct and thus mutually exclusive. As a site for assessing competing visions of social goods, art occasions reflection on the condition of a community's well-being, that is, its social health. We might assume to know what that condition or diagnosis is, but art, based on this account, brings those assumptions into open view, or it may challenge widely held assumptions on the state of affairs. Accordingly, the moral ambiguities of art need not signal or reinforce moral pessimism, that what one knows and does are always discontinuous (and nonoverlapping) from what others know and do. Instead, that art engenders plural moral responses can be taken as indicative of the need for an epistemology that is mindful of the importance of humility, fallibility, capaciousness, and self-correction.[70]

We might draw an analogy with the ambiguity of discerning human goods within the context of natural law ethics and feminist responses to this ambiguity. Drawing from Thomas Aquinas's understanding of how practical truth is gained, Lisa Sowle Cahill notes that the "process of discerning human goods and normative human relationships" is "never free from error and bias."[71] This is so if we see competing accounts of human goods and relationships as something other than expressions of incommensurable difference or the manipulative venting of emotions.[72] This, Cahill thinks, is an essential takeaway from a feminist approach to natural law ethics: "What the feminist debate about difference brings to [natural law] theory, or emphasizes within it, is that mutual understanding and agreement on goods is not achieved in some sphere above or beyond difference, but only from reflection which begins within determinate historical communities with particular experiences of goods and evils, and particular visions or hopes of change."[73] For Cahill, particularity is the necessary condition for the discernment of the "objectivity of values,"[74] and particularity in this sense is not a private account of the good; it is only a partial account of the good.[75] The distinction warrants suspicion of any claim to the good as universal while, at the same time, warranting a regard for any claim to the good as potentially adding to a fuller picture of what the good is and ought to be. As Cahill summarizes, "Appeals to experience are used constructively in feminist moral argument to shift the balance within given patterns of interpretation of the human condition. And appeal to 'experience' introduces some dimension of women's situation which an existing construct diminishes or leaves out of account."[76]

Taking cues from a feminist approach to moral reasoning, we can say that art's moral pluralism—the conflicting ways that art is perceived—reflects the fact of historicity. Historicity, however, need not be taken as evidence that the aesthetic acts of looking, reading, and listening are simply (or only amount to) matters of difference. A feminist approach to moral reasoning pushes us instead to regard our particular histories more accurately as social commentaries, or accounts of how we, as individuals and members of particular communities, have been and continue to be socially (culturally, politically, economically) positioned.[77] We can therefore view our various histories as revealing contrasting yet mutually enriching, or mutually correcting, perspectives on human well-being. On this view, while differing moral responses to art (i.e., the reality of art's moral pluralism) are attributable to the differing histories that inform moral perception, they disclose differences over a common social object or concern: the question of how we should live together, or which goods are important for life together and which are less so, which goods have been ignored or undervalued, who has been the beneficiary of particular goods and who has not, and so forth. While there will always be differences by virtue of our historicity and while we should therefore expect different moral responses to art, these differences are nevertheless held together by a single thread, a shared social question, whether explicitly or implicitly.

So, let us imagine a local arts group holding an open exhibit inviting the public "to fall in love" with art.[78] Though the exhibit attracts a sizable audience and can be considered a success in that sense, reaction to the exhibit is mixed. A number of attendees express excitement that such an exhibition is being held in the neighborhood, since an "arts scene" has been for the most part absent; such absence does not make the neighborhood "bad" but perhaps less desirable than the trendier downtown neighborhoods. Other attendees, however, are more tentative in their assessments, quite anxious that this is a harbinger of the kind of changes to come in the neighborhood: specifically, an influx of younger professionals and with them higher rents and luxury condos, which would make the neighborhood that much more difficult to live in for many of the longtime residents, particularly Black and immigrant residents. Others still are put off by the artworks on display, thinking they are ungodly, and are worried about their negative influence (the influence of radical "wokeism") on the neighborhood's children, while others strongly disagree, believing that such artworks are exactly what the neighborhood needs; they are countercultural, politically and socially attentive, speaking to "the moment," or so they claim. In all of these reactions, their differences reveal much about what persons in the neighborhood think are requisite social goods; these reactions therefore are not necessarily a rejection of the value of social life, of being in community. And what each constituency cares about—their differing or pluralistic assessments, or worries or dislikes, on the one hand, and praise or appreciation of the exhibition, on the other hand—offers occasions for reflection on the variables, factors, and goods that may have been missed in one's own conception of what constitutes the best social life. Thus, rather than assuming that such pluralism is a reflection of "the incommensurability of the premises from which the participants in modern ethical discourse argue their cases,"[79] such pluralism can be regarded as arising from a shared premise or, more specifically, a shared social question and a collective investment in that social question. That commonality is what makes it possible to see such differences as partial accounts rather than mutually exclusive accounts of a community's state of affairs and therefore the possibility of regarding the kinds of inferential moral statements or arguments being made to one another not as argumentative dead ends but instead as capable of changing or enlarging another's mind (or, at the very least, being explicable to another who might differ).[80] By the same token, it is that commonality that makes epistemic humility and the habit of being attentive to others, even if one holds a differing position, commendable and defensible. So long as difference is not equated with mutually exclusive positions but partially revelatory ones, then the virtue of intellectual hospitality ought to be the correlate to difference.[81]

In short, art's moral pluralism, its moral successes as well as failures, occasions partial views of the whole, without which the whole could not be adequately discerned.[82] According to Iris Marion Young, taking as many of these partial views into consideration is what makes phronesis possible: "A public that makes use of all such social knowledge in its differentiated plurality is most likely to make just and wise decisions."[83] Discernment by way of particularity requires the skills or habits of moral reasoning that are both dialogical and dialectical, however.[84] Art's moral pluralism reminds us of the necessity of such habits, that is, the habits of noticing, expecting, and appreciating difference as a means of acknowledging and addressing cultural, social, and ethical blind spots if justice is to be pursued.

But does this not imply that art is a source of moral lessons after all, a position that I have been working against? The implication is unavoidable, though it requires specifying that art is not a source of moral lessons by virtue of art's content (artist's intentionality or what is depicted in the art object itself) and how it presents such content (aesthetic form and technique). Just as we might talk about the social determinants of health, we can talk about the social determinants of the act of looking, reading, and listening, which reconfigures what it might mean to say that art is a source of moral lessons. If it has lessons to tell, those lessons are not restricted to whatever the content of the artwork might be and how it is aesthetically presented but also reside, perhaps more significantly, in the pluralism of moral responses that the artwork elicits. This does not make art morally immaterial so long as such pluralism can be explained in part by competing and yet mutually corrective accounts of the good as described above.

My concern throughout has been making sense of the recurring phenomenon of art failing to effect specific moral outcomes, or why we tend to respond so differently to art, if we are moved toward particular moral judgments and actions at all. If this phenomenon is on account of how our perceptions are reflective of or formed by our particular relational identities or loyalties, then any moral lesson that art provides should be found in that fact rather than in the artwork itself. Rather than schooling us morally or training us for moral discernment, art, its moral pluralism, indicates the need for moral habits or skills that are central to moral discernment that cannot be had through aesthetic encounters or practices per se. Art's moral pluralism may bring our attention to the importance of such skills, but it is not art itself (and our experience of it) that is generative of such skills; acquiring those skills will require something other than looking, reading, listening, and creating; it will require practicing humility, self-correction, and openness to contrary points of view. Art's moral pluralism, then, draws attention to the importance of particular social virtues that can only be acquired external to aesthetic experiences themselves, that is, through the training in or practice of nonaesthetical practices.

TAKING ART AND ETHICS REALISTICALLY IN A FRACTURED WORLD

At the start of this chapter, I indicated that in order to better account for art as morally consequential and, correlatively, as a source in theological ethics in light of my account of the dispositional self, we will need a clearer account of what it means to be persons whose agency is a function of our disposition. That clarity comes in the relationship between our moral perception, on the one hand, and the social practices that we defer to, on the other hand. This linkage refines the nature of our moral perception and the conditions from which it acquires its meaning. We are disposed to perceive in correlation to the authority we intentionally give to (or in some cases simply assume of) particular social practices. To put it differently, first, what we perceive is a matter of our disposition or, as Edwards would say, a matter of our inclinations and consent, likes or dislikes, or what we approve of or reject. But, second, how we are inclined, as Stout would say, is a matter more specifically of the kind of social relationships (and norms that define these relationships) that form who we are, that is, our identity (these social relationships reflect the discursive practices that initiate us into a particular way of observing the world, of making sense of it).

If what we are disposed to perceive is tightly woven into our social practices, this would suggest that a change in perception will require ethical transformation; they go hand in hand. Stout suggests as much when observing that our social practices are artifices or human constructions (like "drapery" or "wardrobe" for our imaginations) and thus subject to experimentation, "trying out new arrangements on a limited basis to see what comes of them."[85]

This is important for him insofar as it provides a pathway to work through our moral disagreements, such as the ones that Burke and Paine were locked into on the nature of political life. Their seemingly intractable disagreement (tradition and gradualism versus democratic revolution) was rooted in different perceptions of the world, reflecting their diverging relational loyalties. But such disagreement is only intractable to the extent that we are unwilling to examine critically our social practices and imagine and risk trying out new ones. But inasmuch as Stout appeals to Walt Whitman's and Henry David Thoreau's examples of relentless reimagining and experimentation of what and how life in the world can be in *Leaves of Grass* and *Walden*, respectively, we might be tempted to think that art can foster the kind of ethical transformation, or social experimentation and thus perceptual transformation, that we need to negotiate our differences.[86]

That prospect is an enticing one, particularly in contemporary Christian theology. Social retrievals of liturgical practices provide yet another example of how aesthetics is regarded as critically important to ethical transformation and the inculcation of social practices that are democratic and solidaristic. As David Albertson and Jason Blakely propose, with forceful assurance,

> Catholic liturgy is a set of practices whose highest aim is communion with God and neighbor. Among other things, the Mass is a public prayer that reconstitutes the social body by reconciling each to the other and all to God. Communion with God works against alienation from one's neighbor, from creation and from oneself. At every Mass, Catholics offer perfect strangers a "sign of peace" and greet them as family. . . . Communal sharing reaches its climax in the radically democratic act of God feeding all of God's people without exception. All are joined in their individual bodies by the one Body of Jesus; all who participate in this meal are made radically interdependent upon each other, organs of a single creature. In effect, they resolve not to be themselves without the other. As Pope Francis is fond of repeating, "no one is saved alone."[87]

But their confidence in the morally formative power of Christian worship is not total. Echoing Copeland's proviso that we noted earlier, they finally admit, though sounding reluctant to do so, that "of course nothing in Catholic liturgy automatically generates communion with one's neighbor. . . . But the same practices, lived faithfully, perennially produce arresting examples of creative communal living."[88] Indeed, but this is true only when the sustained intentionality is there and when such practices are lived faithfully.[89]

We might draw a similar lesson from Edwards but in a more theologically distinctive manner. How we perceive self and world is expressive of social relationships and their discursive practices. For Edwards, God is, of course, our ultimate authority who imputes himself to us (via God's indwelling Spirit) and thus draws us to participate in his own divine life. Such participation is a matter of being inclined or consenting to God's glory. (The flip side of such participation is that it is a consequence of receiving God's grace.)[90] But such inclination or consent (or, more specifically, religious affection) is not a matter of merely perceiving or experiencing God, self, and the world in a certain way; more properly, it is perceiving or experiencing in a manner that is appropriate to the social relationships that reflect the kind of relationality that God approaches humanity and the entirety of creation. Hence, as noted in passing at the end of chapter 4, the reason for Edwards's preeminent concern over whether one's affections (or disposition) were in fact religious by examining one's moral practices. Love of God means simultaneously love of neighbor; the converse, according to Edwards, is "self-seeking, self-exaltation, and opposition to others," the root of injustice.[91] For those who are self-centered,

> their love is far from being of so extensive and universal a nature, as a truly Christian love is. They are full of dear affections to some, and full of bitterness towards others. They are knit to their own party, them that approve of 'em, love 'em and admire 'em; but are fierce against those that oppose and dislike 'em. "Be like your Father which is in heaven: for he maketh his sun to rise on the evil and on the good. . . . For if ye love them which love you, what reward have ye? Do not even the publicans the same?" (Matt. 5:45–46).[92]

But in case one might think that one ought to love one's own family less on account of the universal push of Christian love, Edwards warns that neglecting one's family is just as problematic as opposing our enemies. "Some shew a great affection to their neighbors, and pretend to be ravished with the company of the children abroad; and at the same time are uncomfortable and churlish toward their wives and other near relations at home, and very negligent of relatives, duties."[93] The essential relevant point here is that for Edwards, by virtue of God's authority or sovereignty, the Christian life is one in which we are disposed to perceive the world in a particular way, but such perception is situated within particular social practices or relational norms or priorities: care for one's own and care for the stranger. Thus, all of our moral commitments ought to be measured against such perception and the kind of benevolent social relationships within which such perception proves its meaning.[94]

It is worth noting that Edwards approaches moral (redeemed) perception and its correlative relational embodiment aesthetically, that is, in terms of the symmetry of relations or their beautiful proportions.[95] So, for those who fall short of Christian love, there is "a strange partiality and disproportion."[96] Contrastively, of those who embody Christian love there is "the same beautiful proportion" that we find in "the original," that is, Christ. "There is symmetry and beauty in God's workmanship. The natural body, which God hath made consists of many members; and all are in a beautiful proportion: so it is in the new man, consisting of various graces and affections."[97] But the beauty of Christian love is made possible to the extent that we receive the primary beauty of God's love and are made to participate in that love and beauty.[98] Thus, right moral perception is made possible by the love—its practices—that grace makes possible. Contemplation of secondary beauty, the beauty of creation, has only limited effect without transformative participation in God's primary beauty.

It is this emphasis on ethical transformation that warrants closer attention and appreciation. Art may foster solidarity but not without transformation toward that end, which underscores art's social dependence rather than its autonomy. This is not to say that art is only a social fact, as Theodor Adorno might warn.[99] If art is to be more than a product of social circumstance or an expression of the social conditions of a particular moment, then art, according to Adorno, must oppose society. Through its "artistic form," art can embody a "heterogeneous moment," can be a "not being-for-itself," and thus can "[attack] its traditional foundations"; it is then that art becomes a political or social counterforce.[100] But the question that I believe warrants sustained consideration is the extent to which art's social resistance can have purchase among a people who are not already experiencing the stirrings of resistance. In other words, in the absence of ethical transformation, or at least a social movement toward such transformation, to what extent can it "aid and shape" the world anew? Adorno's primary concern tends to fall on the artist's responsibility to create art that is always oppositional to dominant culture. But absent a more careful consideration of the social and moral conditions for the receptivity of such art (or any kind of art for that matter) and thus the experiential state of art's audience, claims that such art will be successful or have the effect intended will fall short conceptually and descriptively.

Art's moral salience cannot be divorced from the link between moral perception and social practices. If our moral perception is ineluctably tied to particular social practices or relationships, then in order to change our moral perception we will need we need to change our social practices. But do our social practices require changing? What kind of social practices ought we to embody?

Determining such evaluative and normative questions requires more than attending to art. More specifically, if we want art to contribute to such judgments, then we will have to be the kind of people who are capable of making such judgments. Consider the following scenario. Perhaps, as Alasdair MacIntyre imagines, "when for the first time, as a result of some chance encounter some particular great work of art makes a sufficiently disturbing and singular impact on someone who has hitherto found nothing in art to care about, she or he will be compelled to recognize that, but for that chance event, they might have spent their whole lives not caring about what they should have been caring about."[101] But why would one be so compelled to think that is what they ought to have cared about all along? Consider further one who feels the pull of classical music, regarding it as a good, and thus feels compelled to attend to it, to learn how to judge it, and so forth. But how would one know to follow what might be discerned in classical music, to think it ought to be prioritized over other moral considerations we might have and hold dearly? MacIntyre asks, "What would someone be doing who recognized that such goods can be very great goods, but decided that for him they have to be set aside, because their pursuit would distract him from doing what he takes it to be his moral duty to do?"[102] In either the former or latter scenario, a judgment is being made, and such judgment is not simply being made for them (as if the artwork imposes its standard on them), but it is being informed by and assessed through the kind of person they already are, or "what kind of person [they] will have to become."

But theirs is surely only one of many possible accounts of how we ought to perceive self and world. And just as one who is startled by, say, a Chopin sonata but decides to resist its revelations because of the kind of person she believes she is or believes she should become, there are surely others who are willing to have what they listen to issue forth a negative judgment on what they believe is the "measure of human goods, goods that contribute to our flourishing"[103] But which path should we take? Who is right? How should we decide? To claim, as MacIntyre does, that determination of evaluative and normative judgments are matters of the kind of person we are or should be may indeed be true; this is a position, or at least a version of it, that I have staked out throughout this book, without which, I have argued, we lack the conceptual framework to understand the pluralism of moral responses that art typically elicits. But such a position does not necessarily mean that the determination of evaluative and normative judgments requires, as MacIntyre thinks, adopting a "traditionalist" tradition of the virtues in order to make such determinations coherently.[104] Grappling realistically with the morally pluralistic responses that art garners signals an alternative path, an alternative set of virtues and social practices.

Given that we live in a world of differing moral visions and that such differences often express themselves as competing or opposing visions and strikingly so in the presence of art, it would not be difficult to regard art as only a site that mediates such differences and conflict. Art, then, would hardly recommend itself as a constructive moral guide; it is better to slide back into how we typically think of art as matters of play, pleasure, or delight. However, while art alone may not be able to guide us in the adjudication of moral disagreements, art certainly underscores the reality of such disagreements, and to the extent that it does, that is precisely what makes art morally useful. How so?

Art's moral pluralism is either no more than private expressions of how persons feel (a matter of their self-expression, personal desires or tastes, and individual choice) or is a reflection of our varied moral perceptions.[105] My contention has been for the latter, though in large measure the dichotomy between the two choices is a false one, as I have endeavored to demonstrate in this book, at least from an Edwardsean perspective. How one feels is very much up to how one is disposed or inclined, that is, to the state of one's inclination or affections; thus, how one might feel and thus choose is never unencumbered and self-generating. Accordingly, while art's moral pluralism reflects the varied moral perceptions that are brought to bear on the practices of reading, looking, and listening, such moral pluralism does not simply reflect "a cacophony of disparate claims."[106] As proposed in the preceding section, moral perceptions are sustained by (or gain their meaning within and from) particular social practices. This warrants thinking about our moral perceptions as indicative of the kind of social identities and loyalties we have and the patterns of relationships that give such identities and loyalties their normative force. Such a way of thinking about our moral perceptions warrants, in turn, thinking about our disparate moral perceptions as particular social snapshots, or stills of how a person and their community think of themselves socially, how they are socially positioned or regard themselves in relation to others, and thus their assumptions about justice and the good life. And when such disparate moral perceptions as social stills or photographs are assembled and viewed together, they provide a kaleidoscopic view and diagnosis of the state of our collective life. Thus, in this way we need not take all moral perceptions as morally commendable. Some moral perceptions may indeed be morally problematic, deserving critique and suspicion. We might find morally deplorable, for instance, the defacing of a sculpture meant to celebrate Black lives and promote antiracism.[107] But such a judgment, as appropriate as it is (at least in my view), is separable from how the moral perceptions motivating such aesthetic defacement ought not to be ignored but instead should be attended to seriously, for unless we take such motivating perceptions seriously, we would lack a clear-eyed view of the state of our affairs: that racial resentment is real and persists even in a self-described progressive community and that such resentment may reflect the deep unease of changing economic prospects and demographics (and thus the anxiety that comes with the dissolution of long-standing social and cultural hierarchies and diminished reverence for certain institutions such as those related to law enforcement). This judgment thus raises a host of difficult but necessary questions: Is such resentment intransigent? What kind of collective or common life is possible or not possible (or what would it take to form a common life)? And how shall we understand social progress?

Our moral discourse may indeed be fractured, and art's moral pluralism may serve to reinforce the point. Divergent moral opinions, discordant moral judgments, and even violence are not uncommon consequences of art. Add to those consequences responses of indifference, willful rejection, or condemnation of the object of one's looking, listening, or reading, and the pluralism that art effects only deepen. The reality of such pluralism or fracture upends what we might think is possible with good or great art, even beautiful art, or a classic or even socially conscious art or art that intends participation rather than intense personal contemplation. Good persons who are unmoved by what they aesthetically perceive and persons of questionable if not outright vile moral character who are enthused by what they are looking at, reading, or listening to are recurring images that I have struggled to make sense of throughout this book. But the reality of such pluralism—art's moral failures and successes—need not indicate that our moral discourse is hopeless, mired in mutually exclusive moral visions. There is much to be gained from attending to the reality of such fracture, acknowledging it soberly, and understanding its relational grounding, or so I hope to have shown. Taking such a reality seriously compels us to ask what is possible in the midst of such fracture, recommends social virtues appropriate to the persistence of such fracture, and thus draws us toward a more pragmatic, piecemeal, and provisional approach to moral reasoning and cooperation. It is this lesson in moral realism that makes art—our attunement to its moral pluralism—a particularly valuable source for the task of ethics. Art may not be powerful enough on its own to be an agent of moral transformation and social change, but it may, in its successes and failures, show us the kind of transformation that is needed or, more cautiously, possible (and the conditions required for such transformation to take hold) in a morally pluralistic world. At the heart of this change would be humility, not as a "habit of self-effacement" but instead a "selfless respect for reality."[108]

NOTES

1. Recall from chapter 4, Edwards, "Dissertation I," 417–35.
2. This is a premise underlying the notion of art that is considered "classic." See Cahill, *Sex, Gender, and Christian Ethics*, 70–71, which refers to Tracy, *Analogical Imagination: Christian Theology and the Culture of Pluralism*, 14, 102, 134.
3. Edwards, "A Treatise Concerning Religious Affections, in Three Parts," 291.
4. Wall, "Ethics, Knowledge, and the Need for Beauty," 758 (emphasis added).
5. Flores, *The Aesthetics of Solidarity*, 38.
6. Flores, 1.
7. Flores, 7.
8. In this context, consider Flores's aim to defend Roberto Goizueta's ethical assessment of the Guadalupe story from critics, such as Jorge Aquino, who think his rendering of emphatic fusion via the Lady of Guadalupe and Juan Diego relationship masks the problem of structural injustice. It is interesting that Flores aims to defend Goizueta not by rereading his account of Guadalupe in the Holy Week celebrations of San Fernando Cathedral in San Antonio, Texas, but instead through an interpretation of the play *The Miracle of Tepayac*. See Flores, *The Aesthetics of Solidarity*, 32; and Goizueta, *Caminemos con Jesús*, 30 and chap. 4.
9. Flores, *The Aesthetics of Solidarity*, 3, 24.
10. On experience as a theological-ethical source, see Gustafson, *Ethics from a Theocentric Perspective*, 115–56. See also Farley, "The Role of Experience in Moral Discernment," 134–51.
11. While it should be obvious by now that I think Eaton gets many things right about aesthetics and ethics, in raising this question I am signaling an area in which I diverge from her. I will parse out this divergence later in this chapter.
12. The following use of a literary example is in keeping with my earlier view that art can enhance particular notions, a position that will be elaborated in the following section. Thus, my use of literature here is a good example of the kind of work that literature and other art forms can do, but as I will show, it is also a good example of what art cannot do with respect to the moral life.
13. Wall, "Ethics, Knowledge, and the Need for Beauty," 760–61.
14. Smith, *On Beauty*, 442.
15. Smith, 443.
16. See, for instance, Wall, "Ethics, Knowledge, and the Need for Beauty," 761, 763–64, 774.
17. By moral theories I mean theories that tell us what persons are like and thus how they do what they do as well as normative theories that "tell us what to do." See Baier, *Postures of the Mind*, 232–33. Accounts of aesthetics and ethics we have encountered throughout this book are premised typically on both kinds of moral theories, descriptive and normative, in their attempts to argue for the moral salience of the arts; the

arguments are not simply "art is morally salient" but also "we ought to value art because art contributes to the moral life in this or that way."

18. Some accounts including that of William Spohn, discussed in chapter 1, are more explicit than others on this point given their view of the moral life as story shaped. Maria Antonaccio's advocacy of what she calls a reflexive model of literature, as we also saw in chapter 1, is similarly explicit since it corresponds to an account of moral reasoning that is indebted to Iris Murdoch's moral philosophy. Murdoch is rather explicit on this matter herself: "Art then is not a diversion or a side-issue, it is the most educational of all human activities and a place in which the nature of morality can be *seen*." Murdoch, "The Sovereignty of Good over Other Concepts," 85.
19. For instance, Merkle, *Discipleship, Secularity, and the Modern Self*, Part II, esp. chapters 5–9, where she proposes the "dance of discipleship." See also Pramuk, *The Artist Alive*. The turn to dance and music is distinguishable from those who prefer the narrative/literary arts over other kinds of art forms such as Spohn and Antonaccio (and Murdoch).
20. Currie, "Realism of Character and the Value of Fiction," 164.
21. Currie, 170.
22. Putnam, "Literature, Science, and Reflection," 87–90, cited in Eaton, *Aesthetics and the Good Life*, 159.
23. Currie, "Realism of Character and the Value of Fiction," 163.
24. Putnam, *Bowling Alone*, 134–36.
25. Putnam, 19.
26. See, for instance, Beuys, "Art Is Social Capital," 195 and 197. Beuys, an influential late twentieth-century German artist and key to the Fluxus art movement, argued in this interview that art, its creativity and appreciation and embrace as such, created alternative models of social connectedness that countered the corrosive models of relationship and thus "capital" in prevailing economic and political models, institutions, and systems. For more on Bueys's art and legacy, see Greenberger, "Why Jospeh Beuys's Mysterious Art Continues to Inspire—and Incense."
27. De Gruchy, *Christianity, Art and Transformation*, 200.
28. De Gruchy, 201.
29. De Gruchy, 204.
30. De Gruchy, 207.
31. Lee, "How the Arts Generate Social Capital to Foster Intergroup Social Cohesion."
32. Copeland, "Body, Representation, and Black Religious Discourse," 187.
33. Copeland, 189.
34. Copeland, 188.
35. Copeland, 194 (emphasis added).
36. ArtsFund, "Social Impact of the Arts Study." The bridging role of the arts is resonant with Robert Putnam's observation that social capital can both create in-group cohesiveness and mitigate out-group antagonism. See Putnam, *Bowling Alone*, 22–23.
37. ArtsFund, "Social Impact of the Arts Study," 4.
38. ArtsFund, 4 (emphasis added).
39. ArtsFund, 5.
40. The example of "social practice art," or art that fosters partnerships with the goal of social change, is yet another example of the importance of such reliance. An exhibit on social practice art in Chicago, *Toward Common Cause: Art, Social Change, and the MacArthur Fellows Program at 40*, almost failed to take place because its organizers struggled to secure

the kind of partnerships among artists that social practice art aims to foster. According to one of its organizers, this is why museums tend not to sponsor exhibitions of such an art form. See Loos, "Genius at Work."

41. Eaton, *Merit, Aesthetic and Ethical,* 135–36.
42. Eaton, 136.
43. Eaton, 135.
44. Eaton, 137.
45. Eaton, 136.
46. Eaton, 144.
47. Eaton, 141.
48. Eaton, 141 (emphasis added).
49. But that ought not to be taken to mean that certain kinds of moral lessons, or how certain moral lessons are aesthetically framed or presented, will resonate necessarily with particular experiential situations. So, consider the following comparison that Eaton makes: "Though the ethical content of some of Jan Vermeer's and Norman Rockwell's paintings are superficially alike, the intrinsic properties of their works makes all the difference. Rockwell's works are 'childish' and for that reason work better with the morally immature than do Vermeer's. It is intrinsic properties as well as subject matter (use of light, relation of shapes, ambiguities) that made it possible for a war crimes judge at the World Court in The Hague to report that it was the Vermeers in that city's Mauritshuis that regularly restored his faith in humanity" (Eaton, *Merit, Aesthetic and Ethical,* 145). But this assumes that the judge would have found Rockwell paintings uninspiring even if he had the chance to look at the paintings. And even if he had the chance and still maintained his indebtedness to Vermeer paintings, Eaton is perhaps too quick to think that Rockwell paintings work best for the "morally immature" given their straightforward representationalism rather than, say, a more challenging abstraction. Eaton takes a similar position with respect to children's books, such as the *Little Engine That Could,* to which she attributes its success with children to the kind of aesthetic form it takes. But are not children's books also appealing to adults and Norman Rockwell works also appealing to the morally mature, while adults, as much as teens and young adults, are enamored with "YA" novels? (On a side note, and recognizing that a personal anecdote cannot be taken as universally valid, on a recent visit to the Norman Rockwell Exhibition in Arlington, Vermont, my two children, ages nine and eleven at the time of this book's writing, were barely impressed with the pictures he painted between 1939 and 1953 in this small, quaint New England town. No matter my saying how interesting and "cool" they were, all I could manage out of them was something to the effect of the dutiful, perfunctory "they're nice." So much for Rockwell's aesthetic features appealing more to the "morally immature," perhaps.) My point is that saying art's success is linked to its resonance with one's lived experiences is not necessarily indicative of certain kinds of art being successful because they resonate with what are purportedly corresponding "life situations" (Eaton, *Merit, Aesthetic and Ethical,* 148). Life situations are indeed critical to art's success, but to go one step further and say that certain kinds of artworks (or certain aesthetic presentations) connect with particular life situations is descriptively too simplistic and conceptually begins to move in the opposite direction of the claim I am trying to make, that the power of art depends on one's experiential situation irrespective of the art in question (content or form). Those who are sad may not necessarily recoil at looking at muted color landscapes, as some may fear. See Stoppard, "What Should Hang on the Walls of a Hospital?"

50. We might find such an instance in Cooper, "Love Means Drawing Your Boyfriend 1000 Times."
51. Murdoch, "The Sovereignty of Good over Other Concepts," 82.
52. Eaton, *Merit, Aesthetic and Ethical*, 143 (emphases added).
53. Consider the government-funded project to add artwork (paintings and murals) in many parts of Mexico City. As one resident remarked of the artwork in her neighborhood, "'I love that the colors are so strong. . . . 'It gives it a lot of life.'" And yet, it is reported that the aim of the artwork—to decrease crime and violence—has not necessarily succeeded, with eight out of ten residents expressing that they feel unsafe. It is noteworthy that the positive response to the artwork is cojoined with residents' positive response to newly lit streets, further underscoring the question of whether a causative link can be made between art in the neighborhood and the increase or decrease of violence. Is it the brightly lit streets that residents enjoy or the art that surrounds them, or perhaps is their positive regard for the art due to the coinciding of better lit streets? Regardless, that the increase in artwork throughout many blighted Mexico City neighborhoods has not led to a marked turnaround in crime, especially femicide, underscores the challenges of conceptualizing the moral salience of art. As another resident remarked, "'Paint helps a lot, but sadly it can't change the reality of social problems. . . . A mural isn't going to change whether you care about the woman being beat up on the corner.'" See Lopez, "Frida Kahlo, Aztec Gods."
54. Stout, *Democracy and Tradition*, 218.
55. Stout, 219.
56. Stout, 220. Reports of Japanese athletes who fell just short of the gold medal at the 2021 Summer Olympics in Tokyo and profusely apologizing to their fellow Japanese citizens for such "failure" are indicative of the formative nature of social practices and its corresponding norms. "From an early age, Japanese athletes 'are not really supposed to think like they are playing sports for themselves. . . . Especially in childhood, there are expectations from adults, teachers, parents or other senior people. So it's kind of a deeply rooted mindset.' . . . In some respects, these athletes have offered an extreme form of the apologies that are everyday social lubricants in Japanese culture." Rich, "Second Best in the World, but Still Saying Sorry."
57. Stout, *Democracy and Tradition*, 221.
58. Stout, 212.
59. For an assessment of Stout's defense of democracy and defenses of this defense, see Tran, "Assessing the Augustinian Democrats."
60. Stout, *Democracy and Tradition*, 221.
61. Stout, 219.
62. Stout, 219.
63. Stout, 220.
64. Stout, 219.
65. Gustafson, *Ethics from a Theocentric Perspective*, 115. Sociality is taken up under the theme of participation in Gustafson, "Participation."
66. Stout, *Democracy and Tradition*, 216.
67. Stout, 222.
68. Stout, 217.
69. As Justice Stewart asserted with respect to sexually obscene content, "I know it when I see it." See his concurring majority opinion in *Jacobellis v. Ohio* (1964), 378 U.S. at 197.

70. Darlene Fozard Weaver makes a similar case for the epistemological importance of moral diversity but within the context of contemporary Roman Catholic debates on a variety of highly charged social issues, especially surrounding LGBTQ+ recognition. See Weaver, "Christian Formation and Moral Pluralism"; and Weaver, "Church Ethics for a Morally Diverse World."
71. Cahill, "Nature, Change, and Justice," 291.
72. This is how MacIntyre would characterize difference in modernity, as functions of irrational emotivism. See MacIntyre, *After Virtue*, chap. 2 and 3. See also Stout, *Democracy and Tradition*, 123.
73. Cahill, "Natural Law," 82.
74. Cahill, 89.
75. Cahill claims this as a Thomistic fact: "'Practical truth,' the truth of practical reason, 'arises only within contingent states of affairs,' and by means of an 'inevitable choice between competing options.' Aquinas thus generalizes the basic principles of the natural law from inclinations and patterns of behavior that all societies experience as contributing to human flourishing (preserving life, rearing young, cooperating socially) (ST 1–2, q. 94, a. 2), with applications depending in part on circumstances and cultural settings." Cahill, "Toward Global Ethics," 333.
76. Cahill, "Natural Law," 86.
77. On social positionality as a form of social commentary or critique, see Young, "Difference as a Resource for Democratic Communication." See also Young, *Justice and the Politics of Difference*, 185–86, 189, and chap. 4.
78. I am riffing on a similar event near my hometown at a local arboretum inviting the public to "fall in love" with its trees and gardens.
79. Stout, *Democracy and Tradition*, 123. This is Stout's description of MacIntyre's characterization of modern moral discourse.
80. As Iris Marion Young notes, "Group differences are manifest not only in different needs, interests, and goals, but also in different social locations and experiences. People in different groups often know about somewhat different institutions, events, practices, and social relations, and often have differing perceptions of the *same* institutions, relations, or events." Young, *Justice and the Politics of Difference*, 186 (emphasis added). The key here is that while there may be differing perceptions, they pertain to common "objects" that concern all persons within a community (i.e., they all have vested interests in the same "institutions, relations, or events").
81. I take intellectual hospitality as the companion to David Hollenbach's virtue of intellectual solidarity. See Hollenbach, *Christian Ethics and the Common Good*, chap. 6. Hollenbach's intellectual solidarity builds on John Courtney Murray's emphasis on conversation as the key to holding differences together. See Heyer, "The Idea of the Common Good."
82. For Brian Stiltner, this is precisely why the common good is not threatened by moral pluralism, "'because different communities center on the pursuit of different components of the complex human good . . . and because no one association can claim to be a perfect community.'" Stiltner, *Religion and the Common Good*, 178, cited in Heyer, "The Idea of the Common Good," 7–8.
83. Young, *Justice and the Politics of Difference*, 186.
84. I am alluding to Cahill, "Nature, Change, and Justice," 291.

85. Stout draws the decoration/clothing imagery from Burke. See Stout, *Democracy and Tradition*, 223–24.
86. On Stout's indebtedness to Whitman in particular, see Stout, *Democracy and Tradition*, 19–41.
87. Albertson and Blakely, "From Here to Utopia." Cf. Bordeyne, "The Ethical Horizon of Liturgy"; Morrill, *Anamnesis as Dangerous Memory*; Saliers, "Liturgy and Ethics"; Saliers, "Afterword"; Saliers, "For the Sake of the World"; and Tillard, *Flesh of the Church, Flesh of the Christ*.
88. Albertson and Blakely, "From Here to Utopia." We might say that their reluctance is ultimately tempered by their commitment to what Xavier M. Montecel refers to as the "correlational model" of liturgy and ethics: "This model proceeds on the basic assumption that there is or ought to be a meaningful correlation between the practice of liturgy and the shape of human life. There is, in other words, a transferability of meanings between the realm of liturgical action and the realm of moral action." Montecel, "Liturgy, Virtue, and the Foundations of an Ecclesial Ethics," 402. But to the extent Albertson and Blakely think that at minimum liturgy can provide "arresting examples of creative communal living," they seem to shift from a correlational model to what Montecel refers to as the "pedagogical model" of liturgy and ethics: "As members of that body [a church that worships together liturgically], we are trained by liturgy into a Christian way of seeing and way of being." Montecel, "Liturgy, Virtue, and the Foundations of an Ecclesial Ethics," 403.
89. Thus, this is not a discounting of the importance of Christian worship; far from it. But it is to suggest that the directionality of worship to ethical transformation is not as direct as Albertson and Blakely suggest. I would propose that it is more of a sustaining role, an affirmation of the transformative work that is under way.
90. Elizabeth Agnew Cochran employs the language of reception in her characterization of Edwards's account of Christian virtue. See Cochran, *Receptive Human Virtues*.
91. Edwards, "A Treatise Concerning Religious Affections, in Three Parts," 358.
92. Edwards, 368.
93. Edwards, 368.
94. This is a rephrase of Stout, *Democracy and Tradition*, 222. See also Edwards, "A Treatise Concerning Religious Affections, in Three Parts," 393.
95. Edwards, "A Treatise Concerning Religious Affections, in Three Parts," 365.
96. Edwards, 367.
97. Edwards, 365.
98. For a systematic account of beauty and God's nature in Edwards's thought, see Delattre, *Beauty and Sensibility in the Thought of Jonathan Edwards*.
99. De Gruchy, *Christianity, Art and Transformation*, 198–99.
100. Adorno, "Aesthetic Theory," 359, 363. Compare this with James Baldwin's claim: "Art is here to prove, and to help one bear, the fact that all safety is an illusion. In this sense, all artists are divorced from and even necessarily opposed to any system whatsoever." Baldwin, "The Artist's Struggle for Integrity," 51. Thus, art has the capacity to be reactionary to or be an indictment of both liberal- and conservative-leaning values, as exemplified by the art of Neo Rauch. See Meaney, "The Antagonist."
101. MacIntyre, *Ethics in the Conflicts of Modernity*, 144.
102. MacIntyre, 146.

103. MacIntyre, 144.
104. On the traditionalism of MacIntyre's advocacy of the virtues, see Baier, *Postures of the Mind*, 246–62; and Stout, *Democracy and Tradition*, 118–39. See also Okin, *Justice, Gender, and the Family*, chap. 3.
105. This is the dichotomy that MacIntyre sets up in trying to make the case for the necessity of Aristotelian virtues in *Ethics in the Conflicts of Modernity*, 141–46.
106. Stout, *Democracy and Tradition*, 118.
107. See, for instance, Hogan, "Vandal Splatters Gray Paint on George Floyd Bust in Union Square [New York City]."
108. Murdoch, "The Sovereignty of Good over Other Concepts," 93.

CODA

ON SIN AND ART'S MORAL PLURALISM

One might point out that the kind of pluralism I have identified in this book with respect to art's effects is explainable, perhaps rather plainly, by the reality of sin. More specifically, to the extent that our disordered will distorts our moral vision, art's moral failures (its unpredictability in actualizing a particular moral intent or end), should be expected. Such an opinion would for sure not be without Edwardsean warrant. As we have seen, for Jonathan Edwards sin is an inwardness to preserve only one's own life, one's own interests, and an undue flattery of what one thinks one knows and is able to do; consequently, sin is "destructive in its nature."[1]

Such a view of the self under the yoke of sin has a long legacy and not just among Christian thinkers. Iris Murdoch too takes the position that we are "naturally selfish," so much so that we are "predisposed to certain patterns of activity." One can imagine Edwards nodding in agreement when she further states, "The psyche is a historically determined individual relentlessly looking after itself. . . . It is reluctant to face unpleasant realities."[2] Beauty and art may interrupt this inwardness, hence her feeling, as noted at the end of chapter 1, that a good artist may not be a wise person but nevertheless may have a head start in the direction of moral change.[3] However, unselfishness and seeing the world as it exists is a struggle: "The difficulty is to keep attention fixed upon the real situation and to prevent it from returning surreptitiously to the self with consolations of self-pity, resentment, fantasy and despair."[4]

With that in mind, it may very well be the case that art's moral failures—our inability to find and grasp the right moral meanings in it or to be affected by its social aims (at least with art that has such aims or intentions)—are indicative of our selfishness, our penchant for misperception. We therefore should not assume, as Murdoch can be quick to do, that perceiving art—especially great art, as she puts it, or even something as aesthetically simple as a flying kestrel—necessarily initiates a process of unselfing.[5] Maybe for some persons that has indeed been the case; catching a glimpse of a new art exhibit while walking past a gallery during a lunch break provided the occasion to obsess less about their projects, daily tasks, or worries, providing them with a much-needed mental and emotional reset. But as Murdoch also hints, such unselfing is not routine, and unselfing can be mistaken for the way that perceiving art can also draw our attention to other desires, feelings, or even anxieties; on this account, art would not necessarily draw our attention away from ourselves but instead would draw it toward other parts of ourselves that may be equally self-involving. The "brooding self"—over a ding to one's reputation, to invoke Murdoch's example—may not be less brooding after perceiving great art, or a "hovering kestrel," but may find inspiration to overcome one's source of hurt by scheming for ways to eliminate one's competition. Aesthetic perception is therefore not inevitably "a self-forgetful pleasure,"[6] and the tug of inwardness or selfishness on our moral psyche ought not to be underestimated, even more so given the ways this tug toward one's own self can be exacerbated, reinforced, and encouraged by sinful social structures.[7] So, as I have been arguing all along, we should expect that art leads to a variety of moral outcomes, that it is necessarily a site for differences of opinion and also moral discord rather than consensus and mutual understanding. Great and beautiful art may not necessarily lead to moral goodness; it may lead just as much to vice.

But when under the influence of grace, the situation is different, perhaps radically different, or so one might argue further (though those who follow Murdoch would demure on the notion of divine grace per se; her preference is for the "Good" and thus a moral philosophy that retains central characteristics of such a notion of divine grace but without the divine.)[8] While for the unregenerate its misperceptions and moral failures are the rule, for the regenerate art will be morally successful. Art's moral successes are therefore what we should expect as a rule, and art's moral failures should only be counted as exceptions to that rule.

This may indeed be taken sympathetically from an Edwardsean point of view. We saw in chapter 4 how Edwards cast doubt on what a beautiful object, shape, or countenance can provide in terms of right perception.[9] All creation is a sign (or shadow) of the glory of God,[10] and while persons by virtue of their nature and principles common to their nature could gain some understanding of God's glory, such understanding would always fall short (it will always be a shadow or image) without grace.[11] This is particularly so with respect to scripture. For Edwards, the "manner" in which instruction about scripture is given makes all the difference;[12] if it is not immediately from grace, resulting in "a change of nature," then right understanding is not possible.[13] "When the mind is enlightened spiritually and rightly to understand the Scripture, it is enabled to see that in the Scripture, which was before not seen, by reason of blindness."[14]

For Edwards, however, there is no expectation to be had that even the regenerate would be able to perceive correctly as a matter of course, as if it were a kind of "law" of grace. He was ever so vigilant of sin's persistence that he went so far as to caution against assuming that one's perception is righteous even if one seems to be saying all the right things, especially with respect to the Gospel.[15] Citing 1 Corinthians 13:2, Edwards warned that just as Christians in Corinth boasted of their gift of prophecy but lacked love, we too—all of us—are liable of hubris.[16] Thus, we do well to note that even in Christian community, divisions are not to be considered unlikely. As the apostle Paul lamented at the very outset of 1 Corinthians, "For it has been reported to me by Chloe's people that there are quarrels among you, my brothers and sisters. What I mean is that each of you says, 'I belong to Paul,' or 'I belong to Apollos,' or 'I belong to Cephas,' or 'I belong to Christ.' Has Christ been divided?" (1 Corinthians 1:11–13, NRSV).

Knowing what constitutes right or wrong perception is one thing, but it is another thing to be quick to judge that one is in fact perceiving self, world, and God as one should be, an important distinction that has ramifications for the kind of posture we ought to adopt in community. For Edwards, that we perceive rightly could not be known apart from at least close critical introspection, particularly on the quality of our moral practice. This has to be the case, because theologically speaking, while there is a resemblance between graced perception and natural perception (perception by virtue of our common humanity), which speaks to the world (and all of existence for that matter) as God's creative act and thus yearning to be rightly ordered to and in God,[17] that resemblance can also be a liability of sorts, making discernment of graced perception a trickier task than one might want it to be.[18] Thus, some may claim to perceive rightly, but it may only be a semblance. And those who indeed perceive rightly will manifest such perception in the kind of moral practice that necessarily corresponds to it, with sincerity and constancy. The reality of sin only compounds this expectation of moral pluralism; that, in the end, is the rule rather than the exception. As Edwards observes,

> Selfishness is a principle natural to us, and indeed all the corruption of nature does radically consist in it. . . . We in this land are trained up from generation to generation in a too . . . selfish spirit and practice; and notwithstanding all our professions of religion, and though there

are many good things done which are worthy to be commended, yet without doubt we do in general come vastly short of what is required of Christians in the New Testament.[19]

Accordingly, the task before us is to recognize the need for humility, resist hubris, and bear one another with patience, all of which befit a reality of discord that endures in the hope of reformation. "Humility, meekness, love, forgiveness, and mercy. These things . . . especially belong to the character of Christians," and the "benefits we thereby receive" are "the relation that it brings us into, to God and one another."[20] But some version of such virtues are also fitting for non-Christians as well insofar as the truth of things will always be limited and partial, a semblance for all persons absent the fullness of grace, of God's own work in bringing all things to Godself, to God's glory.

NOTES

1. Edwards, "Sinners in the Hands of an Angry God," 92–94.
2. Murdoch, "The Sovereignty of Good over Other Concepts," 76–77.
3. Murdoch, "The Sovereignty of Good over Other Concepts," 94.
4. Murdoch, "The Sovereignty of Good over Other Concepts," 89.
5. The text of Murdoch's famous reference to seeing a kestrel and unselfing begins with a reference to Plato's *Phaedrus* and then proceeds thusly: "Beauty is the convenient and traditional name of something which art and nature share, and which gives a fairly clear sense to the idea of quality of experience arid change of consciousness. I am looking out of my window in an anxious and resentful state of mind, oblivious of my surroundings, brooding perhaps on some damage done to my prestige. Then suddenly I observe a hovering kestrel. In a moment everything is alerted. The brooding self with its hurt vanity has disappeared. There is nothing now but kestrel. And when I return to thinking of the other matter it seems less important." Murdoch, "The Sovereignty of Good over Other Concepts," 82.
6. Murdoch, "The Sovereignty of Good over Other Concepts," 83.
7. On sin and social structures (or social sin), see Heyer, *Kinship across Border*; Daly, *The Structures of Virtue and Vice*; and Finn, *Moral Agency within Social Structures and Culture*.
8. Murdoch, "On 'God' and 'Good,'" 54.
9. See Edwards, "A Treatise Concerning Religious Affections, in Three Parts," 267.
10. Edwards, "Images of Divine Things," 16.
11. See, for instance, Edwards, "A Divine and Supernatural Light," 108–9; and Edwards, "A Treatise Concerning Religious Affections, in Three Parts," 276.
12. Edwards, "A Treatise Concerning Religious Affections, in Three Parts," 268.
13. Edwards, 285.
14. Edwards, 280.
15. Edwards, 278. Hence Edwards's refined attunement to the resemblance of natural goodness and spiritual goodness: "Thus sometimes, under common illuminations, men are

raised with the ideas of the natural good that is in heaven. . . . So there are many things exhibited in the gospel, concerning God and Christ, and the way of salvation, that have a natural good in them, which suits the natural principle of self-love. . . . All that love which natural men have to God, and Christ and Christian virtues, and good men, [however,] is not from any sight of the amiableness of the holiness, or true moral excellency of these things; but only for the sake of the natural good there is in them." Edwards, "A Treatise Concerning Religious Affections, in Three Parts," 277. On the scope of natural capacities for moral goodness, see Edwards, "Dissertation II." The resemblance between the natural and supernatural does not negate the legitimacy and necessity of the former but does demand that judgments of goodness—that is, whether one is indeed led by genuine moral perception and, correlatively, genuine religious affections—requires, as I noted in chapter 4 and reiterate below, close discernment of one's motivations, intentions, and actions.

16. Edwards, "A Treatise Concerning Religious Affections, in Three Parts," 278–79. For a particularly vivid description of the tug of sin and the struggle against it, see Edwards, "Images of Divine Things": "Just thus, oftentimes sinners under the gospel are bewitched by their lusts. They have considerable fears of destruction and remorse of conscience that makes 'em hang back, and they have a great deal of exercise between while, and some partial reformations, but yet they don't fell away. They won't wholly forsake their beloved lusts, but return to 'em again; and so whatever warnings they have, and whatever checks of conscience that may exercise 'em and make [them] go back a little and stand off for a while, yet they will keep their beloved sin in sight, and won't utterly break off from it and forsake [it], but will return to it again and again, and go a little further and a little further, until Satan remedilessly makes a prey of them. But if anyone comes and kills the serpent, the animal immediately escapes. So the way in which poor souls are delivered from the snare of the devil is by Christ's coming and bruising the serpent's head." Edwards, "Images of Divine Things," 18.
17. Edwards, "Dissertation I."
18. Edwards, "Dissertation II," 609–18.
19. Edwards, "Charity and Its Fruits," 271.
20. Edwards, "A Treatise Concerning Religious Affections, in Three Parts," 346.

BIBLIOGRAPHY

Adorno, Theodor W. "Aesthetic Theory." In *Aesthetics: A Comprehensive Anthology*, edited by Steven M. Cahn and Aaron Meskin, 358–75. Malden, MA: Blackwell Publishing, 2008.

Adorno, Theodor W. *The Culture Industry*. Abington, UK: Routledge, 2001.

Albertson, David, and Jason Blakely. "From Here to Utopia: What Religion Can Teach the Left." *Commonweal*, May 24, 2021. https://www.commonwealmagazine.org/here-utopia.

Alexander, Kathyrn B. *Saving Beauty: A Theological Aesthetics of Nature*. Minneapolis, MN: Augsburg Fortress, 2014.

Antonaccio, Maria. "The Consolations of Literature." *Journal of Religion* 80, no. 4 (October 2000): 615–44.

Antonaccio, Maria. *Picturing the Human: The Moral Thought of Iris Murdoch*. New York: Oxford University Press, 2000.

Aquinas, Thomas. *Summa Theologica*. 5 vols. Translated by the Fathers of the Dominican Province. New York: Benzinger Bros., 1948.

Aquinas, Thomas. *Treatise on the Virtues*. Translated by John. A. Oesterle. Notre Dame, IN: University of Notre Dame Press, 1966.

Arenson, Karen W. "An Artwork at Yale May Not be Real, but the Furor Is." *New York Times*, April 23, 2008. https://www.nytimes.com/2008/04/23/nyregion/23yale.html.

ArtsFund. "Social Impact of the Arts Study: How Arts Impact King County Communities." 2018. https://www.artsfund.org/wp-content/uploads/2018/11/ArtsFund_2018_SIS_11.6.pdf.

Baier, Annette. *Postures of the Mind: Essays on Mind and Morals*. Minneapolis: University of Minnesota Press, 1985.

Baldwin, James. "The Artist's Struggle for Integrity." In *The Cross of Redemption: Uncollected Writings*, ed. Randall Kenan, 50–58. New York: Vintage International, 2010.

Baldwin, James, Emile Capouya, Lorraine Hansberry, Nat Hentoff, Langston Hughes, and Alfred Kazin. "The Negro in American Culture." *CrossCurrents* 11, no. 3 (Summer 1961): 205–24.

Barbeau, Jeffrey W., and Emily Hunter McGowin, eds. *God and Wonder: Theology, Imagination, and the Arts*. Eugene, OR: Cascade Books, 2022.

Barrett, Lisa Feldman. "Are Emotions Natural Kinds?" *Perspectives in Psychological Science* 1, no. 1 (March 2006): 28–58.

Barrett, Lisa Feldman. *How Emotions Are Made: The Secret Life of the Brain.* New York: Houghton Mifflin Harcourt, 2017.

Baumgarten, Alexander G. Ästhetik. 2 vols. Translated by Dagmar Mirback. Hamburg, Germany: Feliz Meiner, 2007.

Bell, Clive. *Art.* New York: Frederick A. Stokes, 1914.

Berman, Art. *From the New Criticism to Deconstruction: The Reception of Structuralism and Post-Structuralism.* Urbana: University of Illinois Press, 1988.

Bernstein, J. M. "Introduction." In *The Culture Industry*, by Theodor W. Adorno. Abington, UK: Routledge, 2001.

Beuys, Joseph. "Art Is Social Capital: Toward Economy of Social Art." Interview by Dusan Bjelic in *Dijaløzí*, March 1982. https://www.academia.edu/9717364/Art_is_Social_Capital_Toward_Economy_of_Social_Art_Interview_with_Joseph_Beuys.

Bois, Yve-Alain. "Painting as Trauma." *Art in America* 76, no. 6 (1988): 130–73.

Bordeyne, Philippe. "The Ethical Horizon of Liturgy." In *Sacraments: Revelation of the Humanity of God*, edited by Philippe Bordeyne and Bruce T. Morrill, 119–36. Collegeville, MN: Liturgical Press, 2008.

Bowley, Graham. "What If Trump Really Does End Money for the Arts?" *New York Times*, March 16, 2017. https://www.nytimes.com/2017/01/30/arts/design/donald-trump-arts-humanities-public-television.html.

Braidwood, Ella. "The Love Boom: Why Romance Novels Are the Biggest They've Been for 10 years." *The Guardian*, December 13, 2022. https://www.theguardian.com/books/2022/dec/13/love-boom-romance-novels-biggest-10-years-young-readers.

Bromwich, David. *Moral Imagination: Essays.* Princeton, NJ: Princeton University Press, 2014.

Brown, Frank Burch. *Religious Aesthetics: A Theological Study of Making and Meaning.* Princeton, NJ: Princeton University Press, 1989.

Burch, Audra D. S. "How 17 Outsize Portraits Rattled a Small Southern Town." *New York Times*, January 19, 2020. https://www.nytimes.com/2020/01/19/us/newnan-art-georgia-race.html.

Butler, Judith. *Precarious Life: The Power of Mourning and Violence.* Brooklyn, NY: Verso, 2004.

Cahill, Lisa Sowle. "Nature, Change, and Justice." In *Without Nature? A New Condition for Theology*, edited by David Albertson and Cabell King, 282–303. New York: Fordham University Press, 2010.

Cahill, Lisa Sowle. "Toward Global Ethics." *Theological Studies* 63, no. 2 (2002): 324–44.

Cahill, Lisa Sowle. "Natural Law: A Feminist Reassessment." In *Is There a Human Nature?*, edited by Leroy S. Rouner, 80–93. Boston University Studies in Philosophy and Religion 18. Notre Dame, IN: Notre Dame University Press, 1997.

Cahill, Lisa Sowle. *Sex, Gender, and Christian Ethics.* Cambridge: Cambridge University Press, 1996.

Campbell, Sarah Fay. "Seeing Newnan: Outsize Portraits of Everyday People." *Newnan-Times Herald*, May 29, 2019. https://times-herald.com/news/2019/03/seeing-newnan-outsize-portraits-of-everyday-people.

Carroll, Noël. "Art, Narrative, and Moral Reasoning." In *Aesthetics and Ethics: Essays at the Intersection*, edited by Jerrold Levinson, 126–60. Cambridge: Cambridge University Press, 1998.

Cassidy, Laurie. "Picturing Suffering: The Moral Dilemnas in Gazing at Photographs of Human Anguish." In *She Who Imagines: Feminist Theological Aesthetics*, edited by Laurie Cassidy and Maureen H. O'Connell, 103–23. Collegeville, MN: Liturgical Press.

Castronovo, Russ. *Beautiful Democracy: Aesthetics and Anarchy in a Global Era.* Chicago: University of Chicago Press, 2007.

Cates, Diana Fritz. *Aquinas on the Emotions: A Religious-Ethical Inquiry*. Washington, DC: Georgetown University Press, 2009.

Cates, Diana Fritz. "The Religious Dimension of Ordinary Human Emotions." *Journal of the Society of Christian Ethics* 25, no. 1 (Spring/Summer 2005): 35–53.

Cavell, Marcia. "Taste and Moral Sense." In *Ethics and the Arts*, edited by David Fenner, 293–302. New York: Garland, 1996.

Cep, Casey. "Reading the Old Testament while Pregnant." *New Yorker*, July 7, 2021. https://www.newyorker.com/books/second-read/reading-the-old-testament-while-pregnant.

Choi, Ki Joo. "The Role of Perception in Jonathan Edwards's Moral Thought: *The Nature of True Virtue* Reconsidered." *Journal of Religious Ethics* 38, no. 2 (June 2010): 269–96.

City News Service. "San Diego Proposes Major Budget Cuts to Offset COVID-19 Revenue Losses." KPBS, April 15, 2020. https://www.kpbs.org/news/2020/apr/15/san-diego-proposes-major-budget-cuts-offset-covid-/.

Cochran, Elizabeth Agnew. *Receptive Human Virtues: A New Reading of Jonathan Edwards's Ethics*. University Park: Pennsylvania State University Press, 2011.

Cooper, James. "Love Means Drawing Your Boyfriend 1000 Times." *New York Times*, August 10, 2021. https://www.nytimes.com/2021/08/10/opinion/drawings-of-my-bf-love.html.

Copeland, M. Shawn. "Body, Representation, and Black Religious Discourse." In *Postcolonialism, Feminism, and Religious Discourse*, edited by Laura E. Donalson and Kwok Pui-lan, 180–98. New York: Routledge, 2002.

Cotter, Holland. "Portraits in Zen, from Celestial to Comic." *New York Times*, April 13, 2007. https://www.nytimes.com/2007/04/06/arts/design/06zen.html.

Crain, Caleb. "Why We Don't Read, Revisited." *New Yorker*. June 14, 2018. https://www.newyorker.com/culture/cultural-comment/why-we-dont-read-revisited.

Crisp, Oliver D., and Kyle C. Strobel. *Jonathan Edwards: An Introduction to His Thought*. Grand Rapids, MI: William B. Eerdmans, 2018.

Crocco, Stephen D. "Edwards's Intellectual Legacy." In *The Cambridge Companion to Jonathan Edwards*, edited by Stephen J. Stein, 300–324. Cambridge: Cambridge University Press, 2007.

Cronan, Todd. *Against Aesthetic Formalism: Matisse, Bergson, Modernism*. Minneapolis: University of Minneapolis Press, 2013.

Currie, Gregory. "Realism of Character and the Value of Fiction." In *Aesthetics and Ethics: Essays at the Intersection*, edited by Jerrold Levinson, 161–81. Cambridge: Cambridge University Press, 1998.

Curtin, Deane W. "Varieties of Aesthetic Formalism." *Journal of Aesthetics and Art Criticism* 40, no. 3 (Spring 1982): 315–26.

Dafoe, Taylor. "Arts Leaders Fear Philadelphia's Planned Budget Cuts Will Completely 'Decimate the Grassroots Cultural Scene.'" Artnet News, May 7, 2020. https://news.artnet.com/art-world/philadelphia-mayor-proposes-cutting-arts-1855992.

Dafoe, Taylor. "Bill De Blasio's 2021 Budget Would See a Significant Decrease in Funding for New York's Museums, Already Hit Hard by the Lockdown." Artnet News, April 20, 2020. https://news.artnet.com/art-world/new-yorks-proposed-budget-next-year-see-significant-decrease-funding-museums-1839228.

Dahl, Robert A. *On Democracy*. New Haven, CT: Yale University Press, 2000.

Daly, Daniel. *The Structures of Virtue and Vice*. Washington, DC: Georgetown University Press, 2021.

Dante. *La vita nuova*. Translated by Mark Musa. New York: Oxford University Press, 1992.

Danto, Arthur C. "The Artworld." *Journal of Philosophy* 61 (1964): 571–84.

Davidson, Justin. "High Culture Brought Low." Vulture, June 22–July 5, 2020. https://www.vulture.com/2020/06/the-precarious-future-of-the-performing-arts.html.

de Bolla, Peter. *Art Matters*. Cambridge, MA: Harvard University Press, 2001.

De Gruchy, John W. "Art, Morality, and Justice." In *The Oxford Handbook of Religion and the Arts*, edited by Frank Burch Brown, 418–32. Oxford: Oxford University Press, 2014.

De Gruchy, John W. *Christianity, Art and Transformation: Theological Aesthetics in the Struggle for Justice*. Cambridge: Cambridge University Press, 2001.

Delattre, Roland A. *Beauty and Sensibility in the Thought of Jonathan Edwards: An Essay in Aesthetics and Theological Ethics*. New Haven, CT: Yale University Press, 1968.

Delattre, Roland A. "Religious Ethics Today: Jonathan Edwards, H. Richard Niebuhr, and Beyond," in *Edwards in Our Time: Jonathan Edwards and the Shaping of American Religion*, edited by Sang Hyun Lee and Allen C. Guelzo, 67–86. Grand Rapids, MI: William B. Eerdmans, 1999.

Deleuze, Gilles. *Francis Bacon: The Logic of Sensation*. Translated by Daniel W. Smith. Minneapolis: University of Minnesota Press, 2004.

Dewey, John. "Art as Experience." In *Aesthetics: A Comprehensive Anthology*, edited by Steven M. Cahn and Aaron Meskin, 296–316. Malden, MA: Blackwell, 2008.

Duhart, Bill. "What Is Art All Night? Event Celebrating Togetherness Marred by Shooting in Trenton." Nj.com, January 30, 2019. https://www.nj.com/mercer/2018/06/what_is_art_all_night_and_what_has_it_meant_to_tre.html.

Dyrness, William A. *Visual Faith: Art, Theology, and Worship in Dialogue*. Grand Rapids, MI: Baker Academic, 2001.

Dziemidok, Bohdan. "Artistic Formalism: Its Achievements and Weaknesses." *Journal of Aesthetics and Art Criticism* 51, no. 2 (1993): 185–93.

Eaton, Marcia Muelder. *Aesthetics and the Good Life*. Cranford, NJ: Associated University Presses, 1989.

Eaton, Marcia Muelder. *Merit, Aesthetic and Ethical*. New York: Oxford University Press, 2001.

Edelman, Murray. *From Art to Politics: How Artistic Creations Shape Political Conceptions*. Chicago: University of Chicago Press, 1994.

Edwards, Jonathan. "A Careful and Strict Enquiry into the Modern Prevailing Notions of That Freedom of the Will." In *The Works of Jonathan Edwards*, Vol. 1, *Freedom of the Will*, edited by Paul Ramsey, 135–439. New Haven, CT: Yale University Press, 1985.

Edwards, Jonathan. "Charity and Its Fruits." In *The Works of Jonathan Edwards*, Vol. 8, *Ethical Writings*, edited by Paul Ramsey, 123–397. New Haven, CT: Yale University Press, 1989.

Edwards, Jonathan. "Dissertation I: Concerning the End for Which God Created the World." In *The Works of Jonathan Edwards*, Vol. 8, *Ethical Writings*, edited by Paul Ramsey, *The Works of Jonathan Edwards*, 403–536. New Haven, CT: Yale University Press, 1989.

Edwards, Jonathan. "Dissertation II: The Nature of True Virtue." In *The Works of Jonathan Edwards*, Vol. 8, *Ethical Writings*, edited by Paul Ramsey, 537–627. New Haven, CT: Yale University Press, 1989.

Edwards, Jonathan. "The Distinguishing Marks of a Work of the Spirit of God." In *The Great Awakening*, Vol. 4, *The Works of Jonathan Edwards*, edited by C. C. Goen, 213–88. New Haven, CT: Yale University Press, 1972).

Edwards, Jonathan. "A Divine and Supernatural Light." In *A Jonathan Edwards Reader*, edited by John E. Smith, Harry S. Stout, and Kenneth P. Minkema, 105–24. New Haven, CT: Yale University Press, 1995.

Edwards, Jonathan, "The Great Christian Doctrine of Original Sin Defended." In *The Works of Jonathan Edwards*, Vol. 3, *Original Sin*, edited by Clyde A. Holbrook, 105–437. New Haven, CT: Yale University Press, 1970.

Edwards, Jonathan. "Images of Divine Things." In *A Jonathan Edwards Reader*, edited by John E. Smith, Harry S. Stout, and Kenneth P. Minkema, 16–21. New Haven, CT: Yale University Press, 1995.

Edwards, Jonathan. "Miscellanies" 101. In *The Works of Jonathan Edwards*, Vol. 13, *The "Miscellanies,"* edited by Thomas A. Schafer, 269–270. New Haven, CT: Yale University Press, 1994.

Edwards, Jonathan. "Sinners in the Hands of an Angry God." In *A Jonathan Edwards Reader*, edited by John E. Smith, Harry S. Stout, and Kenneth P. Minkema, 89–105. New Haven, CT: Yale University Press, 1995.

Edwards, Jonathan. "Some Thoughts Concerning the Revival." In *The Works of Jonathan Edwards*, Vol. 4, *The Great Awakening*, edited by C. C. Goen, 289–530. New Haven, CT: Yale University Press, 1972.

Edwards, Jonathan. "To the Rev. Thomas Prince of Boston." In *The Works of Jonathan Edwards*, Vol. 4, *The Great Awakening*, edited by C. C. Goen, 544–57. New Haven, CT: Yale University Press, 1972.

Edwards, Jonathan. "A Treatise Concerning Religious Affections, in Three Parts." In *The Works of Jonathan Edwards*, Vol. 2, *Religious Affections*, edited by John E. Smith, 91–461. New Haven, CT: Yale University Press, 1959.

Elie, Paul. "Everything That Rises: How Racist Was Flannery O'Connor?" *New Yorker*, June 15, 2020. https://www.newyorker.com/magazine/2020/06/22/how-racist-was-flannery-oconnor.

Ellison, Ralph. "The Novel as a Function of American Democracy." In *The Collected Essays of Ralph Ellison*, edited by John F. Callahan, 759–69. New York: Modern Library/Random House, 2003.

Ellison, Ralph. "A Very Stern Discipline." In *The Collected Essays of Ralph Ellison*, edited by John F. Callahan, 730–58. New York: Modern Library/Random House, 2003.

Ewing, Eve L. "Why Authoritarians Attack the Arts." *New York Times*, April 6, 2017. https://www.nytimes.com/2017/04/06/opinion/why-authoritarians-attack-the-arts.html?searchResultPosition=1.

Farley, Edward. *Faith and Beauty: A Theological Aesthetic.* Aldershot, UK: Ashgate, 2001.

Farley, Margaret A. "The Role of Experience in Moral Discernment." In *Christian Ethics: Problems and Prospects*, edited by Lisa Sowle Cahill and James F. Childress, 134-51. Cleveland, OH: Pilgrim, 1996.

Finn, Daniel K., ed. *Moral Agency within Social Structures and Culture: A Primer on Critical Realism for Christian Ethics.* Washington, DC: Georgetown University Press, 2020.

Fiorenza, Elizabeth Schülssler. "The Ethics of Biblical Interpretation: Decentering Biblical Scholarship." *Journal of Biblical Literature* 107, no. 1 (March 1988): 3–17.

Flores, Nichole. *The Aesthetics of Solidarity: Our Lady of Guadalupe and American Democracy.* Washington, DC: Georgetown University Press, 2021.

Florida, Richard. *The Urban Crisis: How Our Cities Are Increasing Inequality, Deepening Segregation, and Failing the Middle Class—And What We Can Do about It.* New York: Basic Books, 2018.

Foster, Hal, Rosalind Krauss, Yve-Alain Bois, and Benjamin H. D. Buchloh. *Art since 1900: Modernism, Antimodernism, and Postmodernism.* New York: Thames & Hudson, 2004.

Francis. *Fratelli Tutti: On Fraternity and Social Friendship.* The Vatican, October 3, 2020. https://www.vatican.va/content/francesco/en/encyclicals/documents/papa-francesco_20201003_enciclica-fratelli-tutti.html.

Francis. *Laudato Si'.* The Vatican, May 24, 2015. https://w2.vatican.va/content/francesco/en/encyclicals/documents/papa-francesco_20150524_enciclica-laudato-si.html.

Friedman, Alexi. "Corzine Proposes Cutting Arts Funding below Required Minimum." *Star-Ledger*, March 15, 2009. http://www.nj.com/news/index.ssf/2009/03/corzine_proposes_cutting_arts.html.

Friedman, Eric. *Reinventing Philanthropy: A Framework for More Effective Giving*. Washington, DC: Potomac Books, 2013.

Fry, Roger. *Vision and Design*. London: Chatto & Windus, 1923.

Gaiger, Jason, and Paul Wood, eds. *Art of the Twentieth Century: A Reader*. New Haven, CT: Yale University Press, 2003.

Gall, David Anthony. "Aesthetic Problems, Realist Solutions." *Journal of Aesthetic Education* 50, no. 1 (Spring 2016): 80–94.

García-Rivera, Alejandra R. *The Community of the Beautiful: A Theological Aesthetics*. Collegeville, MN: Liturgical Press, 1999.

Garsd, Jasmine. "When Does Disaster Photography Cross the Line?" National Public Radio, January 19, 2010. https://www.npr.org/sections/tellmemore/2010/01/disaster_photography_when_does.html.

Gilman, James E. *Fidelity of Heart: An Ethic of Christian Virtue*. Oxford: Oxford University Press, 2001.

Gilson, Erinn C. *The Ethics of Vulnerability: A Feminist Analysis of Social Life and Practice*. New York: Routledge, 2014.

Goen, C. C. "Editor's Introduction." In *The Works of Jonathan Edwards*, Vol. 4, *The Great Awakening*, edited by C. C. Goen, 1–95. New Haven, CT: Yale University Press, 1972.

Goizueta, Roberto S. *Caminemos con Jesús: Toward a Hispanic/Latino Theology of Accompaniment*. Maryknoll, NY: Orbis Books, 1995.

Goizueta, Roberto S. *Christ Our Companion: Toward a Theological Aesthetics of Liberation*. Maryknoll, NY: Orbis Books, 2009.

Goizueta, Roberto S. "Rediscovering Praxis: The Significance of U.S. Hispanic Experience for Theological Method." In *We Are a People! Initiatives in Hispanic American Theology*, edited by Roberto S. Goizueta, 51–78. Minneapolis, MN: Fortress, 1992.

Greenberger, Alex. "Why Joseph Beuys's Mysterious Art Continues to Inspire—and Incense." *ARTnews*, January 5, 2021. https://www.artnews.com/feature/joseph-beuys-who-is-he-why-is-he-important-1234580650/.

Guelzo, Allen. "After Edwards: Original Sin and Freedom of the Will." In *After Jonathan Edwards: The Courses of the New England Theology*, edited by Oliver D. Crisp and Douglas A. Sweeney, 51–62. Oxford: Oxford University Press, 2012.

Gustafson, James M. *Can Ethics Be Christian?* Chicago: University of Chicago Press, 1975.

Gustafson, James M. *Ethics from a Theocentric Perspective*, Vol. 1, *Theology and Ethics*. Chicago: University of Chicago Press, 1981.

Gustafson, James M. "Participation: A Religious Worldview." *Journal of Religious Ethics* 44, no. 1 (2016): 148–75.

Hare, R. M. *Freedom and Responsibility*. New York: Oxford University Press, 1965.

Hart, David Bentley. *Beauty of the Infinite: The Theological Aesthetics of Christian Truth*. Grand Rapids, MI: William B. Eerdmans, 2003.

Hart, David Bentley. "A Sense of Style: Beauty and the Christian Moral Life." *Journal of the Society of Christian Ethics* 39, no. 2 (Fall/Winter 2019): 237–50.

Hauerwas, Stanley. "Agency: Going Forward by Looking Back." In *Christian Ethics: Problems and Prospects*, edited by Lisa Sowle Cahill and James F. Childress, 185–95. Cleveland, OH: Pilgrim Press, 1995.

Hauerwas, Stanley. *A Community of Character: Toward a Constructive Christian Social Ethic.* Notre Dame, IN: University of Notre Dame Press, 1981.

Hauerwas, Stanley. *Dispatches from the Front: Theological Engagements with the Secular.* Durham, NC: Duke University Press, 1994.

Hauerwas, Stanley. *Vision and Virtue: Essays in Christian Ethical Reflection.* Notre Dame, IN: University of Notre Dame Press, 1981.

Havlin, Laura. "Photography and Modern Conflict," *Magnum Photos,* May 22, 2017. https://www.magnumphotos.com/theory-and-practice/photography-and-modern-conflict/.

Heyer, Kristin E. "The Idea of the Common Good: Interdisciplinary Contributions to Catholic Higher Education." *Integritas* 7, no. 1 (Spring 2016): 1–20.

Heyer, Kristin E. *Kinship across Border: A Christian Ethic of Immigration.* Washington, DC: Georgetown University Press, 2013.

Hogan, Gwynne. "Vandal Splatters Gray Paint on George Floyd Bust in Union Square [New York City]." Gothamist, October 3, 2021. https://gothamist.com/news/vandal-splatters-gray-paint-george-floyd-bust-union-square.

Hogan, Linda. "Vulnerability: An Ethic for a Divided World." In *Building Bridges in Sarajevo: The Plenary Papers of Sarajevo 2018,* edited by James Keenan, Kristin Heyer, and Andrea Vicini, 217–22. Maryknoll, NY: Orbis Books, 2019.

Hollenbach, David. *Christian Ethics and the Common Good.* Cambridge: Cambridge University Press, 2002.

Horowitz, Joseph. "The Specter of Hitler in the Music of Wagner." *New York Times,* November 8, 1998. https://www.nytimes.com/1998/11/08/arts/the-specter-of-hitler-in-the-music-of-wagner.html.

Huizenga, Tom. "The New York Philharmonic Plays Pyongyang." National Public Radio, February 26, 2008. http://www.npr.org/templates/story/story.php?storyId=19346628.

Jacobs, Andrew. "The Wild, Wild Lower East Side; Democracy Is Messy. Does That Mean It Doesn't Work? A Look at Community Board 3." *New York Times,* March 3, 1996. https://www.nytimes.com/1996/03/03/nyregion/wild-wild-lower-east-side-democracy-messy-does-that-mean-it-doesn-t-work-look.html.

Jacobs, Julia. "Students' Calls to Remove a Mural Were Answered. Now Comes a Lawsuit." *New York Times,* July 6, 2020. https://www.nytimes.com/2020/07/06/arts/design/university-of-kentucky-slavery-mural-lawsuit.html?searchResultPosition=1.

Jennings, Marianne. "The Absence of Stories: Filling the Void in Ethics." In *Ethics, Literature, Theory: An Introductory Reader,* edited by Stephen K. George, 165–71. Lanham, MD: Rowman & Littlefield, 2005.

Jennings, Willie James. "Anger Is the Engine of Hope Now." *Reflections,* Fall 2020. https://reflections.yale.edu/article/seeking-light-notes-hope/anger-engine-hope-now.

Jennings, Willie James. "Embodying the Artistic Spirit and the Prophetic Arts." *Literature & Theology* 30, no. 3 (September 2016): 256–64.

Jolly, Anne. "Teaching Ethics Should Be a STEM Essential." Middleweb, November 11, 2019. https://www.middleweb.com/25600/teaching-ethics-should-be-a-stem-essential/.

Kant, Immanuel. *Critique of Judgment.* Translated by Werner S. Pluhar. Indianapolis, IN: Hackett Publishing, 1987.

Kant, Immanuel. *Observations on the Feeling of the Beautiful and Sublime.* Translated by John T. Goldthwait. Berkeley: University of California Press, 2004.

Kaufman, Sarah L. "MacKenzie Scott's Multimillion-Dollar Message: Art Is Essential Everywhere, Not Just in Museums and Theaters." *Washington Post,* August 28, 2021. https://

www.washingtonpost.com/entertainment/theater_dance/mackenzie-scott-arts-grants/2021/08/26/266ac8b2-04e3-11ec-8c3f-3526f81b233b_story.html.

Keenan, James F. "Building Blocks for Moral Education: Vulnerability, Recognition and Conscience." In *Conscience and Catholic Education*, edited by David DeCosse, 17–30. Maryknoll, NY: Orbis Books, 2022.

Keenan, James F. "Linking Human Dignity, Vulnerability and Virtue Ethics." *Interdisciplinary Journal for Religion and Transformation in Contemporary Society* 6 (2020): 56–73.

Keenan, James F. "Social Trust and the Ethics of Our Institutions." *Journal of the Society of Christian Ethics* 42, no. 2 (Fall/Winter 2022): 245–64.

Keenan, James F. "The World at Risk: Vulnerability, Precarity and Connectedness." *Theological Studies* 81, no. 1 (2020): 132–49.

Kennedy, Randy. "White Artist's Painting of Emmett Till at Whitney Biennial Draws Protests." *New York Times*, March 21, 2017. https://www.nytimes.com/2017/03/21/arts/design/painting-of-emmett-till-at-whitney-biennial-draws-protests.html.

Kennicott, Philip. "We Used to Think Photos Like This Could Change the World. What Needs to Change Is Who We Are." *Washington Post*, June 26, 2019. https://www.washingtonpost.com/lifestyle/style/we-used-to-think-photos-like-this-could-change-the-world-what-needs-to-change-is-who-we-are/2019/06/26/53c9087a-982d-11e9-830a-21b9b36b64ad_story.html.

Khazan, Olga. "Spanish Woman Botches 'Ecce Homo' Painting in an Attempt to Restore It." *Washington Post*, August 23, 2012. https://www.washingtonpost.com/blogs/blogpost/post/spanish-woman-botches-ecce-homo-painting-in-an-attempt-to-restore-it/2012/08/23/263bd0e2-ed42-11e1-b09d-07d971dee30a_blog.html.

Kinzer, Stephen. "Lilly Heir Makes $100 Million Bequest to Poetry Magazine." *New York Times*, November 19, 2002. http://www.nytimes.com/2002/11/19/books/lilly-heir-makes-100-million-bequest-to-poetry-magazine.html?scp=3&sq=ruth%20lily%20and%20poetry%20magazine&st=cse.

Kranish, Michael. "How Tucker Carlson Became the Voice of White Grievance." *Washington Post*, July 14, 2021. https://www.washingtonpost.com/politics/tucker-carlson/2021/07/13/398fa720-dd9f-11eb-a501-0e69b5d012e5_story.html.

Krauss, Rosalind. "The Im/pulse to See." In *Vision and Visuality*, edited by Hal Foster, 51–79. Seattle, WA: Bay Press, 1988.

Kuklick, Bruce. *Churchmen and Philosophers: From Jonathan Edwards to John Dewey*. New Haven, CT: Yale University Press, 1985.

Lamoureux, Patricia A. "Introduction." In *Seeking Goodness and Beauty: The Use of the Arts in Theological Ethics*, edited by Patricia A. Lamoureux and Kevin J. O'Neill, 1–11. Lanham, MD: Rowman & Littlefield, 2005.

Lauritzen, Paul. *Religious Belief and Emotional Transformation: A Light in the Heart*. Lewisburg, PA: Bucknell University Press, 1992.

Lauter, Estella. "Re-enfranchising Art: Feminist Interventions in the Theory of Art." In *Aesthetics in Feminist Perspective*, edited by Hilde Hein and Carolyn Korsmeyer, 21–34. Bloomington: Indiana University Press, 1993.

Lee, Dahyun. "How the Arts Generate Social Capital to Foster Intergroup Social Cohesion." *Journal of Arts, Management, Law, and Society* 43 (January 1, 2013): 4–17.

Lee, Sang Hyun. *The Philosophical Theology of Jonathan Edwards*. Princeton, NJ: Princeton University Press, 1988.

Loos, Ted. "Genius at Work: 20 MacArthur Fellows Show Their Art in Chicago." *New York Times*, July 13, 2021. https://www.nytimes.com/2021/07/13/arts/design/macarthur-fellows-art-show-chicago.html?searchResultPosition=1.

Lopez, Oscar. "Frida Kahlo, Aztec Gods: Can Art Lift Up a Poor Neighborhood?" *New York Times*, October 14, 2021. https://www.nytimes.com/2021/10/14/world/americas/mexico-city-iztapalapa-murals.html?action=click&module=Well&pgtype=Homepage§ion=World%20News.

Lynton, Norbert. "Expressionism." In *Concepts of Modern Art*, edited by Nikos Stangos, 30–49. New York: Thames and Hudson, 1989.

MacIntyre, Alasdair. *Ethics in the Conflicts of Modernity: An Essay on Desire, Practical Reasoning, and Narrative*. Cambridge: Cambridge University Press, 2016.

MacIntyre, Alasdair. *After Virtue: A Study in Moral Theory*. Notre Dame, IN: Notre Dame University Press, 1989.

Marsalis, Wynton. "Wynton Marsalis on Arts in the After-Times (Future NYC)." Interview by John Schaefer. *Soundcheck*, July 7, 2020. https://www.newsounds.org/story/wynton-marsalis-arts-after-times-future-nyc/.

Marsden, George. *Jonathan Edwards: A Life*. New Haven, CT: Yale University Press, 2003.

Martin, Ryan. *Understanding Affections in the Theology of Jonathan Edwards: The High Exercises of Divine Love*. London: Bloomsbury, 2019.

Matisse, Henri. "Henri Matisse Complete Works 5." Accessed August 19, 2022. https://www.henrimatisse.org/henri-matisse-painting-gallery5.jsp.

Matisse, Henri. *Matisse on Art*. Revised ed. Edited by Jack Flam. Berkeley: University of California Press, 1995.

Matisse, Henri. "Selected Henri Matisse Paintings." Accessed August 19, 2022. https://www.henrimatisse.org/woman-reading.jsp.

McAuley, James. "As Flames Engulfed Notre Dame, a Fire Brigade Chaplain Helped Save the Treasures Inside." *Washington Post*, August 16, 2019. https://www.washingtonpost.com/world/europe/as-flames-engulfed-notre-dame-a-fire-bridge-chaplain-helped-save-the-treasures-inside/2019/04/16/9b7b8fd8-5fcc-11e9-bf24-db4b9fb62aa2_story.html.

McCormick, Patrick T. *God's Beauty: A Call to Justice*. Collegeville, MN: Liturgical Press, 2012.

Meany, Thomas. "The Antagonist." *New Yorker*, October 4, 2021, 20–26.

Meehan, Mary Beth. "Seeing Newnan." 2019–2020. https://www.marybethmeehan.com/portfolio/newnan/.

Merkle, Judith. *Discipleship, Secularity, and the Modern Self: Dancing to Silent Music*. London: T&T Clark, 2020.

Mescher, Marcus. *The Ethics of Encounter: Christian Neighbor Love as a Practice of Solidarity*. Maryknoll, NY: Orbis, 2020.

Mesquita, Batja. *Between Us: How Cultures Create Emotions*. New York: Norton, 2022.

MoMa. "Art and Artists." Accessed August 19, 2022. https://www.moma.org/collection/works/79250.

Montecel, Xavier M. "Liturgy, Virtue, and the Foundations of an Ecclesial Ethics." *Journal of the Society of Christian Ethics* 42, no. 2 (Fall/Winter 2022): 401–16.

Morrill, Bruce T. *Anamnesis as Dangerous Memory: Political and Liturgical Theology in Dialogue*. Collegeville, MN: Liturgical Press, 2000.

Moskowitz, Peter. *How to Kill a City: Gentrification, Inequality, and the Fight for the Neighborhood*. New York: Nation Books, 2018.

Murdoch, Iris. "Art Is the Imitation of Nature." In *Existentialists and Mystics*, edited by Peter Conradi, 243–257. New York: Penguin Books, 1997.

Murdoch, Iris. "On 'God' and 'Good.'" In *The Sovereignty of Good*, 45–74. London: Routledge, 2003.

Murdoch, Iris. "The Sovereignty of Good over Other Concepts." In *The Sovereignty of Good*, 75–101. London: Routledge, 2003.

Newson, Ryan Andrew. *Cut in Stone: Confederate Monuments and Theological Disruption*. Waco, TX: Baylor University Press, 2020.

New York Times. "Inside the Capital Riot: An Exclusive Video Investigation." June 20, 2021. https://www.nytimes.com/2021/06/30/us/jan-6-capitol-attack-takeaways.html.

Nguyen, Mimi Thi. *The Gift of Freedom: War, Debt, and Other Refugee Passages*. Durham, NC: Duke University Press, 2012.

Niebuhr, Gustav. "Anger over Work Evokes Anti-Catholic Shadow, and Mary's Power as Icon." *New York Times*, October 3, 1999. http://www.nytimes.com/1999/10/03/nyregion/anger-over-work-evokes-anti-catholic-shadow-and-mary-s-power-as-icon.html.

Nussbaum, Martha. *Love's Knowledge: Essays on Philosophy and Literature*. Oxford: Oxford University Press, 1990.

Nussbaum, Martha. "Transitional Anger." *Journal of the American Philosophical Association* 1, no. 1 (2015): 41–56.

Nussbaum, Martha. *Upheavals of Thought: The Intelligence of Emotions*. Cambridge: Cambridge University Press, 2001.

Offenhartz, Jake. "'This Isn't Paris!' East Village Community Board Gets Heated over Outdoor Dining." Gothamist, July 14, 2021. https://gothamist.com/food/east-village-community-board-outdoor-dining-debate.

Okin, Susan Moller. *Justice, Gender, and the Family*. New York: Basic Books, 1989.

Palacios-Sánchez, Leonardo, Juan Sebastián Botero-Meneses, Rocio Plazas Pachón, Laura Bibiana Pineros Hernández, Juanita del Pilar Triana-Melo, and Santiago Ramirez-Rodríguez. "Stendhal Syndrome: A Clinical and Historical Overview." *Arquivos de Neuro-Psiquiatr* 76, no. 2 (February 2018): 120–23.

Pierce, Yolanda. "Righteous Anger, Black Lives Matter, and the Legacy of King." Berkley Forum, Berkeley Center for Religion, Peace and World Affairs, June 16, 2018. https://berkleycenter.georgetown.edu/responses/righteous-anger-black-lives-matter-and-the-legacy-of-king.

Posner, Richard. "Against Ethical Criticism." *Philosophy and Literature* 21, no. 1 (April 1997): 1–27.

Pramuk, Christopher. *The Artist Alive: Explorations in Music, Art & Theology*. Winona, MN: Anselm Academic, 2019.

Promey, Sally M. "The Public Display of Religion." In *The Visual Culture of American Religions*, edited by David Morgan and Sally M. Promey, 27–48. Berkeley: University of California Press, 2001.

Putnam, Hilary. "Literature, Science, and Reflection." In *Meaning and the Moral Sciences*, 83–96. Boston: Routledge & Kegan, 1978.

Putnam, Robert. *Bowling Alone: The Collapse and Revival of American Community*. New York: Simon & Schuster, 2000.

Ramey, Paul. *The Just War: Force and Political Responsibility*. Lanham, MD: University Press of America, 1983.

Ransom, John Crowe. "Forms and Citizens." In *The World's Body*, 29–54. 1938; reprint, Baton Rouge: Louisiana State University Press, 1968.

Rawls, John. *A Theory of Justice*. Revised ed. Cambridge, MA: Belknap Press/Harvard University Press, 1999.

Renkl, Margaret. "When a Picture Is Worth a Thousand Tears." *New York Times*, February 17, 2020. https://www.nytimes.com/2020/02/17/opinion/photojournalism-children-nick-ut.html?searchResultPosition=1.

Rich, Motoko. "Second Best in the World, but Still Saying Sorry." *New York Times*, August 5, 2021. https://www.nytimes.com/2021/08/05/world/asia/japan-olympics-apology.html.

Richardson, Joan. *A Natural History of Pragmatism: The Fact of Feeling from Jonathan Edwards to Gertrude Stein*. Cambridge: Cambridge University Press, 2007.

Riis, Jacob. *How the Other Half Lives: Studies among the Tenements of New York*. New York: Dover, [1890] 1971.

Riis, Jacob. "The Tenement House Blight," *Atlantic Monthly* 83 (1899): 760–71.

Rodgers, Thomas. "Picasso Mural Torn from Building after Years of Dispute." *New York Times*, July 30, 2020. https://www.nytimes.com/2020/07/30/arts/design/picasso-fishermen-mural-norway.html.

Rodriguez, Olga R., and Jeffrey Collins. "Statues Toppled throughout US in Protests against Racism." *U.S. News & World Report*, June 22, 2020. https://www.usnews.com/news/politics/articles/2020-06-20/statues-toppled-throughout-us-in-protests-against-racism.

Rojas, Rick. "A Revival Comes to Newark, but Some Worry It's 'Not for Us.'" *New York Times*, August 8, 2017. https://nyti.ms/2uBPEcP.

Rose, Joel. "A Majority of Americans See an 'Invasion' at the Southern Border, NPR Poll Finds." National Public Radio, August 18, 2022. https://www.npr.org/2022/08/18/1117953720/a-majority-of-americans-see-an-invasion-at-the-southern-border-npr-poll-finds.

Rose, Paul Lawrence. *Wagner: Race and Revolution*. New Haven, CT: Yale University Press, 1992.

Ross, Susan A. "Aesthetics and Ethics: Women Religious as Aesthetic and Moral Educators." *Journal of the Society of Christian Ethics*, 38, no. 2 (Fall/Winter 2018): 131–48.

Ross, Susan A. "Women, Beauty, and Justice: Moving beyond Balthasar." *Journal of the Society of Christian Ethics* 25, no. 1 (Spring/Summer 2005): 79–98.

Ross, Susan A. *For the Beauty of the Earth: Women, Sacramentality, and Justice*. Mahwah, NJ: Paulist Press, 2006.

Rubsam, Robert. "The Cinema of Atrocity: Amazon's 'Hunters' and Elem Klimov's 'Come and See.'" *Commonweal*, July 17, 2020. https://www.commonwealmagazine.org/cinema-atrocity.

Saito, Yuriko. "The Aesthetics of Unscenic Nature." *Journal of Aesthetics and Art Criticism* 56, no. 1 (1998): 101–11.

Saliers, Don E. "Afterword: Liturgy and Ethics Revisited." In *Liturgy and the Moral Self: Humanity at Full Stretch before God*, edited by E. Byron Anderson and Bruce T. Morrill, 209–24. Collegeville, MN: Liturgical Press, 1998.

Saliers, Don E. "For the Sake of the World: Liturgy and Ethics." In *Worship as Theology*, edited by Don E. Saliers, 171–90. Nashville, TN: Abingdon, 1994.

Saliers, Don E. "Liturgy and Ethics: Some New Beginnings." *Journal of Religious Ethics* 7, no. 2 (Fall 1979): 173–89.

Sandel, Michael J. *Liberalism and the Limits of Justice*. Cambridge: Cambridge University Press. 1998.

Scarry, Elaine. *On Beauty and Being Just*. Princeton, NJ: Princeton University Press, 1999.

Schwartz, Deanna, and Meghan Collins Sullivan. "Gen Z Is Driving Sales of Romance Books to the Top of the Bestseller Lists." National Public Radio, August 29, 2022. https://www.npr.org/2022/08/29/1119886246/gen-z-is-driving-sales-of-romance-books-to-the-top-of-bestseller-lists.

Sherry, Patrick. *Spirit and Beauty: An Introduction to Theological Aesthetics.* London: SCM Press, 2002.

Smith, John E. "Editor's Introduction." In *The Works of Jonathan Edwards*, Vol. 2, *Religious Affections*, edited by John E. Smith, 1–83. New Haven, CT: Yale University Press, 1959.

Smith, John E. "Religious Affections and the 'Sense of the Heart.'" In *The Princeton Companion to Jonathan Edwards*, edited by Sang Hyun Lee, 103–14. Princeton, NJ: Princeton University Press, 2005.

Smith, Roberta. "In a Mattress, a Lever for Art and Politics." *New York Times*, September 21, 2014. https://www.nytimes.com/2014/09/22/arts/design/in-a-mattress-a-fulcrum-of-art-and-political-protest.html.

Smith, Zadie. *On Beauty*. New York: Penguin Books, 2005.

Spohn, William C. "The Formative Power of Story and the Grace of Indirection." In *Seeking Goodness and Beauty: The Use of the Arts in Theological Ethics*, edited by Patricia A. Lamoureux and Kevin J. O'Neill, 13–32. Lanham, MD: Rowman & Littlefield, 2005.

Spohn, William C. "Spirituality and Its Discontents: Practices in Jonathan Edwards's 'Charity and Its Fruits.'" *Journal of Religious Ethics* 31, no. 2 (Summer 2003): 253–76.

Stamberg, Susan. "Artist Says His Portraits of Day Laborers Are Paintings—Not Statements." National Public Radio, February 13, 2020. https://www.npr.org/2020/02/13/804591711/artist-says-his-portraits-of-day-laborers-are-paintings-not-statements.

Steiner, Wendy. *The Scandal of Pleasure: Art in the Age of Fundamentalism.* Chicago: University of Chicago Press, 1995.

Steiner, Wendy. *Venus in Exile: The Rejection of Beauty in 20th-Century Art.* Chicago: University of Chicago Press, 2001.

Stiltner, Brian. *Religion and the Common Good.* Lanham, MD: Rowman & Littlefield, 1999.

Stoppard, Lou. "What Should Hang on the Walls of a Hospital?" *New Yorker*, July 31, 2021. https://www.newyorker.com/culture/culture-desk/what-should-hang-on-the-walls-of-a-hospital.

Stout, Jeffrey. *Democracy and Tradition.* Princeton, NJ: Princeton University Press, 2004.

Sullivan, Tim, and Stephen Groves. "'We're Sick of It': Anger over Police Killings Shatters U.S." PBS, May 31, 2020. https://www.pbs.org/newshour/nation/were-sick-of-it-anger-over-police-killings-shatters-us.

Svrluga, Susan. "As Colleges Grapple with Racist Legacies, a Monument at Ole Miss Will Finally Go." *Washington Post*, June 19, 2020. https://www.washingtonpost.com/education/2020/06/19/colleges-grapple-with-racist-legacies-monument-ole-miss-will-finally-go/.

Tate Galleries. "Bloomsbury." Accessed November 24, 2023. https://www.tate.org.uk/art/art-terms/b/bloomsbury.

Thiel, John. *Now and Forever: A Theological Aesthetic of Time.* Notre Dame, IN: University of Notre Dame Press, 2023.

Tillard, J.-M.-R. *Flesh of the Church, Flesh of Christ: At the Source of the Ecclesiology of Communion.* Translated by Madeleine M. Beaumont. Collegeville, MN: Liturgical Press, 2001.

Tracy, David. *Analogical Imagination: Christian Theology and the Culture of Pluralism.* New York: Crossroads, 1981.

Tran, Jonathan. "Assessing the Augustinian Democrats." *Journal of Religious Ethics* 46, no. 3 (September 2018): 521–47.

Viladesau, Richard. *Theological Aesthetics: God in Imagination, Beauty, and Art.* Oxford: Oxford University Press, 1999.

Wagner, John. "Trump Says He Found Inspiration for Border Wall at Memorial for Flight 93 Victims." *Washington Post*, September 19, 2018. https://www.washingtonpost.com/politics/trump-says-he-found-inspiration-for-border-wall-at-memorial-for-flight-93-victims/2018/09/19/94cf37bc-bc2e-11e8-be70-52bd11fe18af_story.html.

Wall, Kathleen. "Ethics, Knowledge, and the Need for Beauty: Zadie Smith's *On Beauty* and Ian McEwan's *Saturday*." *University of Toronto Quarterly* 77, no. 2 (Spring 2008): 757–88.

Weaver, Darlene Fozard. "Christian Formation and Moral Pluralism: Challenges and Opportunities." *Studies in Christian Ethics* 33, no. 1 (2020): 27–39.

Weaver, Darlene Fozard. "Church Ethics for a Morally Diverse World." *Journal of the Society of Christian Ethics* 42, no. 2 (Fall/Winter 2022): 273–79.

Weichbrodt, Elissa Yukiko. *Redeeming Vision: A Christian Guide to Looking at and Learning from Art*. Grand Rapids, MI: Baker Academic, 2023.

Weigel, George. "Moral Clarity in a Time of War." In *War and Christian Ethics: Classic and Contemporary Readings on the Morality of War*, 2nd ed., edited by Arthur F. Holmes, 373–90. Grand Rapids, MI: Baker Academic, 2005.

Weiner, Marc. *Richard Wagner and the Anti-Semitic Imagination*. Lincoln: University of Nebraska Press, 1995.

Westphal, Meryl. *In Praise of Heteronomy: Making Room for Revelation*. Bloomington: Indiana University Press, 2017.

Wilkerson, Isabel. "Trouble Right Here in Cincinnati: Furor over Mapplethorpe Exhibit." *New York Times*, March 29, 1990. http://www.nytimes.com/1990/03/29/us/trouble-right-here-in-cincinnati-furor-over-mapplethorpe-exhibit.html?scp=4&sq=maplethorpe%20project%20x&st=cse.

Wolterstorff, Nicholas. *Art in Action: Toward a Christian Aesthetic*. Grand Rapids, MI: William B. Eerdmans, 1980.

Wright, Alastair. *Matisse and the Subject of Modernism*. Princeton, NJ: Princeton University Press, 2004.

Yabroff, Jennie. "The Arts: Exhibits Designed to Shock." *Newsweek*, April 26, 2008. https://www.newsweek.com/arts-exhibits-designed-shock-86277.

Yeager, Diane M. "'Art for Humanity's Sake': The Social Novel as a Mode of Moral Discourse." *Journal of Religious Ethics* 33, no. 3 (2005): 445–85.

Yeager, Diane M. "'Suspended in Wonderment': Beauty, Religious Affections, and Ecological Ethics." *Journal of the Society of Christian Ethics*, 35, no. 1 (Spring/Summer 2015): 121–45.

Young, Iris Marion. "Difference as a Resource for Democratic Communication." In *Deliberative Democracy: Essays on Reason and Politics*, edited by James Bohman and William Relig, 383–406. Cambridge, MA: MIT Press, 1997.

Young, Iris Marion. *Justice and the Politics of Difference*. Princeton, NJ: Princeton University Press, 1990.

INDEX

ABOUT THE AUTHOR

KI JOO CHOI is the Kyung-Chik Han Professor of Asian American Theology at Princeton Theological Seminary. Choi's research and teaching interests span a diverse set of disciplines, from Christian ethics and peace studies to aesthetics and critical ethnic studies. His publications include the monograph *Disciplined by Race: Theological Ethics and the Problem of Asian American Identity*. Choi received his BA and MDiv from Yale and his PhD in theological ethics from Boston College and serves as coeditor of the *Journal of the Society of Christian Ethics*.